The poems of Theocritus are our best witness to a brilliant poetic culture that flourished in the first half of the third century BC. This book considers the context from which these poems grew and, in particular, the manner in which they engage with and re-create the poetic forms of the Greek archaic age. The focus is not on the familiar bucolic poems of Theocritus, but on the hymns, mimes, and erotic poems of the second half of the corpus. Recent papyri have greatly increased our understanding of how Theocritus read archaic poetry, and these new discoveries are fully exploited in a set of readings which will change the way we look at Hellenistic poetry.

Scholars and students interested in Greek and Latin literature, and especially the poetry of the Hellenistic period, will find this an important book. All Greek is translated.

THEOCRITUS AND THE ARCHAEOLOGY
OF GREEK POETRY

THEOCRITUS AND THE ARCHAEOLOGY OF GREEK POETRY

RICHARD HUNTER

University Lecturer in Classics, University of Cambridge,
and Fellow of Pembroke College

CAMBRIDGE
UNIVERSITY PRESS

Published by the Press Syndicate of the University of Cambridge
The Pitt Building, Trumpington Street, Cambridge CB2 1RP
40 West 20th Street, New York, NY 10011-4211, USA
10 Stamford Road, Oakleigh, Melbourne 3166, Australia

First published 1996

Printed in Great Britain at the University Press, Cambridge

A catalogue record for this book is available from the British Library

Library of Congress cataloguing in publication data

Hunter, R. L. (Richard L.)
Theocritus and the archaeology of Greek poetry / Richard Hunter.
p.   cm.
Includes bibliographical references and index.
ISBN 0 521 56040 3 (hardback)
1. Theocritus. Idylls. 2. Greek poetry, Hellenistic – Egypt – Alexandria
– History and criticism. 3. Greek poetry, Hellenistic – Greek influences.
4. Theocritus – Knowledge – Literature. 5. Literary form.
6. Poetics. I. Title.
PA4444.H86   1996
884'.01–dc20   95-32705   CIP

ISBN 0 521 56040 3 hardback

Contents

Preface

Theocritean studies are in a curious state. For one thing, we need a new text. Gow's text is careful and readable, but it becomes increasingly clear that his conservatism has not always served the poet well. Moreover, Gow's *apparatus* is simply not adequate for the serious study of the text and language of the *Idylls*; Gallavotti's third edition goes some way towards remedying these deficiencies, but in Gallavotti also many worthwhile conjectures and suggestions are ignored. As for exegesis, Gow's commentary is an extremely rich one, and the longer I worked on this book the more indebted to it I became; I very much hope that the extent of my debt will be obvious to those familiar with Gow's work, and his name stands second in this Preface after that of Theocritus to indicate just how great that debt is. Nevertheless, Gow's commentary (inevitably) has very clear interests and biases, and an unfortunate result – certainly not Gow's fault – is that many questions in which Gow did not show himself interested have remained unasked. The bulk and sheer quality of his work have, broadly speaking, set the scholarly agenda, but the items of 'any other business' grow ever more numerous. It is to be hoped that the 1994 Groningen conference on Theocritus will prove to have marked a genuine turn of scholarly attention towards some of these pressing issues.

This book is about Theocritus' restoration and re-creation of various poetic traditions, in particular, though not exclusively, the traditions of the archaic age. The focus is not on the 'bucolic Theocritus', but rather on parts of the second half of the corpus as it is conventionally presented in modern editions. I have made no attempt, which would have been doomed from the outset, to be comprehensive in my coverage; 'surface survey' belongs to quite another branch of archaeology. Rather I have tried to open up some of the extraordinary richness and variety of these poems, which have on the whole received less critical attention than the bucolics. Our view of the poetry of the third century is partial and hazy, and too often 'Hellenistic poetry' is treated as an entity in which the whole is easier to grasp, and in some ways more interesting, than the parts; the Theocritean corpus offers our best chance to show how mistaken that view is. Each of Chapters 2 to 6 has at its centre a reading of individual poems, and thus these chapters can be read individually; I hope, however, that they will also be taken together as an exploration of Hellenistic poetics.

Various friends have been willing to take time out of very busy lives to read and offer constructive criticisms of draft chapters, and it is a pleasure to thank Alessandro Barchiesi, Paul Cartledge, Albio Cassio, Marco Fantuzzi, Philip Hardie, and Alexander Sens for the help they have so freely given. I am, as always, also much indebted to many seminar and lecture audiences who have listened to inchoate versions of much of this book, and have often made me rethink and revise, and to the anonymous referees of Cambridge University Press for a number of helpful suggestions. Susan Moore, whom Horace must have had in mind at *Ars Poetica* 438–44, once again proved a sub-editor of great skill and ingenuity.

A shorter, and rather different, version of Chapter 4 (cited as 'Hunter 1995a') is to appear in the collected papers of the 1994 Groningen Conference on Theocritus.

Cambridge
May 1995

Conventions and abbreviations

1 The text of Theocritus is cited, unless otherwise indicated, from Gow's edition. Translations of Theocritus are usually taken from Gow, often with my own adaptations.
2 Editions of and commentaries on Theocritus are cited merely by the editor's name. The principal editions referred to are:
   A. Fritzsche, 2nd edition, Leipzig 1870
   H. Fritzsche and E. Hiller, 3rd edition, Leipzig 1881
   U. von Wilamowitz-Moellendorff, Oxford 1905
   A. S. F. Gow, 2nd edition, Cambridge 1952
   K. J. Dover, London 1971
   C. Gallavotti, 3rd edition, Rome 1993
3 Translations other than of Theocritus are my own, where the translator is not otherwise identified.
4 In the spelling of Greek names, ease of recognition rather than consistency has been the principal aim. Thus, familiar names are usually Latinised, whereas less familiar ones are often transliterated.
5 Modern works cited by author and date only are listed in the Bibliography.
6 Standard abbreviations for (i) collections and editions of texts and (ii) works of reference are used, but the following lists may be helpful:

(i)

Bernand	E. Bernand, *Inscriptions métriques de l'Egypte gréco-romaine. Recherches sur la poésie épigrammatique des Grecs en Egypte* (Paris 1969)
CA	J. U. Powell (ed.), *Collectanea Alexandrina* (Oxford 1925)
CEG	P. A. Hansen (ed.), *Carmina Epigraphica Graeca* (Berlin/New York 1983, 1989)
CPG	E. L. Leutsch and F. Schneidewin, *Corpus*

	Paroemiographorum Graecorum (Göttingen 1839–51)
FGE	D. L. Page (ed.), *Further Greek Epigrams* (Cambridge 1981)
FGrHist	F. Jacoby, *Die Fragmente der griechischen Historiker* (Berlin/Leiden 1923–)
HE	A. S. F. Gow and D. L. Page (eds.), *The Greek Anthology. Hellenistic Epigrams* (Cambridge 1965)
PMG	D. L. Page (ed.), *Poetae Melici Graeci* (Oxford 1962)
PMGF	M. Davies (ed.), *Poetarum Melicorum Graecorum Fragmenta* I (Oxford 1991)
SEG	*Supplementum Epigraphicum Graecum* (Leiden 1923–)
SH	H. Lloyd-Jones and P. Parsons (eds.), *Supplementum Hellenisticum* (Berlin / New York 1983)
SLG	D. L. Page (ed.), *Supplementum Lyricis Graecis* (Oxford 1974)
TrGF	*Tragicorum Graecorum Fragmenta* (Göttingen 1971–)

(ii)

CAH	*The Cambridge Ancient History* (Cambridge 1928–)
Chantraine, *DE*	P. Chantraine, *Dictionnaire étymologique de la langue grecque. Histoire des mots* (Paris 1968)
LfgrE	*Lexikon des frühgriechischen Epos* (Göttingen 1979–)
LIMC	*Lexicon Iconographicum Mythologiae Classicae* (Zürich 1981–)
RE	A. Pauly, G. Wissowa *et al.*, *Realencyclopädie der classischen Altertumswissenschaft* (Stuttgart 1894–1980)

CHAPTER I

Locating the site

TOWARDS THEOCRITUS

This book is designed as a contribution to the study of how Hellenistic poets appropriated their literary heritage and adapted it to the writing of poetry in a new world. The particular focus of this book is not so much on the ever-present engagement with the *Iliad* and the *Odyssey*, but rather on the exploitation and reconstruction of non-Homeric poetry, particularly from what is conventionally labelled the 'archaic age', that is (roughly) the period down to the middle of the fifth century.[1] The poetry of this period is made explicitly central to the third-century poetic enterprise in many ways. Thus, for example, Callimachus adopted the persona of the Ionian iambist Hipponax (second half of the sixth century BC) to introduce his iambic poetry, although some of that poetry went in directions in which Hipponax himself can hardly have moved;[2] recently published papyri – in particular the epinician elegiacs of the so-called 'Victoria Berenices' (*SH* 254–68) – have provided striking confirmation of the extent of Callimachus' engagement with archaic lyric, particularly the poetry of Pindar;[3] the most important new archaic text to have appeared in the last few years – fragments of various elegiac poems of Simonides (*POxy.* 3965) – reveals direct links with more than one poem of Theocritus;[4] the *Phainomena* of Aratus is in part a creative rewriting of Hesiod's *Works and Days* within a Stoicising context; and so on. The reasons for this engagement with the archaic – beyond, of course, the sheer interest of the archaic texts – will have been many. To someone looking back from the third century, particularly

---

[1] For a helpful orientation from an Alexandrian point of view cf. T. Gelzer, 'Die Alexandriner und die griechischen Lyriker', *AAntHung* 30 (1982–4) 129–47. There is a brief but powerful statement in Wilamowitz 1900.16.

[2] For the importance of the figure of Hipponax cf. also Herodas 8.

[3] Cf. Bing 1988; Fuhrer 1992.   [4] Cf. below pp. 26, 97–109; Parsons 1992.10–12.

someone of a scholarly bent and possessed of some historical sense, the 'archaic age' may rather have seemed like the 'pre-Athenian' age. Despite certain phenomena which we will consider presently, the triumph of Athenian culture could have been seen as the death-knell for the rich tapestry of poetic forms to be found in the centuries before that triumph;[5] it was, in any event, undeniable that the extraordinary poetic achievements of one city had replaced the wide geographic spread – from Sicily to Asia Minor – of the poetry and poets of the archaic age.

Athenian poetry was, however, essentially the public drama of the democratic *polis*; although this was extensively studied and edited, and new drama was still written and performed, 'classical' drama may have seemed to offer little scope for creative reworking, particularly to poets whose works would be performed under entirely different conditions from those of the Athenian dramatic festivals. To some extent, then, Attic drama was the inspiration for scholarship, not for high poetry, although we must never forget how much we have lost and how strongly our view of Alexandrian poetry is coloured by subsequent literary history at Rome; the loss of the tragic dramas by the poets of the so-called Alexandrian 'Pleiad' leaves a gaping hole in our understanding of the period.[6] Euripides' *Bacchae* is a central model for Theocritus, Idyll 26,[7] Lycophron's *Alexandra* draws both its metre (iambic trimeters) and much of its stylistic inspiration from Attic tragedy (particularly Aeschylus),[8] and both Euripides and Sophocles seem to have made major contributions to various episodes of Apollonius' *Argonautica*, particularly to the story of Medea. That Menander was the most important influence on all Greek comedy written after him would be hard to deny, and the broader influence of Attic comedy upon new forms such as the mimiambs of Herodas is generally recognised.[9] The importance of the legacy of Attic drama in fact seems to increase as we move into the 'lower' regions of literature, as witness the famous *Fragmentum Grenfellianum* (see below). That the influence of drama should be felt more strongly in 'popular' than in élite culture is

[5] Cf. Wilamowitz 1896.227 (with important reservations about Ionia).
[6] Cf. F. Schramm, *Tragicae Graecae hellenisticae quae dicitur aetatis fragmenta* (diss. Münster 1929); B. Snell, *Tragicorum Graecorum Fragmenta* I, 2nd ed. revised by R. Kannicht (Göttingen 1986) 54–5.
[7] Cf. Cairns 1992.
[8] Cf. S. West, *JHS* 104 (1984) 150. The dating of the *Alexandra* is a notorious problem (third or second century?), but one which can, I hope, here be left out of account.
[9] For discussion and bibliography see Hunter 1995b.

hardly surprising.[10] Moreover, the variety of geographical centres for poetry in the Hellenistic world, the ever increasing importance of patronage, and the burgeoning number of poetic festivals, competitions, and opportunities for *epideixis* in the Hellenistic age may well have seemed more like the picture of poetic production which emerged from archaic texts than the rather monolithic image projected by the later fifth century in which the predominance of Attic tragedy and comedy drove other 'high poetry' from the field.

One particular area of archaic poetry, however, posed special problems of recuperation. This was the world of lyric. Our texts of the lyric poets are just that, 'texts' which formed but one part of a complex performance involving also music and (in the case of choral poetry) dance. The lyric poets sang their poems (or got others to sing them), but as early as the latter part of the fifth century there is evidence for the gradual dissolution of what John Herington has called a 'song culture' and its replacement in part by a 'book culture' and in part by a new kind of specialist music culture in the hands of experts and *virtuosi* whose performances were no longer necessarily tied to specific performance occasions, usually great public or private celebrations.[11] It is to this period also that we can trace the beginnings of a separation, in both theory and practice, between metrical and musical rhythm; the 'natural' assumption that the latter depended upon the former faded, and the latter now went its own way. If the result of these various developments was not quite 'art for art's sake', the link between many forms of lyric poetry and the life of the *polis* was certainly weakened and ultimately broken. By the end of the fifth century the great age of choral poetry (and, in many cases, of the public occasions at which it was performed) was essentially over; the bitter complaints of the conservative Plato about the 'lawlessness' (παρανομία) of contemporary music (cf. *Laws* 3 700a–701a) looked back to a period which was in fact no longer recoverable.[12] For the 'public at large', of course, the world continued to be full of song and dance, but the reality of the change in 'high culture' is not to be denied. Two related symptoms of this change require attention here. As poets concentrated upon the words rather than the music, they naturally tended to write in non-lyric metres; now that they themselves were not necessarily experts in music, only thus could they ensure that the fate of their poems did not depend

---

[10] For these terms, and for a more detailed discussion of this subject, see below pp. 7–10.
[11] Herington 1985.   [12] Cf. Fantuzzi 1980.436–7, 1993a.36–7.

upon the new *virtuosi*. Even in the scanty remains of fourth-century Attic drama, analogous changes may be observable. Attic comedy, for example, seems to have preserved opportunities for a 'lyric' *verbal* style even after its metrical richness had greatly decreased.[13]

The fact that most poetry of the high Alexandrian period is in dactylic hexameters or elegiac couplets is the result of a complex literary and social shift, but in part at least it signals the fact that the rôle of the poet is now much more circumscribed: his business is writing words, that and no more. This gradual separation between the linguistic (which includes the metrical, narrowly understood) and the musical levels is perhaps the most significant development of 'post-classical' poetry. 'Performance', of course, remained a crucial determinant upon the form of poetry, as it continued to be even when 'performance' meant largely 'private reading'. In the fourth and third centuries, the crucial performative context for high poetry was recitation, whether to one's fellow poets or at the court of a patron or at a public 'poetry festival'. The importance of this context is reflected in the increasing dominance of the two most common 'recitative' metres, the dactylic hexameter and the elegiac couplet.[14] Even when poets moved outside these confines – as, for example, the epigrammatists of the first half of the third century not infrequently did –[15] 'lyric' lengths are much more usually used in repeated stichic patterns (cf. Idylls 28–30) than combined into the strophes familiar from the earlier period.[16] It is in fact a prominent feature of the poetic production of the Hellenistic period that poets experimented with stichic composition (i.e. poems written in repeating verses of the same pattern, such as Homer's hexameters or the trimeters of tragedy) in lyric lengths either recovered from the poetry of the past or newly invented, such as the choriambic hexameters in which Philicus, a leading figure of the literary culture at the court of Philadelphus, composed a hymn to Demeter (*SH* 678–80). It is to this fashion that is owed the fact that, in the later grammatical

---

[13] Cf. Hunter 1983a.19–20, 166–7; H.-G. Nesselrath, *Die attische Mittlere Komödie. Ihre Stellung in der antiken Literaturkritik und Literaturgeschichte* (Berlin/New York 1990) 241–66.

[14] Cf. Fantuzzi 1980.440–3, 1993a.52–5; A. Cameron, 'Genre and style in Callimachus', *TAPA* 122 (1992) 305–12. Thus, Halperin's observation (1983.209) that '[Theocritus'] consistent use of the dactylic hexameter suggests that he wished to create an underlying unity among [all his poems] despite their diversity' carries rather less force than might at first appear.

[15] Cf. Parsons 1992.13–16; Fantuzzi 1993a.64–5.

[16] Theocritus, however, does (in my view) seek to produce quasi-strophic effects with his hexameters, cf. below pp. 155–6, and 'verse-paragraphs' are a familiar (though perhaps under-used) notion in the analysis of Hellenistic poetry.

tradition, many verse units are named after poets of the early Hellenistic period.[17] Recitation was presumably also the norm for such compositions, although particular oral, performative effects can hardly be excluded, any more than, for example, we can be sure that no ludicrous cook ever 'sang' iambic trimeters on the Middle Comedy stage.

Running in parallel with these developments, and mutually reinforcing them, came a gradual change in the nature of the transmission of archaic and classical texts. In the early period the words of a Sappho or an Alcman were transmitted both in writing and orally (i.e. by being heard and repeated); the music, on the other hand, was probably learned and passed down only in the latter way. From the middle of the fifth century, however, we have evidence of the development of a system of musical notation, which will have been added to some texts.[18] The growth of the book trade during the fourth century will have meant that increasingly the great poets were being read as unaccompanied 'texts'; it may in any case be doubted just how widespread was an understanding of this musical notation. That some knowledge (as opposed to pure theory) of the music of the classical period did reach third-century Alexandria is suggested by papyri which reveal clear traces of a performing tradition, although it is also clear that the great Alexandrian editors did not include any notation in their editions of the texts, which were presumably based upon earlier 'reading texts' carrying no musical notation.[19] Doubtless much traditional information continued to be transmitted in traditional ways – through performance and re-performance, both formal and informal –[20] and we must not assume that the loss of this part of their heritage seemed to Callimachus and Theocritus to be quite as devastating as it might appear to us; their knowledge of archaic music and dance need not *only* have been a result of their reading[21] or their

---

[17] Cf. esp. F. Leo, *Die plautinischen Cantica und die hellenistische Lyrik* (Abh. Göttingen n.f. 1.7, Berlin 1897) 64–70; Gow–Page, *HE* II p. 459. Leo laid it down as a rule that such naming indicated that the poet in question had used the metre stichically, rather than that he was particularly fond of it. This may well have been true in many cases, but it is unlikely that the same explanation will fit *every* case, and there is hardly the very firm distinction between the two explanations that Leo envisaged.   [18] Cf. West 1992. 261–3, 270–1.

[19] This whole subject is a matter of great debate. I have learned most from Wilamowitz 1900; E. Pöhlmann, 'Sulla preistoria della tradizione di testi e musica per il teatro' in Gentili–Pretagostini 1988.132–44; West 1992. For the relevant texts themselves cf. E. Pöhlmann, *Denkmäler altgriechischer Musik* (Nuremberg 1970) 78–93.

[20] The continuing performance tradition at Sparta (Ath. 14 632f; Herington 1985.206–7) is of particular importance with regard to Idyll 18, cf. below Chapter 5.

[21] The Peripatetic tradition of scholarly monograph will probably have been important here.

reconstructive imagination based upon that reading. As far as metre is concerned, moreover, the situation is somewhat clearer. The fashion for stichic poems in 'lyric' metres, which we have noted above, makes clear (what we would have assumed anyway) that the colometric revolution wrought by Aristophanes of Byzantium upon lyric texts was not a revolution *ex nihilo*.[22] We now possess, in the 'Lille Stesichorus' (*PMGF* 222(b)), a text of one of the lyric canon written out in the second half of the third century and correctly colometrised into dactylo-epitrites; stanzas and triads are marked in the manner which later became conventional. To date, this text remains an important exception, but it is a clear warning against assuming that we know all we need to know about how Alexandrian poets became acquainted with archaic lyric. The other papyri which survive from the pre-Aristophanic era reveal texts still written out as prose,[23] and there is (as yet) no good reason to doubt that this is the form in which Theocritus would normally have read archaic (and classical) poetry; 'how' he heard it performed we cannot know. This form of transmission too may have reinforced the sense of loss felt by those who concerned themselves actively with the poetry of the past, as well as influencing the metrically standard form in which reconstructions of that past poetry were composed. Here again, of course, there is a real danger of over-simplification. The importance for Theocritus of at least the texts of the newer forms of lyric is guaranteed by the *Cyclops or Galateia* of Philoxenus of Cythera, the influence of which upon Idylls 6 and 11 is all but certain, even if it is hard to define because of our ignorance of the details of the dithyramb.[24] This is a salutary warning against the deceptive periodisation that our evidence imposes. Nevertheless, it is likely that this influence remained secondary, and we shall see that the fourth-century poets who seem to have been most influential upon Theocritus composed largely in hexameters and elegiacs.[25]

These developments are still traceable, despite the desperate lacunae in our knowledge, because for the most part they concerned

---

[22] For Aristophanes' work cf. Pfeiffer 1968.184–92. There is much valuable information on Alexandrian practice, as it can be gleaned from the papyri, in Bohnenkamp 1972.103–21.

[23] Useful survey in H. Maehler, *Die Lieder des Bakchylides* (Leiden 1982) 32.

[24] Cf. Gow II p. 118; M. Fantuzzi, 'Mythological paradigms in the bucolic poetry of Theocritus', *PCPS* 41 (1995). The parody in Aristophanes' *Ploutos* seems to date Philoxenus' dithyramb to the very early years of the fourth century. Note also M. L. West's suggestion (*CQ* 20 (1970) 206) that the story of Daphnis (cf. Idyll 1) which Aelian ascribes to 'Stesichorus of Himera' was actually treated by a fourth-century lyric poet of that name; the traditional interpretation is championed by L. Lehnus, 'Note stesicoree: i poemetti "minori"' *SCO* 24 (1975) 191–6.   [25] Cf. below pp. 14–21.

the high poetry which entered the ever-growing book trade. Alongside these developments, however, poetic and musical performances flourished at all levels of society in ways at which we can now only guess. Just as poets now went their own way, largely free from the restraints of the performative occasion, so did the musical *virtuosi* and the popular entertainers; the picture of fourth-century poetry as it emerges from surviving written texts is certainly a very skewed one. No cliché of ancient cultural history is more familiar than the increasing separation of 'popular' and 'élite' culture in the Hellenistic period.[26] Too often the sole evidence adduced for this separation has been what we know of the cultural ambience of the Ptolemaic court. Many modern scholars find it hard to imagine a Callimachus enjoying the Alexandrian equivalent of a 'Royal Variety Performance', and yet we have no reason to assume that the audience for 'élite' culture did not also attend 'popular' performances, for example of the kind dramatised in Idyll 15; the reverse will, of course, not hold good, because in its very nature 'élite' culture defines itself by its self-proclaimed exclusiveness. The differences between the two cultures are not always easy to define, particularly because of our woeful ignorance of the wider musical and poetic world. The rich epigraphic record and the anecdotal compilations of an Athenaeus can tell us that poets competed and musicians played, but, with the partial exception of Attic Middle Comedy, only rarely do we get a glimpse of *what* they wrote or *how* they played.[27]

Of particular importance for the appreciation of Theocritus are the traditions of 'mime', conceived in the broadest generic terms, some scraps of which have reached us from the sands of Egypt.[28] It is clear, for example, that Idylls 2, 3, 14, and 15, like the *Mimiamboi* of Herodas, are in touch not merely with the Syracusan tradition of 'literary mime', represented for us by the fragments of Sophron,[29]

---

[26] Cairns 1992.15–16 issues a proper warning against this over-simplification, but the evidence adduced on the other side is not overwhelming. There is much food for thought in P. J. Parsons, 'Identities in diversity' in A. W. Bulloch *et al.* (eds.), *Images and Ideologies: Self-definition in the Hellenistic World* (Berkeley 1993) 152–70.

[27] For Theocritus' use of the comic tradition cf. below pp. 110–16. Important studies of 'popular' poetry include M. Guarducci, 'Poeti vaganti e conferenzieri dell' età ellenistica', *MAL* 6.2 (1929) 629–65; G. Sifakis, *Studies in the History of Hellenistic Drama* (London 1967); B. Gentili, *Theatrical Performances in the Ancient World. Hellenistic and Early Roman Theatre* (Amsterdam 1979); the introduction by M. Fantuzzi to K. Ziegler, *L'epos ellenistico. Un capitolo dimenticato della poesia greca* (Bari 1988).

[28] The texts are collected in an Appendix to Cunningham's Teubner text of Herodas (Leipzig 1987).   [29] Cf. below pp. 118–19.

but also with wider performance traditions of a 'popular' kind. One of the best known pieces of evidence for these traditions is a notice in Athenaeus:

The player called a *magodos* (μαγωιδός) carries tambourines and cymbals, and all his clothes are women's garments. He makes rude gestures (σχινίζεται), and all his actions lack decency, as he plays the part of adulterous women or bawds (μαστροπούς), or a man drunk and going on a revel to his mistress. Aristoxenus [fr. 110 Wehrli[2]] says that *hilarodia* is serious and derives from tragedy (παρὰ τὴν τραγωιδίαν εἶναι), whereas *magodoi* derives from comedy (παρὰ τὴν κωμωιδίαν). For often *magodoi* took comic scenarios (ὑποθέσεις) and acted them in their own style and manner. (Ath. 14 621c–d)

One text which seems to belong in the context suggested by this passage, and which can be placed alongside the work of Theocritus, is the so-called *Fragmentum Grenfellianum*, preserved on a papyrus of the mid-second century BC.[30] This is the song of an ἀποκεκλειμένη, a woman who has been spurned by her former lover and now complains bitterly outside his house. The setting of the 'song before the door', the *paraklausithuron*, is familiar enough, although it is usually the male partner who is 'locked out' in this way; the *Fragmentum* was indeed presumably performed by a man, as the quoted passage of Athenaeus suggests. Its nearest literary analogue is perhaps the duet of the young 'lovers' in Aristophanes' *Ecclesiazousai* (vv. 952–75), a parallel which may help us to gauge its tone and ancestry. Like the *Fragmentum*, the comic text mixes 'low-life' subject matter with unmistakable reverberations of high poetry.[31] The text of the *Fragmentum* is too long to quote in full, but two extracts may give something of the flavour:

> ἐξ ἀμφοτέρων γέγον' αἵρεσις·
> ἐζευγνίσμεθα· τῆς φιλίης Κύπρις
> ἐστ' ἀνάδοχος. ὀδύνη μ' ἔχει,
> ὅταν ἀναμνησθῶ
> ὥς με κατεφίλει 'πιβούλως μέλλων
> με καταλιμπάνειν
> ἀκαταστασίης εὑρετὴς
> καὶ ὁ τὴν φιλίην ἐκτικώς.

---

[30] For the text see *CA* pp. 177–9; I. C. Cunningham, *Herodae Mimiambi cum appendice fragmentorum mimorum papyraceorum* (Leipzig 1987) 36–8. The fundamental discussion remains Wilamowitz 1896, and I am much indebted to it; also important are O. Crusius, 'Grenfells Erotic fragment und seine litterarische Stellung', *Philologus* 55 (1896) 353–84 and E. Fraenkel, *Elementi Plautini in Plauto* (Florence 1960) 307–18.

[31] Cf. Ussher's notes *ad loc.*; C. M. Bowra, 'A love-duet', *AJP* 79 (1958) 376–81.

ἔλαβέ μ' ἔρως,
οὐκ ἀπαναίνομαι, αὐτὸν ἔχουσ' ἐν τῆι διανοίαι.

(Vv.1–10)

We both took the decision; we were joined. Kypris is the surety of our love. Pain grips me when I recall how he kissed me while he plotted to abandon me, the inventor of inconstancy, he who laid the basis of my love. Desire took hold of me: I cannot deny it; all my thoughts are of him!

ἐὰν δ' ἐνὶ προσκάθει μόνον ἄφρων ἔσει.
ὁ γὰρ μονιὸς ἔρως μαίνεσθαι ποιεῖ.
γίνωσκ' ὅτι θυμὸν ἀνίκητον ἔχω
ὅταν ἔρις λάβηι με· μαίνομ' ὅταν ἀναμνήσωμ'
εἰ μονοκοιτήσω,
σὺ δὲ χρωτίζεσθ' ἀποτρέχεις.   (Vv. 31–6)

Devotion to one person brings madness; solitary love makes you crazy. Know that my spirit is unconquerable when it comes to a fight! I go crazy when I think that I shall sleep alone, but you will run off to someone's bed!

When we place this text beside Idylls 2 and 3, several broad differences are immediately striking. Whereas Theocritus composes in hexameters, the *Fragmentum* consists of a series of lyric lengths, largely dochmiacs and anapaests, usually marked off by word-division and/or phrasing; the closest analogues to this rhythmical technique are to be found in the monodies of the later plays of Euripides, and it is indeed reasonable to assume that this technique has reached the *Fragmentum* through living performance traditions, whereas both the metre and the prosody[32] of Theocritus' Idylls suggest rather the centrality of the written text. Whereas, however, Theocritus' Doric, whatever its precise nature,[33] seems to be an artificial, mimetic construct, the language of the *Fragmentum* makes no concessions to the dialect colouring which would traditionally accompany the rhythms in which it is composed; here too it is tempting to see the difference between a work composed in the light of a historical sensibility and one designed purely with performative success in mind. A similar conclusion may be drawn from a comparison of the vocabulary of the two poets. The language of the *Fragmentum* is marked by a striking

---

[32] In the *Fragmentum* mute plus liquid does not make position, whereas position is much more common than 'Attic correption' in Idylls 2 and 3; for the Theocritean situation in general cf. below p. 30. Particularly telling is the prosodic difference between Κύπρις in 2.130–1 and in the *Fragmentum* (vv. 12, 19 Cunningham).   [33] Cf. below pp. 28–45.

number of words and usages familiar from Hellenistic prose, but not found elsewhere in poetry;[34] its language is thus far closer to that of contemporary speech than is the language of Theocritus. The vernacular is, of course, an important element in the poetic language of Callimachus and Theocritus,[35] but the sheer concentration of such usages in the *Fragmentum* produces an effect far removed from Theocritus' poetic texture; in Wilamowitz's words, 'the metrical form [of the *Fragmentum*] is some two hundred years older than the language'.[36] Whereas the *Fragmentum* offers a powerful evocation of one moment, Idyll 2 ranges over a complex narrative in which scene and time change; characters enter, speak, and leave, and the tapestry of the poem is incomparably richer than is that of the *Fragmentum*. Idyll 3 also includes a 'song' on allusive mythological subjects (vv. 40–51) which finds no parallel in the 'popular' text. No ploy is commoner for the locked-out lovers of Greek epigram and Roman elegy than to appeal to divine or legendary parallels to their situation; of this the *Fragmentum* offers no trace. Moreover, although both Idyll 2 and the *Fragmentum* are, in their different ways, heirs to the tragic tradition of vengeful heroines (especially Medea) and the *pathos* of the *Fragmentum* seems particularly indebted to late Euripides, Idyll 2 deliberately echoes and exploits *specific* passages of (among others) Homer, Sappho, and probably Sophron in a self-conscious 'literary' way which finds no real parallel in the *Fragmentum*.[37] Idyll 2 is actively engaged with its own literary history; the *Fragmentum* is concerned only with the considerable power of its immediate performance.

There can, of course, be no question of turning this comparison into a set of generalisations broadly applicable to the élite poetry of the third century; and yet many of the features of the Theocritean text which are thrown into relief by the *Fragmentum* do in fact recur time and again in the high poetry of the period. No aspect of the poetry of third-century Alexandria has been more discussed than its 'literariness', that is the reworking of specific archaic and classical textual models in such a way as to lay that reworking open to view; it is in fact this

---

[34] Cf. Wilamowitz 1896.220–1.
[35] For Theocritus cf., e.g., Fabiano 1971. For Callimachus Bulloch's commentary on *h.* 5 is particularly important, and cf. also Parsons 1992.16–19.   [36] Wilamowitz 1896.222.
[37] This is not, of course, to deny that, for example, the appeal to the stars and Night (*FG* 11) has many parallels in, say, the epigrams of Asclepiades, or that the equivocation between the fire of love and the burning torches carried by the night wanderer (*FG* 15–16) similarly recurs in 'high' poetry, but it is the evocation of specific prior texts which is in question here, and there can, I think, be little doubt that our two texts operate at very different levels in this regard.

aspect of 'Hellenistic poetry' which has contributed most to the common view of it as an intellectual exercise divorced from any meaningful social or ideological context.[38] Theocritean poems can, of course, be as 'literary' as any that have survived. Idyll 24, for example, begins with a parade of different 'literary genres' which advertises and celebrates the multifaceted heroism of Heracles:

Ἡρακλέα δεκάμηνον ἐόντα ποχ᾽ ἁ Μιδεᾶτις
Ἀλκμήνα καὶ νυκτὶ νεώτερον Ἰφικλῆα,
ἀμφοτέρους λούσασα καὶ ἐμπλήσασα γάλακτος,
χαλκείαν κατέθηκεν ἐς ἀσπίδα, τὰν Πτερελάου
Ἀμφιτρύων καλὸν ὅπλον ἀπεσκύλευσε πεσόντος.
ἁπτομένα δὲ γυνὰ κεφαλᾶς μυθήσατο παίδων·
"εὕδετ᾽, ἐμὰ βρέφεα, γλυκερὸν καὶ ἐγέρσιμον ὕπνον·
εὕδετ᾽, ἐμὰ ψυχά, δύ᾽ ἀδελφεοί, εὔσοα τέκνα·
ὄλβιοι εὐνάζοισθε καὶ ὄλβιοι ἀῶ ἵκοισθε." (24.1–9)

One night when Heracles was ten months old, Alcmena, the lady of Midea, bathed him and his brother Iphicles, who was younger by one night, gave them their fill of milk, and laid them to rest in the bronze shield, that fair piece of armour of which Amphitryon had spoiled Pterelaus when he fell. Touching her children's heads, the woman spoke: 'Sleep, my children, sleep sweetly and wake again; sleep in safety, my two souls, twin brothers. Be happy in your beds and happily reach the dawn.'

The poem begins in proper hymnal fashion with the hero's name, like the 'Homeric Hymn' in his honour:[39]

Ἡρακλέα Διὸς υἱὸν ἀείσομαι, ὃν μέγ᾽ ἄριστον
γείνατ᾽ ἐπιχθονίων Θήβῃς ἔνι καλλιχόροισιν
Ἀλκμήνη μιχθεῖσα κελαινεφέι Κρονίωνι·
(*Homeric Hymn* 15.1–3)

Heracles I shall sing, the son of Zeus, by far the greatest of mortals, whom Alcmene bore in Thebes of the beautiful dances after she had slept with the son of Kronos of the dark clouds.

The hymnal opening of Idyll 24 is followed by the 'homely' touch of v. 3, over which hovers the gluttonous Heracles of comedy: how could a mortal woman 'fill' Heracles with milk? For many critics, Idyll 24 corrects the image of the gluttonous Heracles by turning him into a refined Hellenistic princeling; there is some truth in this, but we

[38] For a brief discussion of this subject cf. Hunter 1993.1–7.
[39] The date of the hymn is uncertain, but there is no compelling reason to think it post-classical.

cannot ignore the later verses which actually direct our attention to the traditional character of the hero (vv. 137–8) and both invite and resist an integration of the traditional and modern representations. Instructively similar is the picture in Idyll 17 of the tipsy Heracles on Olympus, 'having had his fill (κεκορημένος) of fragrant nectar', being escorted to Hebe's bed by Alexander and Ptolemy Soter, not so much the drunken komast as ever the young bridegroom,[40] for on Olympus every night reproduces the pattern of 'the first time'. That Idyll 24, no less than Idyll 17, has a Ptolemaic context is coming to be increasingly appreciated,[41] and in both poems encomium of Heracles is able to encompass the 'comic' side of traditional representations.[42] After comedy, the story of Amphitryon and Pterelaos (vv. 4–5) takes us into the world of epic, but it is a world quickly turned on its head by the lullaby which Alcmena sings, which in turn is revealed as part of a virtuoso reworking of a famous poem of Simonides.[43] When the narrative of the snake-attack begins, the literary texture, if anything, thickens. The confusion in Amphitryon's house has important debts to the events of *Odyssey* 19 and 20[44] and, particularly, to the *Homeric Hymn to Demeter*, an archaic text which is echoed time and again in third-century poetry and provided the obvious model for such extraordinary nocturnal events.[45] Like Heracles, the young Demophoon is a 'late-born' (ὀψίγονος) child (*h. Dem.* 165) and the events in Keleus' house are marked by the eerie light of divine epiphany and a mother's terror (*h. Dem.* 246–9). The whole narrative, however, is a specific reworking of Pindar's version of these events: Pindar told the story at least twice, in Nemean 1 and Paean 20 (= *POxy.* 1792; 2442, fr. 32),[46] testimony to the extraordinarily powerful influence which

---

[40] This, I suspect, is the point of γενειήταν, 'bearded', in v. 33: the divine Heracles is of an age to marry. [41] Cf. below p. 27.

[42] Cf. Hunter 1993.26. F. Griffiths 1979.91 comments, 'in Idyll 17 we find only the abstemious family man devoting himself to wife and progeny'. It is the 'only' which reveals this as a serious under-reading. [43] Cf. below p. 27. [44] Cf. Gow on vv. 38 and 51.

[45] Some of the parallels are noted in Heather White's commentary (p. 40), and cf. Gutzwiller 1981.16, but they are largely ignored by Gow and Dover. Particularly suggestive are: (i) the rôle of Demophoon, τηλύγετος . . . ὀψίγονος τρέφεται (*h. Dem.* 164–5, 219, cf. Theocr. 24.31); (ii) Metaneira's shrieking in fear for her child (*h. Dem.* 245); (iii) her daughters leap from their beds and busy themselves with the child and with lighting the fire etc. (*h. Dem.* 285–91, cf. Theocr. 24.48–53.). I have wondered whether *h. Dem.* 289–91 – Demophoon is inconsolable because 'worse cares and nurses now held him' – support punctuation after γαλαθηνόν in 24.31: *Heracles* never wept when his nurse held him! For this unorthodox punctuation (though on different grounds) cf. White *ad loc.* White well compares 1.28 (the cup) ἀμφῶες, νεοτευχές, ἔτι γλυφάνοιο ποτόσδον.

[46] Lobel (*Oxyrrhynchus Papyri* xxvi, p. 51) observes that it cannot be entirely certain that these fragments are from a 'paean'; could they possibly be from a *hymnos*?

the protean figure of Heracles and his particular modes of heroism had upon Greek aristocratic ideology. The correspondences between Pindar and Theocritus are many and detailed,[47] as also are the clear cases of deliberate *uariatio*. Thus, for example, whereas the Pindaric Alcmena leaps from her bed ἄπεπλος 'without her robe' (*Nem.* 1.50, *Paeans* 20.14), in Theocritus she tells her husband not to bother getting his sandals on;[48] in Theocritus it is the snakes whose eyes blaze (vv. 18–19), in Pindar it is the baby Heracles (*Paeans* 20.13); whereas the Pindaric Heracles throws off his covers and 'reveals his nature' (*Paeans* 20.11–12), in Theocritus Iphicles 'kicked off his woolly blanket in his desire to flee' (vv. 25–6), thereby also (we are to understand) 'revealing his nature'. As in Nemean 1, at least, the extraordinary night is followed by the summoning of Teiresias, who prophesies Heracles' future greatness. Here, then, many texts and many genres are used to express the many-sidedness of Heracles.

It is understandably difficult for many modern readers to conceive how such a dazzling literary texture could function other than solely for the delectation of a learned élite surrounded by the resources of an excellent library. That such an élite formed part, at least, of the poem's audience there is no reason to doubt, particularly as it is clear that the poem has strong links with the Ptolemaic court.[49] Nevertheless, it would be rash to assume that this hymn was intended solely for private study in libraries.[50] Any doubt about the poem's hymnic qualities, generically signalled by its opening and the debt to the *Homeric Hymn to Demeter*, were removed when the publication of the Antinoe papyrus revealed that some thirty verses were missing at the end of the manuscripts and that these verses apparently contained an appeal to the divine Heracles to grant victory to the poet. We cannot, of course, simply infer, as Gow does, that 'the poem itself was written for a competition',[51] because this prayer to the god might be a literary imitation of 'genuine' prayers. Nevertheless, it would be even more rash to assume that the poem was simply an almost context-less 'literary exercise'. Rather, we must seek to understand the social and literary setting which gave rise to such surprising texts.

---

[47] Cf. Gow's notes *passim*; Dover pp. 251–2.
[48] Gutzwiller 1981.17 well observes: 'Alcmene knows the customary dressing procedure of Homeric heroes and fears that her husband will waste too much time following this routine.'
[49] Cf. below p. 27.   [50] Cairns 1992 offers some important general considerations.
[51] Gow on vv. 141ff.

THE POETIC CONTEXT

Theocritus, like many major ancient poets, has concealed his life from us quite successfully. Idylls 15 and 17 must be dated to the period of Arsinoe II's marriage to Ptolemy Philadelphus (probably 278–268 BC), and Idyll 16 can plausibly, though not certainly, be dated to the middle of that decade.[52] The poems which give clear indications of geographical locations are set in three distinct areas – the Greek west, Ptolemaic Alexandria, and Cos – and it is a reasonable deduction from 11.7 and 28.16 that Theocritus came from Syracuse (or at least Sicily), and this was in fact the almost unanimous opinion in antiquity.[53] Outside the poems themselves we get little biographical help for, as Gow observes, 'beyond the name of the poet's parents, the external authorities make . . . no statement which cannot be a deduction from the poems' (1 xxvii). Strong arguments can be put forward for believing that Idylls 13 and 22 presuppose the existence of Books 1 and 2 of Apollonius' *Argonautica*,[54] and that Idylls 17 and 22 presuppose the *Phainomena* of Aratus (which is usually dated c. 275–260).[55] The literary importance of these arguments is, however, not matched by any great chronological precision that they may bring. Nevertheless, it is clearly to the poets of the later fourth and early third centuries that we must look to place Theocritus within his literary world.

Three poets – Erinna, Philitas, and Asclepiades – deserve particular attention as possible forerunners of Theocritean poetic style, although our knowledge of the poetry of two of them is lamentably scanty.

Almost everything about Erinna is disputed – her date (not improbably mid- to late fourth century), her home (perhaps the tiny island of Telos near Rhodes, but other islands have their claims too), even her gender.[56] She is said to have died as a nineteen-year-old *parthenos*, but this may well be an inference from her best-known poem, the *Distaff* (*SH* 401–2), a lament for her friend Baucis who died

---

[52] Cf. below p. 82–7.

[53] The *Suda* observes that some people regarded him as a Coan, which is presumably an inference from Idyll 7; the truth of the inference is defended by Paton in W. R. Paton and E. L. Hicks, *The Inscriptions of Cos* (Oxford 1891) 355–60. It is a curious coincidence that one untrustworthy ancient tradition also made Epicharmus a Coan by descent, cf. Kaibel, *RE* 6.40–1. I have argued below (pp. 118–19) that Idyll 15 also strongly suggests that the poet presents himself as a Syracusan.   [54] Cf. below pp. 59–63.   [55] Cf. below pp. 55–6.

[56] M. L. West, 'Erinna', *ZPE* 25 (1977) 95–119, suggested that the *Distaff* was 'a brilliant pseudepigraphon' by a male poet; the idea is not silly, but there is little positive evidence for it. In particular, the absence of surviving ancient gossip to this effect (*contrast*, e.g., the case of 'Philainis') seems to tell against West.

(aged nineteen?) shortly after her marriage.[57] What is clear, however, is that this poem was much admired in the third century, and admired in terms which recall the aesthetics of the Alexandrian avant-garde. Asclepiades composed an inscription for the work which purports to be Erinna's own words (hence the Doric colouring):

ὁ γλυκὺς Ἠρίννας οὗτος πόνος, οὐχὶ πολὺς μέν
ὡς ἂν παρθενικᾶς ἐννεακαιδεκέτευς
ἀλλ᾽ ἑτέρων πολλῶν δυνατώτερος· εἰ δ᾽ Ἀΐδας μοι
μὴ ταχὺς ἦλθε τίς ἂν ταλίκον ἔσχ᾽ ὄνομα;
(*Anth. Pal.* 7.11 = Asclepiades xxviii G–P)

> This is the sweet labour of Erinna; there is not much of it, as you would expect from a nineteen-year-old girl, but its power[58] exceeds that of many others. Had not Death come early to me, who would have had such a name?

Smallness, sweetness, and effort, *ponos*, here chosen to allow an equivocation between wool-working, women's work *par excellence*, and literary 'labour',[59] all tell a clear story. It is a great pity that we do not know more of this poem.

The Distaff seems to have been a poem in 300 hexameters in which Erinna lamented the death of her friend and recalled the happy times they enjoyed together as children; it is an easy assumption that the poem made considerable use of the familiar *topoi* of 'death as a marriage with Hades' and 'marriage as death', because Baucis seems to have died either soon after her wedding or, if the rhetoric of the epitaphs for Baucis ascribed (probably wrongly) to Erinna is taken literally (*Anth. Pal.* 7.710, 712 = Erinna i–ii G–P), on the very day of her wedding.[60] A substantial, though cruelly torn, fragment of this poem survives on a papyrus of the second century AD (*SH* 401). The

---

[57] Thus, for example, it is clear that *Anth. Pal.* 7.13 (= Leonidas xcviii G–P) on the death of Erinna uses Erinna's own description of the death of Baucis, cf. D. N. Levin, *HSCP* 66 (1962) 197–8.

[58] The exact sense of δυνατώτερος is hard to catch; Gow–Page suggest 'more influential'. Perhaps 'with greater power [to move]'?

[59] It is true that Callimachus uses this word to describe the epic *Capture of Oichalia* (*Epigr.* 6 = lv G–P), or at least allows the poem to describe itself thus, and the tone there may not be free of irony; nevertheless, Asclepiades' epigram fits well with passages such as Theocr. 7.51.

[60] Cf. T. Szepessy, 'The story of the girl who died on the day of her wedding' *AAntHung* 20 (1972) 341–57; M. Alexiou and P. Dronke, 'The lament of Jephtha's daughter: themes, traditions, originality', *Studi Medievali* 12.2 (1971) 819–63. For 'laments' for the bride as she leaves her parents' house cf. M. Alexiou, *The Ritual Lament in Greek Tradition* (Cambridge 1974) 120–2. A very difficult fragment of Pindar's *Threnoi* (fr. 128c S–M) seems to identify a particular kind of lament with Hymenaios who died 'in the act of first love-making', cf. M. Cannatà Fera, 'Peani, ditirambi, treni in Pind. fr. 128c S–M', *GIF* 11 (1980) 181–8; did Erinna use this conceit somewhere in her poem?

dialect of the poem, which was thought worthy of comment even in antiquity, is in essence the Doric of the lyric tradition with a substantial Aeolic element.[61] The latter has generally been seen as deliberate acknowledgement that the poem is to be read within the tradition of Sappho, famous throughout antiquity as the poet of female friendship and the wedding-song; whereas Sappho made extensive use of the hexameter in her wedding-songs, Erinna produces a bitter variation in the same metre for what is a rather different kind of 'farewell'.[62] The Doric in which the poem is written presents a more complex problem. It has been seen as simply the 'natural' language in which this Dorian poet would write,[63] and we can hardly doubt that there was considerably more Doric hexameter poetry written in the fourth century than survives today. On the other hand, the probably rather later case of Theocritus means that we should not exclude the possibility that Erinna's Doric was intended to evoke the traditional language of lyric in which laments (*threnoi*) were written by some of the greatest poets of the archaic period (notably Simonides and Pindar). Erinna's obvious familiarity with, and evocation of, not only Sappho but also the laments of the *Iliad*[64] mean that we can hardly rule out any form of 'literary sophistication' on *a priori* grounds. The choice of the hexameter may be in part because of Sappho (cf. above), in part because of the broad literary developments which have been traced in the preceding pages, or in part because Erinna sets up her emotional suffering as being on a par with the 'epic' suffering of men, and hence must use the weight of the hexameter to give vent to her grief. Whatever the truth, the combination of subject, dialect, metre, and overall length strikes us as an extraordinary forerunner of some of the most familiar features of Alexandrian poetry.

Soon after the publication of the papyrus it was realised that the surviving section of *The Distaff* is loosely structured into sections by recurring laments which function as a quasi-refrain, without however reaching the formal identity of the refrains in Idyll 1 and the Laments of Bion and 'Moschus'; this feature, together with a certain similarity

---

[61] Cf. especially Latte 1968.510–11.

[62] Cf. M. B. Arthur, 'The tortoise and the mirror: Erinna *PSI* 1090', *CW* 74 (1980) 53–65, p. 65; for Sappho and Erinna in general cf. also J. Rauk, 'Erinna's *Distaff* and Sappho fr. 94', *GRBS* 30 (1989) 101–16.

[63] Or, in West's terms (above, n. 56): 'The Doric element is meant to convey that she is an ordinary person, a homely little Telian maid.' The terms of the problem are well put by U. W. Scholz, *A&A* 18 (1973) 33.

[64] Cf., e.g., M. B. Skinner, 'Briseis, the Trojan Women, and Erinna', *CW* 75 (1982) 265–9.

of 'feel' to parts of the Theocritean corpus, established Erinna as an important element in the immediate poetic context out of which Theocritus developed.[65] At the very least, the torn scraps of *PSI* 1090 serve as a reminder that in the latter part of the fourth century the islands of the south-east Aegean and the adjacent coast saw a flourishing literary culture with which Theocritus could have come into close contact if, as seems all but certain, some of his productive life was spent on Cos.

It is indeed from Cos that one of the two other poets to be considered here, Philitas, seems to have come. Like Callimachus and Apollonius after him, Philitas was both a scholar and a poet. His scholarship was concerned largely with explications of Homer and the collection of rare poetical and dialectal forms (*glossai*);[66] Zenodotus, the first Librarian of the Royal Library at Alexandria and the foremost Homeric critic of his day, is said to have been Philitas' pupil. Like Zenodotus after him, Philitas is said to have acted as tutor to the future Ptolemy Philadelphus, who was born on Cos in 308.[67] His influence has been detected all over the poetry of Callimachus,

---

[65] Cf., e.g., Latte 1968.523; C. M. Bowra, 'Erinna's *Lament for Baucis*' in *Greek Poetry and Life* (Oxford 1936) 325–42; Gallavotti 1952.28–34.

[66] Cf. Pfeiffer 1968.88–93; Fantuzzi 1993b.145–7.

[67] For a survey of the chronological uncertainties here cf. Nickau, *RE* 10A.25–6; for the nature and terminology of such 'tutorships' cf. E. Eichgrün, *Kallimachos und Apollonios Rhodios* (diss. Berlin 1961) 183–93. There is, I think, a fair chance that the description of Linus, μελεδωνεύς ἄγρυπνος ἥρως, teaching the young Heracles 'letters' at 24.105–6 glances at Philitas' education of the young Ptolemy. For the general idea cf. F. Griffiths 1979.92 '[the catalogue] may be a masquerade of the courtiers themselves, for here Theocritus writes about the tutorial positions occupied by people like himself'; Thomas 1995. Any teacher of Heracles, particularly Linus, could not afford to nod off, but Callimachus famously praises Aratus' ἀγρυπνία, and Aratus was, like Philitas, both a scholar and a poet; the Aratean *Lives* synchronise Aratus with Philitas, which may go back to an alleged link between them. The idea that Philitas was the originator of the aesthetic ideal of λεπτότης has often been suggested (and is not put to rest by A. Cameron, *CQ* 41 (1991) 534–8). More importantly, however, Philitas was popularly believed to have worked himself to death; his 'epitaph' (Ath. 9 401d-e = *FGE* pp. 442–3) names one of the causes of death as νυκτῶν φροντίδες ἑσπέριοι. Philitas, then, is the watchful 'hero' from a previous generation who observes the deeds of his successors (cf. Ar. fr. *322 K–A). μελεδωνεύς, 'attendant', could also suggest 'someone who takes pains', i.e. 'learned', and μελεδωνός seems to have this sense on a late Hellenistic inscription from Klaros (*BCH* 10 (1886) 514–15) which honours one Gorgos as ὁ πάσης πολύβυβλος ἀφ' ἱστορίης μελεδωνός: a local Philitas? D. O. Ross, *Backgrounds to Augustan Poetry: Gallus, Elegy and Rome* (Cambridge 1975) 22 suggests that μελεδωνεύς may contain a pun on μέλος. At another level, Linus is chosen as the 'inventor' of the Greek alphabet (γράμματα), cf. Diod. Sic. 3.67.1, Zenobius 4.45 (*CPG* 1 p. 97), just as Eurytos 'the good drawer (of bows)', Eumolpos 'the good singer' and Harpalykos 'snatcher' all have names which suggest originating masters of their respective arts. For what it is worth, the *Suda* describes Philitas as γραμματικός <καὶ> κριτικός (Kuchenmüller 1928.36 defends the transmitted text).

Theocritus, and Apollonius, and his poetry is certainly praised by
Callimachus in the *Reply to the Telchines*; that Callimachus and
Apollonius, at least, made some use of his glossographical researches,
there is no reason to doubt.[68]

Philitas' two major poetic works[69] seem to have been the hexameter
Hermes, which (if a marginal scholion in Parthenius is to be believed)[70]
told the story of Odysseus' affair with one of Aeolus' daughters who
was eventually saved from her father's wrath only because one of her
brothers wished to marry her, and the elegiac *Demeter*, which seems to
have told the story of the goddess's grief and wandering. Both poems,
therefore, reflect the same developments which we have already
traced: the predominance of the hexameter and the elegiac couplet,
the engagement with and rewriting of archaic texts (the *Odyssey* and
the *Hymn to Demeter*), a fashion for narrative poetry which was shorter
in length and more concentrated in scope than the 'traditional epic'.
It has often been observed that the plot of the *Hermes*, with its interest
in love and incest, looks forward to many of the 'epyllia' of the later
Hellenistic and Roman periods. Philitas also wrote epigrams and may
have published a collection of *Paignia*. According to Hermesianax in
his catalogue of poetic lovers, the citizens of Cos erected 'under a
plane-tree' a statue of Philitas 'singing of his Battis [or 'Bittis']' (fr.
7.75–8 Powell) and, if any genuine biographical information can be
drawn from this source, this creates a presumption that Philitas wrote
first-person poetry on erotic subjects;[71] to go further, however, would
be as dangerous as to infer from much fuller information that
Theocritus 'was in love with' Amaryllis (cf. Idyll 3). Whether or not
Philitas wrote 'bucolic' poetry has been endlessly discussed, and will
concern us presently. There is little sign in the very scanty fragments
of any dialectal colouring out of keeping with what is regular in these
metres,[72] although his poetry was clearly full of rare vocabulary.
There is also no sign of metres other than hexameters and elegiacs,

---

[68] Cf., e.g., *SH* 673, identifying Philitas as the source of the gloss ἄεμμα at Call. *h.* 2.33.

[69] Fragments in *CA* pp. 90–6; Kuchenmüller 1928; *SH* 673–5.

[70] The latest statement of the sceptical case is P. Knox, 'Philetas and Roman poetry', *PLLS* 7 (1993) 61–83.

[71] Cf. also Ovid, *Trist.* 1.6.2. It must, however, be stressed that the Hermesianax passage is no good basis for biographical arguments.

[72] A possible exception is fr. 18 Powell (= 14 Kuchenmüller) which tells of the 'golden apples' of Dionysos and which is cited by the scholiast on Theocr. 2.120. One tradition of the scholia transmits Doric forms, but Kuchenmüller believed this to be the result of the Theocritean context; whatever the truth, it is obviously tempting to associate this fragment with Theocr. 3.40–2.

and the Roman poets treat him and Callimachus as the Greek elegists *par excellence*; it is, however, an easy guess that the *Paignia* included some metrical 'games'.

The third poet who is important in the present context is Asclepiades of Samos,[73] an older contemporary of Theocritus who is included, together with Poseidippos with whom he often disputes the authorship of epigrams in the Anthology, in the Florentine list of the Telchines, i.e. Callimachus' (real or alleged) opponents; the reason for this may simply be that Asclepiades and Callimachus were known to have expressed apparently divergent views about the merits of the *Lyde* of Antimachus of Colophon, an elegiac catalogue poem of the early fourth century which became a touchstone of taste in Alexandrian literary discussion.[74] Asclepiades' preserved poetic output consists almost entirely of witty and elegant epigrams, largely on erotic themes, which were clearly an important formative influence on the direction subsequently taken by the epigrammatic tradition. They are largely written in the traditional language of Ionian elegy (Samos was an Ionian island), but the epigram on Erinna (cf. above) does not seem to be a unique case of Doric colouring.[75] Such variety was the hallmark of his production, for he also wrote in lyric, and later metricians gave his name to a choriambic verse used by Sappho and Alcaeus and by Theocritus in Idylls 28 and 30. There is in fact a strong circumstantial case for believing that he wrote Aeolic poetry of the kind familiar from Theocritus, and he would therefore be an important model for those poems of Theocritus.[76] There are also signs of hexameter poems (*SH* 218–19), and of choliambs (*SH* 216–17), a metre which was used by Theocritus (Epigram XIX) to celebrate Hipponax, the most famous archaic choliambist, and which enjoyed considerable popularity in the late fourth and early third centuries.[77]

---

[73] For the biographical information etc. cf. Fraser 1972.1 557–61; *HE* II pp. 114–18.

[74] Cf. Call. fr. 398 with Pfeiffer's commentary; P. Knox, *HSCP* 89 (1985) 112–16; N. Krevans, 'Fighting against Antimachus: the *Lyde* and the *Aetia* reconsidered' in Harder–Regtuit–Wakker 1993.149–60. Whereas Callimachus seems to parody Asclepiades in fr. 398, Call. *h.* 5.2 seems to be parodied in an epigram ascribed to either Asclepiades or Poseidippos (*Anth. Pal.* 5.202 = Asclepiades XXXV G–P); it might be tempting to reverse this chronology after the pattern of the *inuitus regina / inuita o regina* paradigm, but for the case which is well stated by A. Cameron, *GRBS* 31 (1990) 298–9: 'In Callimachus the ἄρτι serves a precise and important function . . . in 5.202.4 [it] is entirely otiose . . . The effect of the line derives entirely from its transference *as a whole* from a solemn, hymnic context to a crude, erotic context'. It is, even so, difficult to make much of this in terms of any literary 'dispute'.

[75] Cf. *Anth. Pal.* 7.145 = XXIX G–P (discussed by Wilamowitz 1924.II 117), and *Anth. Plan.* 68 = XXXIX G–P (if indeed that couplet is by Asclepiades).   [76] Cf. below p. 173.

[77] For a survey cf. G. A. Gerhard, *Phoinix von Kolophon* (Leipzig/Berlin 1909) 202–27.

The picture which emerges from the mists of our evidence is in fact of a poet whose range and interests prefigure those of Theocritus in important ways. Concentration upon Theocritus' 'bucolic' poems has tended to obscure the fact that the range and variety of his poems are very characteristic of the poetic milieu of the period; more recent work, however, on the origins of the Theocritean corpus seems likely to redress the balance.[78]

In Idyll 7, which is set on Cos, the narrator, Simichidas, proposes 'bucolic song'[79] to the mysterious goatherd Lycidas:

ἀλλ' ἄγε δή, ξυνὰ γὰρ ὁδὸς ξυνὰ δὲ καὶ ἀώς,
βουκολιασδώμεσθα· τάχ' ὥτερος ἄλλον ὀνασεῖ.
καὶ γὰρ ἐγὼ Μοισᾶν καπυρὸν στόμα, κἠμὲ λέγοντι
πάντες ἀοιδὸν ἄριστον· ἐγὼ δέ τις οὐ ταχυπειθής,
οὐ Δᾶν· οὐ γάρ πω κατ' ἐμὸν νόον οὔτε τὸν ἐσθλόν
Σικελίδαν νίκημι τὸν ἐκ Σάμω οὔτε Φιλίταν
ἀείδων, βάτραχος δὲ ποτ' ἀκρίδας ὥς τις ἐρίσδω.

(7.35-41)

But come; the journey and the day are ours to share. Let us join in bucolic song, and perhaps each of us will benefit the other. For[80] I am a clear mouthpiece of the Muses, and all say that I am the best of singers; but by Zeus I am not quick to believe them. In my own opinion my poetry does not yet surpass that of Sicelidas from Samos or Philitas, but I compete with them as a frog against grasshoppers.

Sicelidas we know to be another name for Asclepiades (presumably one that he used himself), and so the most 'neutral' reading of this famous passage would simply be that Simichidas names Asclepiades and Philitas as two famous poets of the present or recent past. It is, however, in the nature of Idyll 7 that no simple reading is likely to satisfy; moreover, Simichdas' closing 'so I spoke designedly (ἐπίταδες)' and the goatherd's smiling answer (v. 42) strongly suggest that these verses demand a complex response. Interpretations of this reference to these poets cover the full range from seeing here a clear acknowledgement by Simichidas/Theocritus that Asclepiades and Philitas were his principal 'bucolic' models[81] to a symptom of Simichidas' amusing gaucherie, for only an *ingénu* could pair two

---

[78] Cf. the contributions of K. Gutzwiller and A. Griffiths to Harder Regtuit Wakker 1995.

[79] My translation is not intended to imply any particular meaning for βουκολιάζεσθαι in this passage; the matter is, of course, hotly disputed.　　[80] Cf. below p. 22

[81] Cf., e.g. Puelma 1960.158. Puelma rightly notes that v. 41 expresses Simichidas' rivalry with them in terms of the 'bucolic agon'.

poets whose aesthetic views were so completely opposed.[82] If this latter view seems greatly to exaggerate the importance of our evidence for any 'dispute' between Asclepiades and the Alexandrian 'Philitans' (principally Callimachus), the former seems to restrict unnecessarily the range of poetry alluded to. A full discussion of the problems of this vexed poem cannot be attempted here, but some clarification of the rôle of Asclepiades and Philitas may be possible.

That the figure of Lycidas has some connection with Philitas is an old suggestion, and in an important discussion Ewen Bowie[83] has argued that the goatherd is in fact a character from Philitan 'bucolic'; Simichidas is similarly a character from Theocritean 'bucolic', but also in some sense represents the poet and is thus part of an elaborate compliment by Theocritus to the older Coan poet. Bowie is certainly right to insist that, of itself, there is nothing improbable in the idea of Philitan 'bucolic', and if he is correct then it is likely that the song Lycidas sings will be full of Philitan echoes.[84] Be that as it may, some speculative refinement may be possible by considering the sequence of what Simichidas actually says.

Simichidas praises Lycidas as, by popular repute, 'the best syrinx-player among the herdsmen and reapers', a fact which 'warms his heart', although he believes himself to be Lycidas' equal (presumably in playing the syrinx). After proposing bucolic song (vv. 35–6, quoted above), he describes himself as a 'clear mouthpiece of the Muses' who is popularly rated as the best singer (ἀοιδός), although in his view he is not yet the equal of Asclepiades or Philitas.[85] The traditional interpretation of these verses must explain that Simichidas' point is that Lycidas' alleged pre-eminence in the countryside is matched by his own alleged pre-eminence in the city (from which he is coming). The mannered parallelisms and contrasts in phrasing between vv. 27–30 and 37–40 may, however, encourage the notion that some distinction is being drawn between being a 'syrinx-player' and being a 'singer'. Although the two ideas are, of course, closely linked (cf. 11.38–9) and both Lycidas and Simichidas will presently be singing,

---

[82] Cf., e.g., B. Effe, 'Das poetologische Programm des Simichidas: Theokrit, Id. 7, 37–41', *WJA* 14 (1988) 87–91. For humour at Simichidas' expense in general cf. G. Giangrande, 'Théocrite, Simichidas et les *Thalysies*', *AC* 37 (1968) 491–533 (= *Scripta Minora Alexandrina* I 119–61).   [83] Bowie 1985.   [84] Cf. further below p. 27.
[85] My view of the problems in these verses is closest to that of Serrao 1971.22–5. Hutchinson too (1988.206–7) rightly draws attention to the difficulties in the sequence of thought here; his own solution is that 'the poet creates a fissure which displays his conjunction of a historical level with an imaginary'.

this contrast is familiar from Idyll 1, in which the nameless goatherd is a 'syrinx-player' and Thyrsis a 'singer'.[86] καὶ γὰρ ἐγώ in v. 37 may therefore mean, not 'for I too [as well as you]', but rather 'for indeed I'.[87] If this idea is along the right lines,[88] then Lycidas is praised as a 'syrinx-player' because (on Bowie's reading) he is a 'bucolic' character, whereas Simichidas both plays the syrinx – for he too is a bucolic creation (of Theocritus) – and 'sings', like Tityros (v. 72) and Komatas (vv. 88–9), as being a poet (another Hesiod in fact, cf. v. 92). He proposes 'bucolic song' (whatever the precise meaning of the term) because of the rustic setting in which he finds himself (vv. 31–4) and because of Lycidas' presence, but in fact the range of his poetry is wide, as the references to Philitas and Asclepiades and the nature of the song he subsequently sings demonstrate. When he claims that the fame of his songs has perhaps 'reached the throne of Zeus [i.e. Phil-adelphus]' (v. 93), we may be tempted to see not merely an allusion to a (real or hoped-for) patron, but also an echo of Theocritus' own encomiastic verse (cf. 17.131–4); in other words, the poem stresses the width of Simichidas' repertoire, not its narrowly focused 'rusticity'. In such a poem, the picture of Philitas and Asclepiades which we have traced fits very comfortably.

Perhaps the only thing about Idyll 7 upon which most critics agree is that it is 'programmatic' in the broad sense that it both displays and reflects upon important aspects of Theocritus' poetic art as we find it in the rest of the corpus.[89] In the context of this book, one feature of this poem deserves particular note. This is the extraordinary richness of its literary texture, a texture which is woven out of the full range of

---

[86] The author of Idyll 8 seems to draw some distinction between the two activities (cf. v. 4), and I wonder whether Theocritus would have written v. 34 in which 'the syrinx-player sings'. The implications of 4.29–32 are ambiguous.

[87] For the former cf. 28.17, for the latter 5.134, 6.29, probably *Epigr.* IX.3, and Denniston 1954.108–9. In support of the traditional interpretation, Segal 1981.132 adduces the parallelism between v. 37 and v. 92, 'the Nymphs taught me too . . .'

[88] For a quite different interpretation of the difference between συρικτάς and ἀοιδός cf. Puelma 1960.153 n. 28. Gutzwiller 1991.165 addresses the central problem of these verses, but from a quite different angle.

[89] Hutchinson 1988.201–12 comes closest of recent critics to denying even this; he is prepared to concede *almost* (cf. 211 n. 120) nothing to those who see *some kind of* identification between 'Simichidas' and 'Theocritus'.

I am very conscious that I have not read everything which has been written, even in recent years, about Idyll 7, but I hope that the limited scope of my concerns will partially excuse this failing. Some bibliographical assistance can be sought in T. Choitz and J. Latacz, 'Zum gegenwärtigen Stand der "Thalysien"-Deutung (Theokrit, Id. 7)', *WJA* 7 (1981) 85–95 and Krevans 1983. It is this last article which has most stimulated my thinking about Idyll 7; it suffers only from an over-narrow and unexamined concern with the nature of 'pastoral'.

archaic and contemporary poetry. This extraordinary fullness of literary reference, which turns the poem into a kind of echoing chamber of poetic allusion, is matched by the different, interweaving voices which we hear within the poem – Simichidas, Theocritus, Lycidas, Tityrus, Komatas . . . it is as though Theocritus has sought to write literary history in a poetic mode. As such, this difficult poem forms an excellent introduction to the concerns of this book.

There would be little to be gained from cataloguing all the (real or alleged) allusions to earlier poetry which have been uncovered in Idyll 7, but the archaic poets who are most obviously evoked may be listed in rough chronological order.

(i) Homer. The meeting of Simichidas and Lycidas evokes a number of Homeric scenes, but most notably the meeting of Athena and Odysseus in *Odyssey* 13 and that of Odysseus and Eumaios with the rude Melantheus (beside a beautiful spring) in *Odyssey* 17.[90] It is noteworthy that both of these scenes mark important stages on Odysseus' journey (the return to Ithaca, the movement towards the palace itself), just as the narrator's closing prayer to be allowed 'once again to plant the winnowing-shovel upon Demeter's heap' (vv. 155–6) seems to look to Teiresias' prophecy of how Odysseus will finally achieve the end of his wanderings: 'When another traveller falls in with you and takes the thing upon your shoulder to be a winnowing-fan, then plant that balanced oar in the ground and offer to Lord Poseidon the noble sacrifice of a ram and a bull and a boar that mates with sows. Then return home . . .' (*Od.* 11. 127–32, trans. Shewring). Both the *Odyssey* and Idyll 7 portray a journey towards something which is both old and new.

(ii) Hesiod. It has long been recognised that Lycidas' gift of a rustic staff to Simichidas (vv. 43–4, 128–9) replays the Muses' gift of a staff (σκῆπτρον) to Hesiod when they inspired him with song on Helicon (*Theogony* 22–35). Idyll 7 thus joins an impressive list of ancient poems which reworked that Hesiodic scene to present the 'initiation' of a poet or the sources of a poet's song; Callimachus was transported in a dream to Helicon to question the Muses on aetiological matters in the *Aitia*. Lycidas' praise of Simichidas as 'a shoot all fashioned for truth by Zeus' (πᾶν ἐπ' ἀλαθείᾳ πεπλασμένον ἐκ Διὸς ἔρνος), v. 44, has been plausibly connected with the famous declaration of Hesiod's Muses

---

[90] For some discussion cf. U. Ott, 'Theokrits "Thalysien" und ihre literarischen Vorbilder', *RhM* 115 (1972) 134–49; F. Williams, 'Scenes of encounter in Homer and Theocritus', *MPhL* 3 (1978) 219–25; Halperin 1983.224–7.

that they can 'speak many lies which resemble true things and also . . . many things which are real' (*Theog.* 27–8), an utterance which echoes throughout all ancient discussion of the nature of poetry.[91] The spring Bourina (etymologised from βοῦς, 'cow') takes the place of the Hesiodic Ἵππου κρήνη, the 'Spring of the Horse', in which the Muses of Helicon bathe (*Theog.* 6) and which was believed to have been created by a blow from Pegasus' hoof.

(iii) Hipponax and Archilochus. Archaic iambic finds an important place in the song of Simichidas: the description of an Arcadian rite in which Pan is beaten with squills and the threats made against him in vv. 109–14 bear a general resemblance to the harsh world of Hipponax's poetry, but more specifically the 'dismissal' of Philinos seems to rework a passage from the 'Cologne Epode' of Archilochus (*SLG* 478 = Arch. fr. 196a West):[92]

> Νεοβούλη[
> ἄ]λλος ἀνὴρ ἐχέτω·
> αἰαῖ πέπειρα δ. [[93]
>
> ἄν]θος δ' ἀπερρύηκε παρθενήιον
> καὶ χάρις ἣ πρὶν ἐπῆν·
> κόρον γὰρ οὐκ[
>
> ..]ης δὲ μέτρ' ἔφηνε μαινόλις γυνή·
> ἐς] κόρακας ἄπεχε·   (vv. 24–31)

Let some other man have Neoboule; alas, she is all too ripe . . . her maiden's bloom has lost its petals; gone is the charm she once had. She can't get enough . . . a crazy woman. No thanks – let her go to the crows!

> ὦ μάλοισιν Ἔρωτες ἐρευθομένοισιν ὁμοῖοι,
> βάλλετέ μοι τόξοισι τὸν ἱμερόεντα Φιλῖνον,
> βάλλετ', ἐπεὶ τὸν ξεῖνον ὁ δύσμορος οὐκ ἐλεεῖ μευ.
> καὶ δὴ μὰν ἀπίοιο πεπαίτερος, αἱ δὲ γυναῖκες,
> "αἰαῖ", φαντί, "Φιλῖνε, τό τοι καλὸν ἄνθος ἀπορρεῖ."
> μηκέτι τοι φρουρέωμες ἐπὶ προθύροισιν, Ἄρατε,
> μηδὲ πόδας τρίβωμες· ὁ δ' ὄρθριος ἄλλον ἀλέκτωρ
> κοκκύσδων ναρκαῖσιν ἀνιαραῖσι διδοίη·   (7.117–24)

---

[91] Cf., e.g., Serrao 1971.43–52, Goldhill 1991.232–3. Bowie 1985 attractively links this verse to v. 14 as referring to the mimetic verisimilitude of (Philitas' and Theocritus') poetry.

[92] See especially A. Henrichs, 'Riper than a pear: Parian invective in Theokritos', *ZPE* 39 (1980) 7–27. For Hellenistic and earlier interest in Archilochos, whose fame ranked second only to Homer's, cf. S. R. Slings, *ZPE* 79 (1989) 1–8.

[93] West's supplement δὶς τόση, 'twice your age', has been widely accepted here, cf. Hesychius δ 1978.

O Erotes like red apples, shoot with your bows at the lovely Philinos, shoot, since the poor fool has no pity for my friend. Without a doubt[94] he is riper than a pear, and the women say 'Ah, Philinos, your lovely bloom is dropping.'[95] Aratus, let us no longer keep watch at his door and wear our feet out; let the crowing of the dawn cock bring someone else the pain of numbness.

The warning to Philinos, expressed in echoes of poetry which was believed to have caused its objects of ridicule to hang themselves,[96] could hardly be more pointed. As the 'Cologne Epode' ends with a successful seduction 'amidst the blooming flowers' (vv. 42–3), so Idyll 7 ends with a sensual (? and erotic) party 'on deep couches of sweet rushes and amidst the fresh-cut vine-leaves' (vv. 132–4);[97] the similarity may not be accidental. Moreover, the whole frame of an 'initiatory' walk in the countryside may owe something to the legend of Archilochus' initiation which is preserved on a third-century inscription from Paros (*SEG* xv.517).[98] According to this legend, the young Archilochus was despatched by his father to sell a cow and, on his way into town, while the moon was still shining, he met some women who laughed and teased him and left him a lyre in place of the cow; subsequently he realised that these women must have been the Muses. His future fame as a poet was later prophesied to his father at Delphi. If anything, the existence of this legend should warn against an over-narrow interpretation of 'bucolic', for despite this rustic meeting it was not for 'rustic' poetry that Archilochus subsequently became famous. Both Hipponax and Archilochus are celebrated in Theocritus' epigrams (xix and xxi).[99]

---

[94] This is a provisional attempt to translate the difficult καὶ δὴ μάν; textual corruption is not improbable here.

[95] V. 121 perhaps represents the 'ageing' Philinos as the dying Adonis, whose charms will soon do no one any good; cf. the constant repetition of parts of αἰάζειν in Bion's *Lament for Adonis*. The Theocritean verse is like a refrain which 'the women' chant. On the various possible nuances of αἰαῖ cf. Henrichs art. cit. 23–4.

[96] The earliest certain reference to the actual suicide of Lycambes and his daughters appears to be *P. Dublin* inv. 193(a) of the late third century BC (= Test. 10 Tarditi; p. 64 of West's edition), cf. G. W. Bond, *Hermathena* 80 (1952) 1–11; the suicide is not explicit in Dioscorides, *Anth. Pal.* 7.351 (= xvii G–P), but may be thought to be an obvious inference from that poem. For a careful survey of the tradition cf. C. Carey, 'Archilochus and Lycambes', *CQ* 36 (1986) 60–7.   [97] Cf. esp. Bowie 1995 for the erotic interpretation of the end of Idyll 7.

[98] Test. 4 Tarditi. Cf. A. Kambylis, 'Zur "Dichterweihe" des Archilochos', *Hermes* 91 (1963) 129–50. Kambylis stresses that the story cannot derive from Archilochus' own verses, which we would otherwise have expected to be quoted.

[99] That 'the Muses and Delian Apollo' favoured Archilochus (*Epigr.* xxi.4) may simply be a conventional compliment, but we might also think of the rôle of the Muses and of (Pythian) Apollo in the Parian legend of the poet.

(iv) Simonides. Although Lycidas' *propemptikon* for the voyage of his beloved Ageanax to Mytilene most naturally evokes the world of Lesbian poetry, a world which Theocritus re-creates in Idylls 28 and the paederastic 29–30,[100] a recently published papyrus of Simonides' elegiac poems (*POxy.* 3965 = Simonides fr. eleg. 22 West²) strongly suggests that Lycidas' song is heavily indebted to Simonides' paederastic poetry.[101] Lycidas' song thus evokes, *inter alia*, the world of archaic poetry as part of his efforts, seen most clearly in the story of Komatas, to reach back into the past, to bring it forward to the present and make it still part of contemporary experience (vv. 86–9). This indeed is one way of expressing the aim of Theocritus' re-creations of past poetic forms. Elsewhere Theocritus' most extensive evocation of Simonides, both as poet and as legendary figure, seems – as far as our present knowledge of that poet allows us to say – to be in Idyll 16, the poem for Hiero of Syracuse.[102] The famous song of the Simonidean Danae, however, in which she addresses the sleeping baby Perseus as they drift on the open sea (*PMG* 543), seems to be reworked in the lullaby which Alcmena sings in Idyll 24:

> εὗδε βρέφος,
> εὑδέτω δὲ πόντος, εὑδέτω δ' ἄμετρον κακόν·

Sleep, child, may the sea sleep, may my measureless trouble sleep

> ἁπτομένα δὲ γυνὰ κεφαλᾶς μυθήσατο παίδων·
> "εὕδετ', ἐμὰ βρέφεα, γλυκερὸν καὶ ἐγέρσιμον ὕπνον·
> εὕδετ', ἐμὰ ψυχά, δύ' ἀδελφεοί, εὔσοα τέκνα·
> ὄλβιοι εὐνάζοισθε καὶ ὄλβιοι ἀῶ ἵκοισθε."   (24.6–9)

Touching her children's heads, the woman spoke: 'Sleep, my children, sleep sweetly and wake again; sleep in safety, my two souls, twin brothers. Be happy in your beds and happily reach the dawn.'

The similarity would be unremarkable, but for other points of contact between the two poems. Like Heracles, Perseus was the son of Zeus and a mortal woman, and was destined to become a slayer of snaky monsters[103] and to found a dynasty. The 'bronze-bolted' box in which

---

[100] Cf. Krevans 1983.214–15. Bowie 1985 also raises the possibility that Philitas wrote poetry set on Lesbos.

[101] I have discussed this in greater detail in 'One party or two?: Simonides 22 West²', *ZPE* 99 (1993) 11–14. Bowie 1995 adds further possible reflections of Simonides in Idyll 7.

[102] Cf. Chapter 3 below.

[103] For what it is worth, I suspect (though cannot demonstrate) that the description of the snakes in v. 14 evokes descriptions of the sea-monster coming to devour Andromeda; this train of thought may also help with φαγεῖν in v. 16, though other problems still remain there (cf. A. Griffiths 1995). If this is on the right lines, then the impulse may have come from

Danae and Perseus drift is δαιδάλεος, 'elaborately wrought', like the 'beautiful' (v. 5) shield in which Heracles and Iphicles sleep,[104] and the gentle rocking of the shield-cradle corresponds to the movement of the sea (κινηθεῖσα λίμνα, *PMG* 543.4).[105] This shield has often been connected with a story from Aelian (fr. 285 Hercher) found in the *Suda* that the infant Ptolemy Soter was exposed by Lagus in a bronze shield and was protected and fed by an eagle. The date and origin of the story is unknown, but it is hardly improbable that it dates at least from Soter's lifetime.[106] It is now generally accepted that the young Heracles represents at some level the young Philadelphus,[107] who here replays a scene from his father's legend. By recalling Perseus, who was Heracles' great-grandfather, in the context of Heracles' own childhood, Theocritus thus emphasises dynastic continuity and the repetition of virtue from generation to generation, themes which were particularly dear to Ptolemaic ideology (cf. esp. 17.56–7). The use of material from a different, but similar, myth in the telling of a story is a familiar literary technique, but here this mingling serves more than purely literary purposes.

There can be little doubt that Idyll 7 is also replete with allusions to contemporary and near-contemporary poetry. Set on Cos, the poem could hardly fail to evoke Philitas, and the scholiast on v. 6 cites a verse of that poet which mentions the spring Burina (fr. 24 Powell); it is most unlikely that that was an isolated coincidence. If Bowie's hypothesis, or something like it, is correct, then the song of Lycidas may be full of Philitan echoes, and Theocritus' archaic models will have been mediated to him through prior reworkings in Philitas. Asclepiades too is an obvious poet in whom to seek parallels within

Pind. *Nem.* 1.63, Heracles' killing of sea-monsters (for which see Bond on Eur. *HF* 400–2). Perseus appears already on the archaic Heracles' shield (*Aspis* 216–37); the description there of the snakes which hang from each Gorgon's belt (vv. 233–6) is at least suggestive in the context of Idyll 24. Heracles and Perseus are paired in an elaborate *ekphrasis* at Ach. Tat. 3.6–8.

[104] δαιδάλεον in v. 42 of Amphitryon's sword may pick up (? unconsciously) Simonides' adjective; cf. also γαλαθηνόν (v. 31), a word which Simonides uses of Perseus.

[105] This may be thought to support A. Griffiths' change of δίνησε to κίνησε in v. 10 (*CQ* 22 (1972) 109). If the transmitted text is correct, it must be defended, not as Gow defends it, but as the transference of a verb appropriate to the military use of shields to the more domestic use found here; the verb would thus call attention to Theocritus' literary strategy. This strategy of rewriting the grandeur of epic and high lyric in a domestic mode has been well catalogued in the literature on this poem, cf., e.g., Horstmann 1976.57–71, Gutzwiller 1981.10–18, Zanker 1987.176–81. I wonder also whether ἐδίνασεν at Pind. *Paeans* 20.13 is relevant (cf. above pp. 12–13). [106] Cf. *RE* 23.1603–4.

[107] Cf., e.g., L. Koenen, *Eine agonistische Inschrift aus Ägypten und frühptolemäische Königsfeste* (Meisenheim 1977) 79–86; F. Griffiths 1979.91–8; Zanker 1987.179–81; Weber 1993.241–2.

Idyll 7, and a number of passages carrying more or less persuasive force have been adduced.[108] What is not at issue, however, is that the literary texture of Idyll 7 carries special force for the rest of Theocritus' poetry also. Part of the purpose of this book will be to investigate that texture.

THE LANGUAGES OF THEOCRITUS

The Theocritean corpus is in many ways the most remarkable ancient poetry collection to have survived. It clearly contains the work of more than one poet, spread over perhaps as much as three centuries of antiquity. Both in extent and in the order in which the poems are presented in modern editions, the collection has some links with what can be reconstructed of ancient texts of this poet, but is in fact largely the creation of the Renaissance:[109] 'the early history of the transmission of the text of Theocritus is still almost a complete mystery'.[110] Antiquity read more 'Theocritus' than we can, and the papyri suggest that no canonical sequencing of poems imposed itself upon ancient readers, although what we think of as the 'bucolic' poems do seem usually to have been grouped together. In this situation of an obscure pre-history combined with the striking variety of types of poem which the corpus offers, the temptation to look for meaningful sub-groupings within these thirty (or thirty-one) poems is almost irresistible. What we know of the circumstances of poetic production in the third century makes the hypothesis of independent composition and circulation for each poem a likely one, and yet some notable parallels exist – most famously perhaps in the *Aitia* of Callimachus and the *Mimiamboi* of Herodas – for individual 'poems' which also clearly belong in a wider 'collection' and exploit that fact for particular poetic effects. Moreover, strong literary arguments can be adduced for believing that certain poems within the corpus have a special relationship with each other: Idylls 6 and 11, and 13 and 22,[111] are the most obvious cases. Whether or not there was a Theocritean 'poetry book' (or 'books') has been extensively debated;[112] many scholars (not unreasonably) would like to believe that the poetry books of the Octavianic and Augustan periods had

---

[108] Most striking is *Anth. Pal.* 12.166 (= Asclepiades xvii G–P) with 7.118–19.

[109] For a helpful brief summary cf. Dover xv–xviii; at greater length Gow i xxx–lxix, Gutzwiller 1995.   [110] A. W. Bulloch, *CQ* 37 (1987) 505.   [111] Cf. below pp. 59–63.

[112] Cf. the helpful survey in Gutzwiller 1995, and in general Krevans forthcoming.

Greek forebears, and the obviously artful arrangement of Virgil's *Eclogues* is particularly suggestive, given the primary position of Theocritus as a model for those poems. The corpus of Catullus too offers some kind of *very* rough analogy to that of Theocritus; the place that metrical difference holds in Catullus is to some extent occupied in Theocritus by variety of subject-matter and generic affiliation, and Catullan scholarship also has been much concerned with the archaeology of poetic order. Such activity must always have a double purpose. The first is the literary-historical aim of reconstructing any authorial ordering of the poems and the meaning of such an ordering; this exercise must never forget that poems by the same poet with (what seem to us) significant shared characteristics were not necessarily grouped together by that poet. The second purpose is to use 'grouping' as a heuristic device for the exploration of meaning within individual poems. However uncertain our conclusions on the first question are likely to be, the second exercise remains potentially fruitful, and it is this with which I shall largely be concerned.

Both the nature of third-century poetry as a whole and the particular shape of the Theocritean corpus suggest that, at least at the first stage, a 'generic' approach to the grouping of poems in terms of the inherited system of social and poetic forms is unlikely to be successful.[113] Although it is obvious, for example, that some Idylls share a 'bucolic' subject-matter and/or setting, whereas some are 'mythological' narratives or dramatic scenes set in an urban environment, the shared elements are numerous enough to suggest that no clear picture is likely to emerge from such an approach. Rather, the first steps towards 'grouping' must be through an examination of metre and language.

Metrical studies have established that there is considerable variety of technique within Theocritean hexameters.[114] Thus, for example, Idylls 1, 3, 4, 5, 6, and 7 conform, broadly speaking, to the norms of the Callimachean hexameter, norms which are strongly enough marked to differentiate these verses clearly from the practice of

---

[113] Cf. above pp. 4–6.
[114] I draw most upon Kunst 1887; Di Benedetto 1956.56–8; M. Brioso Sánchez, 'Aportaciones al estudio del hexametro de Teocrito', *Habis* 7 (1976) 21–56, 8 (1977) 57–75; Fantuzzi 1995. As many of the available studies (especially Kunst and Brioso Sánchez) operate with groups rather than individual poems, there is always the danger that a different system of grouping would produce different results. I hope, however, that the broad conclusions which I have drawn are not seriously misleading.

Homer and the epic tradition;[115] Idyll 11 ('Polyphemus in love'), however, freely infringes these norms, and this, when taken together with the subject of that poem, makes the suspicion that the poet is there seeking a specific mimetic effect – the Cyclops as an imperfect metrician – hard to resist. So too, Idyll 15 ('The Adonis Festival') seems to use metre as an important tool in its mimetic presentation of two uneducated women.[116] Of the other poems with which this book will largely be concerned, Idylls 10, 12, 13, 16, 17, 22, and 24 observe the Callimachean norms no more than does the Hellenistic mainstream outside Callimachus. As for the internal structure of the hexameter and the relative predominance of dactyls over spondees, detailed metrical studies show these poems behaving in a broadly uniform way, which is also consistently different, and 'more conservative', than the 'bucolics': it is thus clear that Theocritus felt the need for more than one metrical style, and the central theme of this book will be how Theocritus engages creatively with that archaic tradition with which the metrical technique of the 'non-Callimachean' hexameters seems to align him.

This is, moreover, not merely a matter of metre, but involves prosody as well. So-called 'Attic correption', whereby a syllable containing a short vowel followed by a combination of mute and liquid consonants is treated as 'open' or 'light' and scanned short, is a helpful diagnostic here. The less free a poet is with this licence, the more 'Homeric' his verse. Theocritus is in general considerably freer in his use of 'Attic correption' than the other third-century poets, but it is again in Idylls 12, 13, 16, 17, 22, and 24 that he is closer both to other poets and to the Homeric position.[117] The possible implications of this difference are clear when we consider that Apollonius' epic is very sparing with this licence and that Callimachus broadly follows Homeric practice in his *Hymns*, but is much freer in the epigrams.[118] This feature seems to be one of the many 'generic signals' which site a poem within particular traditions; the fact that such linguistic signals are often difficult for the modern reader to appreciate must not be allowed to diminish a recognition of their importance. Such signals may, however, be ambiguous: the group of poems considered here

---

[115] For a description of these norms cf., e.g., N. Hopkinson, *Callimachus, Hymn to Demeter* (Cambridge 1984) 51–5; A. S. Hollis, *Callimachus, Hecale* (Oxford 1990) 15–23.

[116] Cf. below p. 119.

[117] Cf. Kunst 1887.64–96; S. R. Slings, *ZPE* 98 (1993) 31–7. For the subject in general cf. P. Maas, *Greek Metre* (Oxford 1962) 75–7; Fantuzzi 1988.155–63.

[118] Cf. Hopkinson on Call. *h.* 6.35.

covers mythological narrative, encomium, and erotic monologue, and it would be rash to assume that similar metrical or prosodic technique will carry similar meanings throughout. Although it seems a not unreasonable working hypothesis that these 'traditional' poems use metre to display their links with the poetic heritage, whereas the 'bucolics' advertise their modernity, there is always the danger that the (perhaps chance) constitution of our present corpus may distort at least one aspect of these differences. Within organised 'poetry books' meaning can indeed be created by networks of difference and similarity between poems, but the history of the Theocritean corpus suggests that we should at least be cautious in this case. What may be fairly clear in the case of the individual poem becomes much more uncertain in the context of poetic grouping. Moreover, our ignorance of even the basic parameters of Theocritean chronology offers the further danger that we may not take adequate account of evolution over time. Nevertheless, the obvious success of metrical analyses of poetic difference should encourage us to pursue linguistic difference as well.

Linguistic difference within the Theocritean corpus, however, poses far more difficult problems than metrical difference; such problems may indeed be intractable, but no issue is in fact more important for the appreciation of this poet. We may assume that, in any language, linguistic detail conveys poetic meaning, but this is particularly the case in Greek, in which different types of poetry (Homer and Aristophanes, say) used quite different linguistic registers and the 'intrusion' of one register into an alien context was a very marked linguistic event. Moreover, the Hellenistic scholarly concern with dialect glosses and poetic language will have made contemporary poets particularly sensitive to these issues. The fact that the language of most 'high' poetry was traditionally determined by generic, rather than geographic, considerations (i.e. 'Doric' for choral poetry, 'Ionic' for epic etc.) was an obvious focus for the attention of the new poets. Thus, for example, one of the leading poets under Philadelphus, Philicus, gave his *Hymn to Demeter* (*SH* 676–80) an Attic dialectal colour appropriate to the setting at Eleusis.[119] It is clear, therefore, that the central linguistic problem which faces the editor of the text of Theocritus, namely the constant need to choose between metrically equivalent forms of the same word which differ only in dialectal

[119] Cf. Latte 1968.541–3.

affiliation, also carries fundamental implications for poetic meaning. No reader of Theocritus can fail to be impressed by his obvious care in the selection and juxtaposition of words, and it is not unreasonable to assume that he will have taken similar care with matters of form and dialect.

Some problems may, of course, seem of greater moment than others. Thus, for example, it is obviously crucial whether the first word of Idyll 22 is ὑμνέομεν or the almost universally transmitted 'Doric' ὑμνέομες;[120] the poet announces a hymn, which is a traditional poetic form, but does he do so in the traditional Ionic language of the 'Homeric Hymns' or with a Doricising form which results in a wholly new tension between language and 'genre'? The varieties of Callimachean form and dialect suggest that, for Theocritus also, assumptions based upon the 'normal' patterns of form and language in classical Greek poetry may be very dangerous. In other passages, however, it may seem less important to be able to decide between two, equally Doric, forms of, say, the infinitive; when faced with such a problem Gow's counsel of despair is understandable:

Problems of this kind . . . though troublesome to an editor, are not so to a modern reader. The nuances which might decide Theocritus between μαστίζοιεν and μαστίσδοιεν, between ἀείδειν and ἀείδην and ἀείδεν, are now too subtle to be grasped, and if we were sure, as we are not, which Theocritus chose, we could not appreciate the reasons for, or the effect of, his choice . . . And since to tinker with the text in such details is as likely to deprave as to improve it, I have in general been content to follow Wilamowitz.[121]

Although Gow's statement of our ignorance is broadly accurate, his assertion that such matters are not 'troublesome' to the modern reader ought to be completely false. In the face of the advance of the *koine*, third-century inscriptions reveal an impressive survival of both weak and strong Doric forms across wide geographic areas;[122] linguistic difference was a living issue for Theocritus' ancient readers, and so our insecurity about this aspect of his text can only be infuriating. Theocritus himself gives obvious prominence to questions of dialect through direct reference to dialectal difference (e.g.

---

[120] No one, to my knowledge, has suggested ὑμνεῦμες, which is also metrically possible. For the dialectal superscription to Idyll 22 cf. below p. 45.

[121] Gow I lxxv. Cf. also *HE* I xlvii: ' . . . vagaries of dialect affect neither the meaning nor, to a modern reader, the poetical value of the poems'.

[122] Cf. Buck 1955.176–7; Ruijgh 1984.66–8; V. Bubeník, *Hellenistic and Roman Greece as a Sociolinguistic Area* (Amsterdam/Philadelphia 1989).

12.13–14,[123] 15.87–95,[124] 18.48[125]). In the opening verses of Idyll 1, a poem whose programmatic meaning does not depend upon assumptions about its position in any original Theocritean 'poetry book', the cumulative effect of distinctive Doric forms seems to be to convey the 'new' sound of 'new' poetry:[126]

ἁδύ τι τὸ ψιθύρισμα καὶ ἁ πίτυς, αἰπόλε, τήνα,
ἁ ποτὶ ταῖς παγαῖσι, μελίσδεται, ἁδὺ δὲ καὶ τύ
συρίσδες· μετὰ Πᾶνα τὸ δεύτερον ἆθλον ἀποισῆι.
αἴ κα τῆνος ἕληι κεραὸν τράγον, αἶγα τὺ λαψῆι·

Sweet is the whispering music of that pine-tree by the springs, goat-herd, and sweet too is the music of your syrinx. After Pan you will take second prize: if he chooses the horned he-goat, you will receive the she-goat.

Not dissimilar perhaps are the repeated Doric vowels of the opening verses of Callimachus' *Hymn to Athena*, which also announce the arrival not just of the goddess, but also of a new poetic form:

ὅσσαι λωτροχόοι τᾶς Παλλάδος ἔξιτε πᾶσαι,
  ἔξιτε· τᾶν ἵππων ἄρτι φρυασσομενᾶν
τᾶν ἱερᾶν ἐσάκουσα, καὶ ἁ θεὸς εὔτυκος ἕρπεν·[127]

All you bath-pourers of Pallas, come out, come out! Just now I heard the snorting of the sacred horses! The goddess is ready to appear.

Readers of Theocritus, then, are meant to be attuned to dialectal nuance. Interpretation of those nuances is, of course, no easy matter. Thus, for example, Theocritus uses two forms of the masculine and neuter dative plural of πᾶς, namely the common Greek πᾶσι(ν) and also πάντεσσι.[128] Both forms are found in Homer, the latter perhaps as an 'aeolic' feature in the epic language.[129] Such datives in -εσσι are a familiar feature of the traditional language of epic and lyric, but are also attested on Doric inscriptions from both the mainland and the colonies of the West (both Corinthian and other), are found in

---

[123] Cf. below pp. 193–4.   [124] Cf. below pp. 119–22.
[125] Cf. below pp. 154–5. It is interesting that there are no such examples in the 'pure bucolics': perhaps those poems offer a different kind of mimetic universe.
[126] I am, of course, here assuming that the Doric forms in these verses are largely transmitted accurately; for the problem in general cf. below p. 35, and for an 'Atticisation' of these verses cf. Dover xxxii.   [127] For this reading cf. Bulloch *ad loc.*
[128] It is odd that neither form was needed in the 'pure bucolics'. πᾶσι(ν) occurs at 12.11, 21, 16.102, 17.51, 88, 25.19, 75, and 131, and πάντεσσι at 2.125, 15.105, 111, 16.20, 17.125, 22.163, and 25.14.   [129] For bibliography on this matter cf. Braswell on Pind. *Pyth.* 4.130(c).

Syracusan authors, and are common throughout the Theocritean
corpus.[130] When, therefore, the Carian Delphis boasts to Simaitha,

καὶ γὰρ ἐλαφρὸς
καὶ καλὸς πάντεσσι μετ' ἠιθέοισι καλεῦμαι (2.124–5)

for nimble and fair am I called among all the young men,

what 'flavour' should we assign to the form πάντεσσι? No particular
flavour at all? Or perhaps, particularly next to the Homeric prosody
of καλός with long *alpha*, it is a touch of high style characterising
Delphis' proud boast?[131] At 16.20 the form is placed in the mouth of
one of the misers who reject the need for poets:

πᾶς δ' ὑπὸ κόλπου χεῖρας ἔχων πόθεν οἴσεται ἀθρεῖ
ἄργυρον, οὐδέ κεν ἰὸν ἀποτρίψας τινὶ δοίη,
ἀλλ' εὐθὺς μυθεῖται· "ἀπωτέρω ἢ γόνυ κνάμα·
αὑτῶι μοί τι γένοιτο." "θεοὶ τιμῶσιν ἀοιδούς."
"τίς δέ κεν ἄλλου ἀκούσαι; ἅλις πάντεσσιν Ὅμηρος."
"οὗτος ἀοιδῶν λῶιστος, ὃς ἐξ ἐμεῦ οἴσεται οὐδέν."

(16.16–21)

Everyone keeps their hands on their purses and looks for monetary
gain himself; they would not rub the rust off their money to give
someone a handout, but straightaway they say: 'The shin is further
than the knee: may I myself have a windfall', or 'The gods give *time*
to poets', or 'Who would listen to another? Homer is enough for all',
or 'The best of poets is the one who will get nothing from me.'

The nationality of these misers is not specified, but Idyll 16 will in due
course turn to celebrate a Syracusan patron, and it is not unreasonable
to locate this opening scene there also; is πάντεσσιν intended to sound
like an authentic snatch of Syracusan speech,[132] or does the miser

---

[130] Cf. Magnien 1920.78–9; Bechtel 1923.250–1; Buck 1955.89; Monteil 1968.39; Molinos
Tejada 1990.220. Ruijgh 1984.80 makes the attractive suggestion that the ending of
Δωριέεσσι at 15.93 carries a particular charge (cf. further below p. 120).

[131] Elsewhere in the poems generally regarded as genuine this prosody occurs only at 1.34, for
which cf. below p. 43, and 6.14, 19. Wilamowitz's ἀιθέοισι is adopted by Gow in the OCT
and (silently) by Dover. It may well be correct, and the form is found on an epitaph of the
third or second century (Bernand 62.3), cf. K. Latte, *Gnomon* 23 (1951) 254, Gow II 592.
Nevertheless, I wonder whether the epic and *koine* form can be defended as part of Delphis'
'Homeric' boast; so too, Albio Cassio reminds me that μετά with the dative is exclusively a
poetic construction ('mostly epic' LSJ), and in fact is uncommon in the 'bucolics' (1.39, 91).

[132] Noteworthy in this context also is λῶιστος, which might be a further touch of dialectal
'realism': epigraphic evidence for λωίων is predominantly from Doric cities, cf. LSJ s.v.
Elsewhere in Theocritus the superlative occurs only at 14.3, again in a representation of
conversation; for the colloquial flavour of Idyll 14 cf. Dover 189–90.

perhaps use a 'Homeric' form to ram home his point about the sufficiency of Homer? The latter possibility seems the more likely, particularly in view of the ephelkystic *nu* which would not have occurred in vernacular speech.

In the case I have just considered we are at least certain of what needs explanation. Too often, however, the linguistic 'facts' of the Theocritean text are simply uncertain. The medieval and Renaissance manuscripts of Theocritus are, not to put too fine a point on it, in a dialectal mess, and the papyri show that a similar chaos reigned in late antiquity.[133] The archetype of our manuscripts clearly contained many variants of both word and form, and we can often see in the papyri how one dialectal form is deliberately replaced by another. Change usually takes one of two broad directions. On the one hand, there is gradual and 'accidental' loss of increasingly unfamiliar forms: thus a recently published papyrus of the first century AD has revealed a localised Doric form in Idyll 15 which had completely disappeared from the tradition.[134] On the other hand, there is clear evidence of superficial Doricising of otherwise Ionic texts, to conform to beliefs about 'the genre'. Both types of corruption are standard in the transmission of dialect texts. Comparison of the earlier (i.e. first and second centuries AD) and later papyri suggests that, in the bucolic Idylls at least, the predominant movement is towards the standardisation of what are perceived as Doric forms,[135] but the vagaries of the transmission are such that it would be very dangerous to seek to assume a rigid methodology based upon this observation. Thus, for example, our most extensive Theocritean papyrus, the Antinoopolis papyrus of (probably) the late fifth century AD,[136] often offers Ionic forms against the Doric of the main tradition.[137] As well as the transmitted texts themselves, the ancient and medieval manuscripts often label the dialect in which a poem is written: Idylls 1, 2, 13–18, 20, 21, and 23–6 are each at least once described as 'Doric', whereas Idylls 12 and 22 are ascribed to the 'Ionic *koine*'. The origin of these notices is likely to be diverse, and in some cases they seem to imply a textual construct quite different from that of the poem which they

[133] Cf., e.g., Latte 1968.526–34. The lists of Theocritean papyri in the standard editions should be supplemented from Molinos Tejada 1990.vii-ix and pp. 8–9 of Gallavotti's third edition.
[134] Cf. below p. 121.   [135] Cf. Molinos Tejada 1990 *passim*.
[136] Cf. A. S. Hunt and J. Johnson, *Two Theocritus Papyri* (London 1930).
[137] Cf. G. Darms, 'Die Ionismen des Papyrus Antinoae in der Pharmakeutria des Theokrit', *Glotta* 59 (1981) 165–208.

introduce.[138] Nevertheless, it would be foolish simply to ignore these notices, and we will see some reason for thinking that they are worth taking very seriously in the case of Idylls 12 and 22.

It is not merely the state of the transmission whch seriously complicates the constitution of the Theocritean text. High Greek poetry had never been dialectally 'pure', in the sense that a particular poet would use only the forms currently in use in a particular dialect area. The languages of epic and lyric, for example, are notoriously composite: alternative forms of different dialectal origin happily co-exist, both for the convenience of metrical composition and to mark the language of poetry as different from that of other forms of discourse. So too in non-literary poetry, such as the many surviving dialectal verse inscriptions (often epitaphs) of the archaic and classical periods, the use of non-dialectal 'Homerisms' is a frequent and 'natural' consequence of the use of dactylic verse.[139] A similar situation prevails in what remains of the local poetry of the fourth and third centuries, as for example in the Doric hexameters of Isyllos of Epidauros, to which Wilamowitz compared the language of Theocritus;[140] here, the inherited Ionic language of epic co-exists happily both with a Doricising *koine* and with local forms of the region. With a highly sophisticated poet, such as Theocritus or (even more, perhaps) Callimachus, writing in a period of great linguistic fluidity, we would expect that their language would be either more mixed and less specifically local than that of verse inscriptions or, conversely, more regular and consistent, depending upon the type of poetic effect intended. Broad consistency of dialect within generic parameters, for example, might have been one way in which 'élite' poetry marked itself off from more 'popular' verse. Whatever the truth, it is clear that familiar assumptions about poetic dialect will not get us very far in the case of Theocritus. Moreover, 'Doric' covers a great variety of linguistic phenomena across a very wide geographic area. Although it is certainly possible to identify a 'Doric *koine*' in the third century, the number of different, but equally 'Doric', forms available to Theocritus often makes the identification of 'the dialect' merely the first step towards fixing the text.

---

[138] Cf. H. L. Ahrens, *Philologus* 33 (1874) 405. Halperin 1983.159 attractively suggests that some, at least, of the *tituli* derive from a time when poems which were not obviously 'Doric', i.e. 'pastoral', had to be identified as such; this would help to explain the absence of *tituli* from Idylls 3–11, particularly as that for Idyll 1 is only very weakly attested.

[139] For a preliminary study cf. K. Mickey, 'Dialect consciousness and literary language: an example from ancient Greek', *TPhS* 1981.35–66.

[140] Cf. *Isyllos von Epidauros* (Berlin 1886) 25–8.

As far as the 'bucolic' poems are concerned, however, many (though by no means all) thorny problems would be solved if a recent suggestion of C. J. Ruijgh were in fact correct. In an article published in 1984, Ruijgh suggested that the genuine 'Doric' poems[141] were in fact composed in the language of an *emigré* Cyrenean élite living in Alexandria; this language was basically Cyrenean Doric, tempered by an admixture of forms influenced by the Attic *koine*. That the 'mythical' marriage song of Idyll 18 is written in the dialect that Callimachus himself spoke is an intriguing idea, but Ruijgh's suggestion must remain a speculative hypothesis, not least because it depends upon the assumption (never spelled out by Ruijgh) that the manuscript transmission is both stable and generally reliable.[142] Ruijgh's suggestion has encountered important linguistic objections which cannot be rehearsed in full here,[143] but if it were the case that the language of this major group of poems was not merely uniform but also broadly true to a particular historical sub-dialect, then this would be a major gloss upon the standard critical view of Theocritus in which it is rather variety and the juxtaposition of linguistic and motival material of very varied origin which are seen to characterise the whole corpus. This standard critical position has been well described by Gianfranco Fabiano:

What seems chiefly to characterise Theocritus' poetic language is the instability of the system at every level, from the least phonetic unity, which always enjoys a considerable autonomy inside the changeable convention of the dialect, to the structure of the *Idylls* as complex syntheses of different literary genres. In Theocritus' poetry it is usual to meet with extravagant elements which apparently derive from other fields and clash with the fundamental character of the poem where they appear . . . As Doric is no strictly local dialect, the

---

[141] Ruijgh's categories (1984.56) are taken over from Gow (see below p.38); thus the poems with which he is concerned are Idylls 1–7, 10, 11, 14, 15, 18, and 26.

[142] Rightly noted by Molinos Tejada 1990.49. The principal hallmarks to which Ruijgh pointed were feminine participles in -οισα, the ablatival suffix -θε rather than -θεν, and -ες rather than -εις as the ending for the 2nd person singular of the verb. It is, however, at least worrying that -ες rather than -εις is nowhere guaranteed metrically (Monteil 1968.43, Gow on 1.3) and, on the basis of one inscription and a notice in Eustathius, Ruijgh perhaps exaggerates the importance of this as a diagnostic feature of Cyrenean; the caution of Molinos Tejada 1990.279–81 seems fully justified. As for participles in -οισα rather than -ουσα, the former belongs to the traditional language of Doric lyric, as we can see from the Lille Stesichorus (cf. below p. 44), but its place in the transmission of Theocritus is not nearly so secure as Ruijgh implies: the very exiguous evidence of the earlier papyri in fact supports -ουσα no less than -οισα, which is then standardised in later texts, cf. Molinos Tejada 1990.56, 158. For the dialect of Idyll 15 cf. below pp. 119–23, and for Idyll 18 below pp. 153–5.

[143] Cf. Molinos Tejada 1990; Abbenes 1995.

Doric element alone is already so differentiated that it makes up an unlimited reserve of expression: from common-Doric forms, which may be occasionally endowed with the dignity of choral-lyric tradition, to strictly local and provincial Doric forms. In the idylls where the Doric element prevails phonetic surprises follow one another without any apparent rule[144] . . . Theocritus' language, no matter what the dialect [i.e. the basic character of a particular poem], is almost always made dynamic in a series of oppositions between Homerisms and rough Doric forms, high artificiality and colloquialisms, realism in some details and refusal of a consistent realistic poetics, personal tone and literary stimuli.[145]

If Fabiano's description is broadly accurate, then this too will be a serious hindrance to how much we may hope to achieve by the application of consistent philological method to the text of Theocritus, for the poetry itself is designed to defeat 'method'. With either Ruijgh or Fabiano, however, we are forced back to the details of the text, and thus to the reliability of the transmission.

In the face of apparent chaos, editors of Theocritus are forced to make choices, and the best modern editor, A. S. F. Gow, divided the poems of the corpus into five dialectal groups:[146]

(i)   Genuine poems in Doric: Idylls 1–7, 10, 11, 14, 15, 18, 26.
(ii)   Dubious or spurious poems in Doric: Idylls 8, 9, 19–21,23, 27.
(iii) Poems prevailingly in Epic dialect with an admixture of Doric:
       Idylls 13, 16, 17, 24.
(iv)   Poems in Epic and Ionic: Idylls 12, 22, 25.
(v)   Poems in Aeolic: Idylls 28–31.

Gow's division is merely a systematisation of what was already a long-standing critical consensus, but with the obvious exception of the Aeolic group, the basis for it is as much *a priori* assumptions about 'genre' as judgements concerning the transmission of individual poems.[147] Such assumptions have led to dialectal decisions which in turn lead to the classification which Gow proposes; the danger in such circularity is obvious. Thus it is, for example, that all modern editions remove several unanimously transmitted Doric forms from the text of Idyll 22, not just because of the manuscript superscription 'in Ionic

---

[144] Perhaps an unconscious echo of Wilamowitz on Isyllos, 'die Formen wechseln so regellos . . .' (*Isyllos von Epidauros* (Berlin 1886) 25).

[145] Fabiano 1971.528–9, 533.

[146] Gow I lxxii. Gow never really spells out the criteria he is using, and this is one of the reasons why I have thought it useful to treat this matter at some length.

[147] Cf. Latte 1968.526–34; Halperin 1983.143–56.

koine', but because of assumptions about the linguistic construct which is appropriate for a hymn. That generic considerations should play a rôle in linguistic decisions is inevitable and only proper; what is improper is the assumption that particular generic considerations imposed particular and traditional linguistic choices upon a third-century poet. All that we know of the period might seem to suggest the very opposite. Even if our conclusions will not in the end differ radically from those of Gow, the basis for this classification must be made much clearer than it has been to date.

As for the poems in Gow's third and fourth groups, poems which we have already seen to share certain metrical similarities, the most useful way to proceed is through phenomena whose certain presence in, or absence from, the text is guaranteed by metre. Di Benedetto was able to demonstrate that the 'bucolic' poems show marked differences in the range and type of metrically guaranteed 'Homeric' forms which they admit, and so it may be hoped that clear differences between Gow's various groups will emerge. The aim of the investigation will be, on one hand, to seek to confirm the grouping suggested by metrical tests, and on the other to seek to establish certain 'facts' about the language of the poems in question, which may then provide guidance in the linguistic areas which are not subject to firm demonstration. I begin with two features, one general and the other specific, to illustrate different aspects of the issues involved. Both phenomena, however, illustrate the crucial fact that what is at stake here is not merely a matter of linguistic or dialectal colour, but rather the 'meaning' conveyed by a particular style: it is stylistic features which site a poem within particular traditions.

A familiar feature of high Greek poetry is the apparent 'omission' of the definite article from positions where it would certainly be expected in prose; the greater the freedom with which the definite article is omitted, the more 'marked' the style. Broadly speaking, Theocritus uses the definite article far more in the 'bucolic' poems and the 'mimes' (Idylls 2, 14, 15) than in the poems of Gow's third and fourth groups, in which his usage does not differ radically from that of Homer.[148] As we would expect, no single explanation will account for the phenomena. Thus, for example, among the 'bucolics'

---

[148] Cf. W. G. Leutner, *The Article in Theocritus* (diss. Johns Hopkins 1907), especially 18–24; A. Svensson, *Der Gebrauch des bestimmten Artikels in der nachklassischen griechischen Epik* (Lund 1937) 65–9. My remarks draw largely upon the statistics in Leutner.

Idyll 7 displays a relatively high number of 'Homerisms',[149] and so it
is reasonable to associate its relatively low use of the article with
its generally 'poetic' style. Idyll 18, however, displays very few
'Homerisms',[150] and its very low use of the article may be a feature
which is mimetic of high lyric.[151] Within Gow's third and fourth
groups Idylls 16, 17, 22, 24, and 25 broadly follow Homeric practice –
with Idyll 17 (the *Encomium of Ptolemy*) being the 'most Homeric' –
whereas Idylls 12 and 13 are rather freer in their use, although not as
free as the 'Doric' poems (with the exception of Idyll 18). An obvious
preliminary conclusion would be that, whereas most of the 'bucolics'
and the 'mimes' seek to mark their difference from inherited poetic
norms and/or reproduce elements of 'real speech',[152] the other poems
stand, to a greater or less degree, within the inherited diction of high
poetry. Some support for this conclusion may perhaps be found in the
relative freedom with which the article is used in the prefatory epistle
of Idyll 13 and in the stichomythic exchange between Polydeuces and
Amycus in Idyll 22; within a broadly archaising linguistic mode,
these passages seek to catch some of the flavour of personal
communication.

The use of the definite article thus allows broad stylistic distinctions
between groups of poems; my second example is a more specific
matter of verbal form which will, however, be seen to point in a
similar direction.

Idyll 12 is a monologue by an infatuated *erastes* to an apparently
less than infatuated *eromenos*.[153] The opening word is ἤλυθες, 'you have
come', which is repeated in anaphora at the head of v.2. This trisyllabic
aorist belongs to the traditional language of epic (from which it passed
as an alternative form into high lyric). In the Theocritean corpus it
appears in the simple form only here and at 22.183 (the battle of
Lynceus and Castor) and 25.164 (Heracles' narrative of his victory
over the Nemean lion), and in compounds at 22.85 (the fight of
Polydeuces and Amycus) and three times in Idyll 25 (vv. 86, 121,
182).[154] Elsewhere in the corpus the aorist is always either ἦλθον or
the metrically equivalent Doric form ἦνθον, and it is hard to believe
that the absence of the trisyllabic form from the 'Doric' poems can be

---

[149] Cf. Di Benedetto 1956.55.   [150] Cf. Di Benedetto 1956.54.
[151] For the lyric models of Idyll 18 cf. below pp. 150–3.
[152] The most 'articular' poems (on Leutner's statistics) are the 'Goatherd's Monologue' (Idyll
3) and the rustic conversations of Idylls 4, 5, and 10.
[153] For a full treatment of this poem cf. below pp. 186–95.
[154] Elsewhere in the bucolic corpus only Bion fr. 12.3 (in mythical narrative).

accidental. Within our corpus of poems its presence at the head of Idyll 12 thus acts as a rather striking linguistic marker, although we must again bear in mind the dangers of over-interpretation that the very existence of the corpus poses (cf. above p. 31). The 'meaning' of this marker lies probably not merely in the dialectal colour of the poem, but also in the character of the speaker who, as we shall see, lives very much in the past. It is the archaising tone of the form which explains its distribution through the corpus. Both Idyll 12 and Idyll 22 are identified in the manuscripts as 'Ionic', and Idyll 25, as we shall see, consistently follows the traditional language of epic; 12 and 22 are certainly not free from linguistic uncertainty (cf. below), but there is some reason to think that Idyll 12 at least begins with a dialectal marker of an emphatic kind. In a later chapter we will explore the literary affiliations which support this linguistic argument.

While it is important not to overestimate the possible value of such phenomena by, for example, assuming consistency of dialect through a poem on the basis of a single observable feature, it is also clear that clusters of such phenomena will be our best guide in this area. The third person singular imperfect of the verb 'to be' is usually the Doric ἦς, which can of course never be guaranteed against ἦν, but the epic–Ionic forms ἦεν and ἔην occur in Idylls 17, 22, 24, and 25, but nowhere else;[155] the epic and *koine* pronominal adjective σφέτερος occurs in Idylls 12, 13, 17, 22, 24, and 25, but in none of the 'bucolics' or 'mimes' except for Idyll 21, which there are good grounds for believing to be non-Theocritean; ὄφρα, 'in order that', occurs only at 16.30, 25.190, and 27.6, where it may be added to the already impressive case for the non-Theocritean authorship of that poem; so too another familiar word from the high *koine* of epic and lyric, ἠδέ, 'and', occurs certainly in Idylls 16 (v. 87), 17 (v. 124), 22 (v. 39 and perhaps 58), and 25 (v.139), but otherwise only in Idylls 20 (v.43) and 23 (v.52), which there are good grounds for believing to be post-Theocritean.[156] This distribution should at least make us wary of accepting Meineke's ἠδέ into the text of 1.106,[157] although it would be

---

[155] ἦεν: 22.130, 25.211; ἔην: 17.13, 24.133, 25.218.

[156] The use at 20.43 may be mock high-style.

[157] Meineke's emendation in fact produces a Homeric verse-end (*Il.* 21.351). If we ignore Longolius' translation of Plutarch, then the folklore of bees and adulterers could as happily be adduced in favour of the transmitted ὧδε as for Meineke's emendation: Daphnis would then mockingly advise Aphrodite to go somewhere where the bees will *not* get her. 'Oaks', whatever other function they may serve (cf. scholiast and commentators *ad loc.*), may look to *h. Aphr.* in Aphrodite's account of the child she will bear to Anchises. Be that as it may, the significance of κύπειρος remains obscure.

very dangerous to seek to remove all apparently 'anomalous' cases. Thus, for example, whereas the epic σφέων occurs only at 17.24 and 22.10, σφισι is found once in the clearly genuine 'bucolics' (7.33), as well as in the non-bucolics;[158] Idyll 7 is perhaps the most 'Homerising' of the bucolics, and this is a good instance of that.[159] The Doric ποτί is common throughout the corpus and was a feature of the traditional language of epic and high lyric, but πρός is also common in Idylls 22 and 25 and occurs, whether as preposition or prefix, in each of Idylls 3 (v. 19), 5 (v. 93), 8 (v. 34), 9 (v. 18), 12 (v. 32), 17 (v. 52), 18 (v. 55), 21 (v. 18) and 23 (v. 6),[160] as well as in the fragments of Epicharmus and Sophron. Idylls 9, 21, and 23 may no longer preserve Theocritean norms, and reasons for regarding Idylls 12, 17, 22, and 25 as linguistically quite different from the 'bucolics' are now emerging, but Idylls 5 and 18 are otherwise strongly Doricising.[161] So too the Attic–Ionic and *koine* ἄν (rather than κε or κα) occurs certainly in Idylls 16, 22, 24, and 25, and in 'bucolics' whose authenticity is very doubtful,[162] but otherwise only in χὥταν at 7.53; as ἄν is a standard feature of the epic–lyric tradition,[163] it is possible that χὥταν helps to mark the stylistic affiliations of Lycidas' song.[164] Similarly, the epic–lyric genitive σέθεν is found not only in Idylls 17 (vv. 46, 135), 25 (v. 162), the Aeolic 29 (vv. 32, 37), and the almost certainly spurious 27 (vv. 43, 45), but also once in Idyll 4 (v. 38), where Gow suggests that it 'is perhaps an indication of the more serious tone';[165] at the very least the verses contain a brilliant juxtaposition of the 'high' and the 'low':

ὦ χαρίεσσ' Ἀμαρυλλί, μόνας σέθεν οὐδὲ θανοίσας
λασεύμεσθ'· ὅσον αἶγες ἐμὶν φίλαι, ὅσσον ἀπέσβης.

O lovely Amaryllis, you alone we shall not forget even in death; as dear to me as my goats were you at your departure.

---

[158] 16.12, 47, 17.84, 22.83, 25.18, 190.   [159] Cf. Di Benedetto 1956.55.

[160] At 21.18 and 23.6 προσ- could be replaced by ποτ-.

[161] Cf. Di Benedetto 1956.54. At 3.19 it seems likely that euphony is as important as metrical necessity (πότπτυξαι is not an easy word), and at 18.55 ποτ' ἀὥ could in fact replace πρὸς ἀὥ, cf. Molinos Tejada 1990.332. πρὸς ἀὥ is in fact a phrase ascribed to Sophron (fr. 166 Kaibel), and πρός is found once in the indirect tradition of Alcman (*PMGF* 70a); at *Epigr.* XXI.3 the tradition divides between ποτ' ἀὥ and πρὸς ἀὥ in a poem of uncertain dialectal colour.

[162] Cf. Gow on 8.35; Molinos Tejada 1990.362.   [163] Cf. Nöthiger 1971.47–9.

[164] Cf. above p. 26.

[165] Dover xlii notes that τεῦς rather than σέθεν would produce word-break after a fourth-foot spondee, but metrical 'convenience' is hardly a sufficient explanation in a poet such as Theocritus.

It is clear, therefore, that there is some linguistic sense in gathering the poems of Gow's third and fourth groups, at least to differentiate them from the first group of 'Doric' poems.

Up to this point I have been concerned with linguistic features which are metrically guaranteed, but other phenomena can hardly be left completely out of account. An interesting example is the relative distribution of -ουσι and the Doric -οντι in the third person plural of thematic verbs; for what it is worth, the transmission is generally unanimous and stable with regard to these alternative forms,[166] with -οντι naturally predominant in the 'bucolics' and 'mimes',[167] whereas both forms are found in the other poems and seem to have co-existed in the inherited language of high poetry.[168] The two forms are, however, not always interchangeable as the Doric form cannot add ephelkystic *nu*. Thus at 12.23, 16.5, 69, 72, 81, 17.78, 97, 22.174 and 178 -ουσιν would avoid the hiatus offered by -οντι; that no such example exists from the 'bucolics' and 'mimes' can hardly be accidental.[169] Whether or not the Doric form can be elided (as apparently in archaic lyric) is disputed,[170] and becomes important at 1.35 where the two men portrayed on the wonderful cup 'wrangle with words', νεικείουσ' ἐπέεσσι (in a unanimous transmission). Here there is a very strong case for the epic–*koine* form. Not only is the phrase itself a Homeric one[171] and the verb appears in an epic form (νεικείω rather than νεικέω), but there is here a particular reworking of the trial scene from the Homeric Shield of Achilles, a scene which is the Homeric forebear of the dispute of the Theocritean lovers, just as the cup as a whole offers a 'bucolic' version of the Shield as a whole:

> ἔνθα δὲ νεῖκος
> ὠρώρει, δύο δ' ἄνδρες ἐνείκεον εἵνεκα ποινῆς
> ἀνδρὸς ἀποφθιμένου·   (*Il.* 18.497–9)

---

[166] 12.23 and 31 are important exceptions, cf. below p. 45.

[167] Again Idyll 27 is a noteworthy exception.

[168] Cf. Nöthiger 1971.56–60 and, reaching rather different conclusions, Braswell on Pind. *Pyth.* 4.18(d).

[169] Wilamowitz's κατατρίψουσιν ἀκρέσπερον for the transmitted κατατρίψοντι ἀκρέσπερον at 24.77 seems very likely. At 17.38 φαντὶ ἀδεῖν Wilamowitz similarly proposed φασὶν. Note also 16.19 τιμῶσιν ἀοιδούς.

[170] At 22.19 ἀπολήγοντ' is universally transmitted, but it is hard to resist Meineke's ἀπολήγουσ'. Some critics explain (some or all) of the apparent examples in Pindar and Bacchylides as middles with elision of -αι, rather than actives with elision of -ι.

[171] Cf. Molinos Tejada 1990.132. ἔπος in fact is otherwise found only at 13.54, 17.136, 25.66 and 77, and 28.24, and may have carried the wrong stylistic and dialectal associations for the 'bucolic' poems.

> There a quarrel had arisen, and two men were quarrelling over the
> compensation for a man who had been killed.

The momentary flavour of Homeric style suggests the depths of the
lovers' suffering as they 'struggle in vain' (v. 38).[172]

The number of possible linguistic tests, both positive and negative,[173]
is very great, but I hope that enough material has now been gathered
to allow tentative conclusions about the language of the poems to be
studied in this book. Idylls 15 and 18 are 'Doric' poems and will be
considered separately in the appropriate place.[174] Idylls 16 and 17
appear to be written in a version of the inherited *koine* of high poetry in
which epic–Ionic and Doric elements exist side by side;[175] the number
of alternative forms attested by high lyric is, however, such as to warn
against over-systematisation. Welcome confirmation of the linguistic
form in which this lyric tradition was available to Theocritus has
recently come in the shape of the 'Lille Stesichorus', a major papyrus
text dating from the middle of the third century BC, or slightly later,
and hence written perhaps within a generation of Theocritus' period
of activity. Like Theocritus, Stesichorus was classed by the grammatical
tradition as a 'Doric' writer (cf. Test. B 21 Davies), and the Lille text
can help us to see what this classification might mean.[176] The forms
presented by the Lille text can act as a guide, no more, to what
Theocritus might have regarded as the traditional language of lyric
poetry. Much uncertainty remains of course – are we to read ἀείδωμες
or ἀείδωμεν in 16.4,[177] ἤνθον or ἦλθον in 16.9? –[178] but the parameters
of our uncertainty are now clearer than they were. Idylls 13 and 24
are frequently grouped with 16 and 17, and to some extent this is fair,
but it is also clear that 13 and 24 show noticeably fewer of the 'epic'

---

[172] In view of the programmatic nature of this poem, it is tempting also to believe that there is at
least a suggestion that the men compete for the woman's favour in an 'amoibaian
(ἀμοιβαδίς) song contest'; if so, ἔπη will also suggest 'hexameters'.

[173] By a 'negative' test I mean one which notes the complete absence of a particular feature from
the group of poems under examination. Thus, for example, outside the 'bucolics' and 'Doric
mimes' there are no first and second declension accusative plurals with short vowels (-ος,
-ος), no examples of λῆν, 'to wish' (cf. Dover xxxix), and no metrically guaranteed 'Doric
futures', cf. Magnien 1920.115–16; Monteil 1968.45; Molinos Tejada 1990.294–6.

[174] Cf. below Chapters 4 and 5.　　　[175] For this language see especially Nöthiger 1971.

[176] On the language of the Lille text cf. P. J. Parsons, *ZPE* 26 (1977) 11–12; C. Gallavotti,
Bollettino dei Classici 1977.1–30; M. Haslam, *GRBS* 19 (1978) 47–52; J. M. Bremer in J. M.
Bremer, A. M. Taalman Kip, and S. R. Slings (eds.), *Some Recently Found Greek Poems* (Leiden
1987) 129–30.

[177] An interesting comparison here is with the transmitted Doric verbal forms in the opening
verses of Idyll 13: are these intended to catch the flavour of friends talking together?

[178] The Lille text offers the Doric form in vv. 180 and 303.

elements of traditional poetic diction than do the other poems considered here. While metre suggests that there is some sense in grouping them together, in the matter of language Idyll 13 at least seems to stand close to the more 'Homerising' of the bucolics, such as Idyll 7. With Idyll 22, however, we appear to be in qualitatively different territory. On the one hand the text offers an impressive number of metrically guaranteed epic–Ionic forms, particularly in the treatment of pronouns and pronominal adjectives, which seems to support the manuscript description of the language as 'Ionic' and to differentiate it clearly from that of Idylls 16 and 17. On the other hand, the manuscripts present a fair number of universally transmitted Dorisms, and in this they are supported by the papyri, including *POxy.* 1806 which is a *relatively* early Theocritus papyrus (late first century AD). None of these Doric forms is, however, protected by metre, and modern editorial practice has been to produce a uniformly Ionic text, in keeping with the inherited hymnic form.[179]

As for Idyll 12, we have seen that it begins with a striking departure from the language of the Doricising poems, and also admits other phenomena which are avoided in this latter group. The manuscripts offer a very mixed picture, although with one exception[180] the only papyrus text, the late Antinoopolis papyrus, offers a consistently Ionic language. As with Idyll 22, no Doric form is metrically protected.[181]

---

[179] Molinos Tejada 1990.38, however, is inclined to keep an open mind about the Doric forms, in view of the text offered by the earliest papyri.

[180] ἀραιᾶς in v. 24.

[181] A particularly intriguing example is the transmitted μᾶλον 'apple', in v. 3. Adoption of the Ionic μῆλον, a form which can mean 'sheep' as well as 'apple', allows a quasi-pun with ὄις in v. 4 to be more strongly felt. μᾶλα, 'flocks', however, in the 'Lille Stesichorus' (v. 241) rather complicates the question; cf. Gallavotti 1984.7–8; A. C. Cassio, 'Iperdorismi callimachei e testo antico dei lirici (Call. *Hy.* 5, 109; 6, 136)' in *Tradizione e innovazione nella cultura greca da Omero all'età ellenistica. Scritti in onore di Bruno Gentili* (Rome 1993) 903–10.

CHAPTER 2

'All the twos': Idyll 22

HYMNS OF PRAISE

Hymnal writing is one of the more remarkable extant products of the élite poetry of the third century; even when allowance is made for the inevitably distorted picture which the accidents of survival transmit, hymnal and 'para-hymnal' poetry in the extant work of the major poets of the century is a striking phenomenon. From Callimachus are preserved five hexameter hymns and one elegiac – much the largest continuous body of his work to have survived. The sole extant epic of this period, the *Argonautica* of Apollonius, is framed as a 'Hymn to the Argonauts', that is a hymn on the traditional 'Homeric' model in which the central mythic narrative has been greatly extended, but in which the hymnic frame remains.[1] This structure is reinforced by many hymnic elements within the main body of the narrative, not merely included hymns, such as that of Orpheus to Apollo (*Arg.* 2.701–13), but also briefer references that recall the hymnic status of the whole.[2] Within the Theocritean corpus, Idyll 22, with which I shall be concerned in this chapter, presents itself unambiguously as a hymn (ὑμνέομεν v. 1 – ἡμετέροις . . . ὕμνοις v. 214), and it seems to be written in the largely Ionic 'epic' dialect of the *Homeric Hymns*;[3] Idyll 24 (the *Herakliskos*) and Idyll 26 (*Lenai or Bakchai*), which are to various degrees 'Doricising', are both clearly at least para-hymnal.[4] In Idyll 17 (*Encomium of Ptolemy*) the poet presents his activity as 'hymning' (v. 8), and the poem is replete with hymnal *topoi*.[5] Idyll 16 (*Charites or Hieron*)[6] also begins by presenting itself as a ὕμνος (vv.

---

[1] For similarities in the hymnal endings of *Arg.* and of Theocr. 22 cf. below p. 46.
[2] Note 2.161–3 – a hymn to Polydeuces; cf. below p. 143.   [3] Cf. above p. 45.
[4] For 24 cf. the fragments and scholion on the end of the poem preserved by the Antinoopolis papyrus (vv. 140–72), and the opening Ἡρακλέα has an obvious parallel in the opening of the fifteenth Homeric hymn (to Heracles), cf. above p. 11.; for the hymnal form of the narrative itself cf. Gutzwiller 1981.12ff. For Idyll 26 cf. Cairns 1992.
[5] Cf. further below pp. 79–82.   [6] Cf. below Chapter 3.

1–4), but then surprises us by posing the question 'Who deserves / will take any notice of my ὕμνος ?' (vv. 5–7). By the end of the poem the answer is clear – note v. 103 ὑμνεῖν . . . Ἱέρωνα – although we, and Hieron, are teased with the deferral of 'hymns' until after his victory and his acceptance of the poet's 'Graces'. Hymnic form is, of course, merely one constituent of this extraordinary poem, but the subject-matter shows that it is by no means the least important constituent – Hieron, at least, would not have thought so. Both 16 and 17 are Doricising idylls, and it is not unreasonable to connect their dialect in part with the traditions of choral lyric, as well as (in the case of 16) the locality concerned.[7] The 'Adonis-song' which occupies the last part of Idyll 15 has many hymnal features, but is not a hymn of the traditional kind.[8]

In varying degrees these 'hymns' are the literary manifestation of hymnal writing and performance as these flourished at all levels of Hellenistic society, and occasionally we are afforded glimpses of other areas of this activity by the chance survival of papyri or inscriptions. The Hellenistic world was, after all, full of gods and godlike men requiring praise. The hymnal poems of Callimachus and Theocritus reveal a persistent interest in the distinctions between men and gods and how those distinctions are broken down in the case of great rulers (and patrons); contemporary statuary too negotiates these boundaries by presenting rulers as different from 'ordinary men' in ways which not merely complicate identification for modern scholars (is this a god or a ruler?), but clearly also helped to fashion the new boundaries.[9] The 'Homeric hymn', which identified the areas of a god's power and placed him or her within the overall scheme of the divine, seems in retrospect an obvious vehicle for describing these shifting boundaries of power. Moreover, this concern with distinctions between the praise of men and the praise of gods is to be connected not merely with the political realities of third-century monarchies, but also with the scholarly enterprise of collecting and classifying the poetic heritage.[10] One important means of distinguishing between different kinds of 'praise poetry' is through the status of the recipient, and in this area

---

[7] Cf. above p. 44.   [8] Cf. below pp. 127–37.

[9] Cf. Smith 1988. Smith 45 notes that the Ptolemies made greater use of 'divinising attributes' than did other Hellenistic monarchies; the Pharaonic inheritance, of course, made the Ptolemies at least representatives of the divine. Cf. further below pp. 79–82.

[10] For the classification of lyric poetry in general, and hymns in particular, cf. H. Färber, *Die Lyrik in der Kunsttheorie der Antike* (Munich 1936); A. E. Harvey, 'The classification of Greek lyric poetry', *CQ* 5 (1955) 157–75, at pp. 166–7; Pfeiffer 1968.130.

fine 'academic' distinctions, for example between 'hymns' and 'encomia', could carry real political charge. We must not, however, overstate the nature of these changes visible in the poetry of the third century. From its earliest days Greek poetry shows a pressing concern with the distinctions between men and gods, and the necessity of getting right the language appropriate to each. The importance of Pindar's encomiastic poetry to the language of Alexandrian poetry is rightly a critical commonplace, and no gnomic theme occupies so large a space in the epinicians as the importance of fitting one's praise to the status of the victor being honoured. Moreover, from a literary point of view, it is easy enough to see in the prominence of hymnic poetry a further familiar feature of the third century, namely the exploration of popular and 'sub-literary' forms as vehicles for élite poetry. This is perhaps clearest in the case of the 'Adonis-hymn' of Idyll 15 which, of all the poems mentioned in this survey, seems to be stylistically closest to the cult hymns preserved on papyrus and stone. The reasons for this lie, of course, within the nature of that poem as a whole.[11]

'Literary' hymns (including the rhapsodic 'Homeric hymns') are regularly dismissed as 'secular', in the sense that they do not perform any of the cultic or 'religious' functions that 'real' hymns perform.[12] Archaic hymns, so the argument goes, may have been performed at religious festivals, but they do not form part of the negotiation between man and god which is the true mark of cult; the performance of narrative hexameter poetry was simply one of the ways in which the gods were honoured, not a necessary part of religious observance. A fortiori, Hellenistic narrative hymns are in no real sense 'religious'. A stronger version of this thesis adds that, in any case, the gods and their myths celebrated in Hellenistic 'literary' hymns now no longer meant what they had once meant; myths are simply the raw material for poetic narrative, not the expressions of deep social and intellectual structures.[13] In support of this thesis is adduced what Marcel Detienne called 'the invention of mythology', one manifestation of which is the writing and cataloguing of myth and legend such as we know Hellenistic poets to have practised in their scholarly lives and

---

[11] Cf. below Chapter 4.

[12] For a helpful summary of those functions cf. J. M. Bremer, 'Greek hymns' in H. S. Versnel (ed.), *Faith, Hope and Worship. Aspects of Religious Mentality in the Ancient World* (Leiden 1981) 193–215. There is also much relevant material in *AION* 13 (1991), which is devoted to 'L'inno tra rituale e letteratura nel mondo antico'. For further remarks on the function of hymns cf. below pp. 79–82.   [13] What follows reuses material from Hunter 1992.29–34.

used in their poetry; such activity, which helped to free mythic stories from their original social and cultic contexts, both bestowed new life upon these stories and erased their social 'meaning'. Moreover, it is a common view that the 'mythic thinking' of the archaic and classical periods had, by the third century, given way to some extent to different modes of thought which were, if not more rational, at least closer to modes that we ourselves would recognise. Thucydides, the sophists, and Plato are, of course, the major figures here. That important changes had taken place is hard to deny, though the work of Geoffrey Lloyd in particular has shown us how misleading simplistic models of the replacement of 'non-scientific' by 'scientific' ways of thinking can be. That 'myths' in Hellenistic poetry are no more than codified stories, available to poets as narrative material, ignores the powerful evidence for continuity, as well as change, in Greek religion and cult. Moreover, it would be very naive to imagine that even the poetry of the Alexandrian library was produced in a social and intellectual vacuum. Such a view depends, at the very least, upon fragile inferences from the texts themselves, a misleading view of poetic production in this period which exploits the (undeniable) 'éliteness' of these texts to create a set of poets with no contact whatsoever with the ordinary, public performance of poetry, and finally – and most importantly – some very questionable assumptions about the nature of ancient religion and cult. Moreover, the context of the Alexandrian court itself, in which it is not unreasonable to place the majority of Callimachus' and Theocritus' hymnic poems,[14] would seem to rob the alleged dichotomy of any interpretative power it may have possessed. In this context the language, forms, and hierarchies of cult and religion were used to express power relations of a kind which *we*, with our very different ways of thinking, normally label 'secular'.[15] As the heirs of the Pharaohs, the Ptolemies inhabited a space in which everything was 'religious', and we can hardly assume that their Greek subjects, particularly the learned men of the court, were quite oblivious to this.

In the archaic period ὕμνος and ὑμνεῖν refer to 'song' across the full

---

[14] For the Ptolemaic context of Idyll 22 we must rely upon general considerations such as the importance of the Dioscuri in Ptolemaic cult (cf., e.g., Gow II 385, Fraser 1972.I 207, Hunter 1995c) and the appropriateness of some of the poem's themes to the self-presentation of the Ptolemies recognisable elsewhere, cf. Hunter 1993.160–1. For Idyll 24 cf. above p. 27, F. Griffiths 1979.91–8.

[15] For the limitations of this dichotomy see esp. S. R. F. Price, *Rituals and Power* (Cambridge 1984), although Price's concern is largely with the imperial cults of the eastern Roman empire.

range of narrative and lyric forms.[16] Hesiod, the poets of the 'Homeric hymns', and the pre-Socratics all use this vocabulary to designate their own activities. The earliest reference to one of the extant Homeric hymns is a famous chapter of Thucydides (3.104) which cites the *Hymn to (Delian) Apollo* as προοίμιον 'Απόλλωνος and ascribes this poem to Homer. It is clear both from this description and from many of the hymns themselves that they functioned as rhapsodic introductions to 'epic' narrative, but were sometimes greatly extended by the inclusion within this 'proem' of a major narrative. This proemial function is explicitly recognised by Theocritus when he prefaces his narrative of the exploits of Polydeuces and Castor with a rewriting of the *Hymn to the Dioscuri*.[17] The other key fact about ὕμνοι was their subject. 'In the old days,' says the Athenian Stranger in Plato's *Laws* (3 700b1), 'hymns were a form (εἶδος) of song consisting in prayers to the gods', and this link between 'hymns' and the divine never disappeared; the later rhetorical division between hymns to gods and encomia to men may thus have crystallised out of ordinary spoken usage at a relatively early date (cf. Pl. *Rep.* 10 607a4, Arist. *Poetics* 1448b27).[18] (The song of Thyrsis about τὰ Δάφνιδος ἄλγεα in Idyll 1 is both a βουκολικὰ ἀοιδά and a ὕμνος, but Daphnis is a very unusual figure, who though not apparently immortal, was certainly on close terms with the immortals).[19] As far as the form of 'hymns' is concerned, it may have been broadly true that in the early period 'cultic hymns' tended to be lyric performances by choirs whereas 'rhapsodic hymns' were hexameter performances by a single rhapsode, but the distinction can be seen breaking down well before the Hellenistic period;[20] from the fourth century onwards survive a number of hexameter 'hymns' whch clearly occupied a genuine place in cultic performance.

There is no reason then to doubt that the Alexandrian poets would have called the 'Homeric hymns' ὕμνοι, although there are also no

---

[16] For what follows cf. Wünsch, *RE* 9.140–83; T. W. Allen and E. E. Sikes, *The Homeric Hymns* (London 1904) xliii–liv.   [17] Cf. below pp. 52–7.

[18] Cf. S. Koster, *Antike Epostheorien* (Wiesbaden 1970) 114–16. It is noteworthy that the Plato passage draws an explicit contrast between hymns and encomia, on the one hand, and Homer as an example of ἡ ἡδυσμένη Μοῦσα on the other. On the meaning of ὕμνος cf. also below p. 75.

[19] A Daphnis who used to sing βουκολικοὶ ὕμνοι makes a dedication to Pan in Theocritus, Epigram 2. If the noun has special force there, it too may refer to the kind of song offered in Idyll 1.

[20] See also the discussion of how performance affects this distinction in A. Aloni, 'La *performance* di Cineto' in *Tradizione e innovazione nella cultura greca da Omero all'età ellenistica. Scritti in onore di Bruno Gentili* (Rome 1993) 129–42.

compelling grounds for assuming that the origins of our collection go back as far as the lifetime of Theocritus. The fact that the hymns of Callimachus obviously form a unified collection of some kind would clearly be a poor basis for such an assumption;[21] Callimachus, with his obvious interest in poetic arrangement, hardly needed the stimulus of a model collection. As for the authorship of the 'Homeric hymns', Thucydides' confidence in their authenticity was probably widespread, except in the narrower circles of literary scholarship, where scepticism may be found until a relatively late date;[22] such scepticism was, however, not universal,[23] and I see no clear sign that Hellenistic poets exploited doubt about the authorship in their rewritings.

The Homeric hymns have left very little trace in the papyrus record and do not seem to have been the subject of extensive Alexandrian exegesis.[24] This apparent neglect, however, contrasts strangely with their obvious importance as model texts for the Alexandrian poets and, at least, for Ovid after them.[25] To consider only Theocritus, Idyll 22 is crucially indebted to the *Homeric Hymn (33) to the Dioscuri*, as well as to parts of the *Iliad* and the *Odyssey*, to the *Cypria*, and to Pindar's tenth Nemean ode; to this list would be added the second book of Apollonius' *Argonautica*, could we only be sure of the relative chronology.[26] Idyll 24 seems to depend largely upon Pindar's account of the same events in Nemean 1 and Paean 20, but it is the *Homeric Hymn to Demeter* which provides the main archaic model for the nocturnal events in Amphitryon's house, thus serving also as a generic marker within the poem.[27] This recuperation of the archaic hymnic voice was, in one sense, not a task of recuperation at all, because the chain of rhapsodic transmission had never been broken; nevertheless, the hymnal voice was peculiarly important for poets so concerned with the cultural past.

Poems which reconstruct and adapt the past are, in two senses, a

---

[21] For Callimachus' hymns as a collection cf., e.g., the contributions of Haslam and Henrichs to Harder–Regtuit–Wakker 1993, and N. Hopkinson, *Callimachus, Hymn to Demeter* (Cambridge 1984) 13.

[22] Cf. the commentary preserved on a second-century AD papyrus as *POxy.* 2737, fr. 1.19–27 (= Ar. fr. 590 K–A) which refers to οἱ εἰς Ὅμηρον <ἀναφερόμενοι> ὕμνοι. A mid first-century BC papyrus cites *h. Dem.* as a poem by Orpheus (cf. Richardson 1974.66–7). The absence of reference to the hymns in the Homeric scholia presumably also reflects their doubtful status.

[23] *PHibeh* 173 (cf. S. R. Slings, *ZPE* 79 (1989) 1–8) of the mid third century BC preserves parallel verses of Homer and Archilochus, including very probably *h. Dem.* 480. Note also *SH* 78 (Philodemus citing 'Homer in the *Hymns*').

[24] That they were not completely neglected is suggested by two places where *h. Ap.* seems to have affected the Homeric text, cf. S. West, *The Ptolemaic Papyri of Homer* (Cologne/Opladen 1967) 32–5.

[25] Cf. Richardson 1974.67–73; S. Hinds, *The Metamorphosis of Persephone. Ovid and the Self-Conscious Muse* (Cambridge 1987).   [26] Cf. below pp. 59–63.   [27] Cf. above p. 12.

kind of historical writing. The past, here represented by an earlier text, is seen through the new text, so that both ends of a historical process are displayed; Thomas Greene has usefully labelled this the 'historical self-consciousness' of poems.[28] More particularly, hymns tell of the birth of gods or the establishment of their powers or of incidents in the timeless past which exemplify that power. Like mythological narrative in general, hymns look to the past for the validation of the present order; the linking of the past to the present is not only a central structuring mode of such poems, but also to some extent their very purpose. Thus the importance of the prior, 'model', texts is not limited to the familiar technique of the generation of meaning through allusion and difference: the originating and validating force of the hymn's narrative is paralleled and exemplified by the originating and validating force of the model text.

HYMNING THE DIOSCURI

The opening 22 verses of Idyll 22 are a close rewriting of the *Homeric Hymn (33) to the Dioscuri*, which I here quote in full:

ἀμφὶ Διὸς κούρους ἑλικώπιδες ἔσπετε Μοῦσαι
Τυνδαρίδας Λήδης καλλισφύρου ἀγλαὰ τέκνα,
Κάστορά θ' ἱππόδαμον καὶ ἀμώμητον Πολυδεύκεα,
τοὺς ὑπὸ Ταϋγέτου κορυφῆι ὄρεος μεγάλοιο
μιχθεῖσ' ἐν φιλότητι κελαινεφέι Κρονίωνι
σωτῆρας τέκε παῖδας ἐπιχθονίων ἀνθρώπων
ὠκυπόρων τε νεῶν, ὅτε τε σπέρχωσιν ἄελλαι
χειμέριαι κατὰ πόντον ἀμείλιχον· οἱ δ' ἀπὸ νηῶν
εὐχόμενοι καλέουσι Διὸς κούρους μεγάλοιο
ἄρνεσσιν λευκοῖσιν ἐπ' ἀκρωτήρια βάντες
πρύμνης· τὴν δ' ἄνεμός τε μέγας καὶ κῦμα θαλάσσης
θῆκαν ὑποβρυχίην, οἱ δ' ἐξαπίνης ἐφάνησαν
ξουθῇσι πτερύγεσσι δι' αἰθέρος ἀίξαντες,
αὐτίκα δ' ἀργαλέων ἀνέμων κατέπαυσαν ἀέλλας,
κύματα δ' ἐστόρεσαν λευκῆς ἁλὸς ἐν πελάγεσσι,
ναύταις σήματα καλὰ †πόνου σφίσιν†· οἱ δὲ ἰδόντες
γήθησαν, παύσαντο δ' ὀιζυροῖο πόνοιο.
χαίρετε Τυνδαρίδαι ταχέων ἐπιβήτορες ἵππων·
αὐτὰρ ἐγὼν ὑμέων καὶ ἄλλης μνήσομ' ἀοιδῆς.

[28] T. M. Greene, *The Light in Troy. Imitation and Discovery in Renaissance Poetry* (New Haven / London 1982) 17.

Muses of the glancing eyes, tell of the sons of Zeus, the Tyndaridai, glorious children of Leda of the lovely ankles, Castor the horse-tamer and blameless Polydeuces. Having lain in love with the dark-clouded son of Kronos, she bore them beneath the peak of the great mountain of Taygetos, children who are saviours of men upon the earth and of seafaring ships, when wintry storms rage over a harsh sea. Men in ships mount the platform in the stern and call in prayer upon the sons of great Zeus with vows of white lambs; fierce wind and the sea-wave drive the ship down, but suddenly they appear, darting through the air on swift wings. At once they calm the blasts of the terrible winds and lay to rest the waves upon the surface of the white sea, [fair signs for sailors].[29] The sailors rejoice at the sight and cease from their wearying toil.

Hail, Tyndaridai, who ride upon swift horses. I shall remember you and another song also.

Theocritus sticks close to his model, while studiously avoiding direct echo or repetition.[30] The date of the *Homeric Hymn* is uncertain – estimates range from the sixth to the fourth century – and so a comparison of the 'religious ideas' of the two poems should not be expected to yield striking results. Moreover, we will expect that the vast majority of motifs and ideas in a Hellenistic hymn will have archaic and/or classical parallels: the language and ideas of hymnic praise are of necessity conservative, because it is part of the point of such praise that its object is thereby placed (or confirmed) in a familiar category of the divine – radical innovation would threaten to defeat the very purpose of praise. Nevertheless, with these provisos, it may be possible to trace certain lines of development in the Hellenistic poem.

Whereas the hymn poet invokes the Muses, Theocritus' opening ὑμνέομεν both focuses our attention on the rôle of the poet and momentarily evokes the 'performance' of the hymn, as does the same word at the head of Callimachus' *Hymn to Artemis*. The anaphoric repetition at the start of the second sentence, ὑμνέομεν καὶ δὶς καὶ τὸ τρίτον, hints perhaps at the sense 'we < utter the word > ὑμνέομεν . . . twice, and even for a third time . . .', thus reinforcing this performative suggestion through the evocation of a choral refrain.[31] Without

---

[29] The text here is quite uncertain.
[30] Cf., e.g., Wilamowitz 1906.184–5; G. Perrotta, *SIFC* 4 (1926) 238–9; Kurz 1982.80–4.
[31] Cf. Dover *ad loc.*, who finds this interpretation 'not impossible'; strangely, Gow does not comment. Dover too rightly sees a problem in the interpretation of vv. 6–8. Most naturally, v. 6 might be taken to refer to storms at sea, in which case vv. 8–9 come as a surprise, although the rôle of the Dioscuri as saviours was certainly not limited to their nautical function (cf. *RE*

entering fully into the 'mimetic' mode familiar from Callimachus' hymns, Theocritus still suggests the excited repetitions which characterise hymnic form. What we have is a kind of brief 'memory' of performance; it is as though the echo of choral performance still hovers faintly over the formality of the ionic hexameters.

There may, however, be another aspect of this repetition. 'A second and a third time' suggests also the division of Idyll 22 itself, as indicated by the hymnal markers in vv. 1, 26, and 135–6, into a 'hymn' to the Dioscuri, a 'hymn' to Polydeuces, and then a 'hymn' to Castor; the final verses form the farewell *coda* to the whole.[32] Whereas the archaic hymn singer usually passes to 'another song' at the completion of his *prooimion*, Theocritus has no subject of song other than the Dioscuri (collectively and as individuals). The poet is no longer primarily 'a poet', who can turn his hand from subject to subject, but rather stands in a much closer relationship with the divinity being celebrated. He offers his poem (or poems)[33] to the Dioscuri (or perhaps to all the dead heroes of the heroic age)[34] as μειλίγματα (v. 221), 'soothing offerings', a word whose special connections with hero cult and the cult of the dead (cf. LSJ s.v. 2) are particularly relevant here. The Dioscuri are not 'dead' (in the conventional sense), but they are *daimones* and we have just seen how dangerous they can be; the poet 'buys' their favour by the propitiatory offering of his poem. Here we have travelled far from the archaic 'servant of the Muses' and have taken important steps towards the Roman *uates*. Not dissimilar perhaps is the conclusion of Idyll 7 in

---

5.1094–7). However the grammar is explained, vv. 7–9 do give the two most prominent cases of the function outlined in v. 6; Theocritus thus creates the appearance of a strict parallelism (genitives at the heads of three successive verses), which is complicated both structurally (the relation between v. 6 and vv. 7–9) and syntactically (the variation between participial phrases and a relative clause). It is tempting to relate this intricacy to the poem's concern with equality and difference, cf. below p. 57. The language of these verses finds a striking parallel in the (late Hellenistic) first hymn of Isidorus to Isis (Bernand p. 633); the poet is listing all of those who are aided by the goddess – καὶ ὅσοι ἐμ πελάγει μεγάλωι χειμῶνι πλέουσι | ἀνδρῶν ὀλλυμένων νηῶν κατὰ ἀγνυμενάων | σώζονθ' οὗτοι ἅπαντες, ἐπευξάμενοί σε παρεῖναι. This is another warning against too hard a distinction between 'literary' and 'real' hymns.

32   It is perhaps a moot point whether vv. 212–13 belong more closely with what precedes (so, e.g., Gallavotti) or what follows (Gow). 'It is no light thing to make war with the Tyndaridai' may apply to both narratives and clearly forms a transition to what follows. Nevertheless, the close reworking of *Nemeans* 10.71–2 (cf. below p. 66), together with the breaking up of the standard hymnic formula οὕτω χαῖρε (*Hom. h.* 3.545, 4.579, 9.7 etc.) which is here divided between narrative and *envoi*, forces us to read these verses very closely with the end of the Castor narrative. Callimachus uses χαῖρε to mark the *envoi* of each of his hymns, and cf. 26.33–8.

33   The closing verses would make an excellent conclusion to a group of poems or a poetry book, but any such hypothesis must remain pure speculation.   34   Cf. below p. 76.

which the farewell to the goddess of the harvest is marked by a ritual act and a prayer for repetition:

ᾶς ἐπὶ σωρῶι
αὖτις ἐγὼ πάξαιμι μέγα πτύον, ἁ δὲ γελάσσαι
δράγματα καὶ μάκωνας ἐν ἀμφοτέραισιν ἔχοισα.

Upon [Demeter's] heap may I plant again the great winnowing-shovel while she smiles on us with sheaves and poppies in either hand.

So too the hymnal conclusion of Apollonius' *Argonautica* expresses a wish that the annual cult of the Argonautic heroes will be marked by repetition of the poem. In these three texts we can see the directions in which Roman poets were to move in constructing their public rôle; in Idyll 22 the principal vehicle for these developments is Theocritus' exploitation of our knowledge of the hymnic tradition.

The most obvious difference between the opening section of Idyll 22 and the *Homeric Hymn to the Dioscuri* is, of course, the sheer length and detail of the Theocritean description of the storm at sea and the intervention of the Dioscuri. This vivid, ecphrastic technique may have general or particular forebears which are now lost to us,[35] but the encomiastic force of the passage is clear: the more frightening the danger, the greater our debt to the Dioscuri. Certain aspects of the later poem also widen the scope of the model text. In the Homeric hymn the gusts over the hostile sea are χειμέριαι, 'wintry', 'stormy';[36] in Theocritus this is replaced by the idea of ships which put out to sea despite contrary indications from the stars – the ships 'do violence to the stars . . .' The prominent rôle of divine signs, set in the heavens to assist men, recalls the theology of Aratus' *Phainomena* (cf. esp. *Phain.* 420 in a scene of shipwreck), and a specific debt to that poet has been convincingly identified in the language of these verses.[37] Aratus describes how the sudden disappearance of 'the Manger' (Φάτνη)

---

[35] The apparent lack of contact with Alcaeus' 'Hymn to the Dioscuri' (fr. 34 Voigt) is both noteworthy and perhaps surprising.

[36] There is perhaps a general reminiscence of Hesiod's account of the problems of autumn sailing (*WD* 674–7).

[37] Cf. E. Maass, *Aratea* (Berlin 1892) 259–60; Effe 1978.65 n. 32; M. Pendergraft, 'Aratean echoes in Theocritus', *QUCC* 24 (1986) 47–54; Sens 1994. Gow II 119 n. 3 remains sceptical. Effe sees the use of Aratus here as part of Theocritus' ironic reversal of Aratus' theology; judgement about this will depend upon the view taken as to the relationship between the soteriology of the opening verses and the grim lesson of the Castor narrative, cf. below pp. 69–70. It is relevant that Apollonius too seems to have used the Aratean shipwreck for his description of Heracles uprooting a tree (*Phain.* 422–4 / *Arg.* 1.1201–4); that scene has, of course, important links with Theocritus, and may help to confirm the Aratean echoes in Idyll 22.

marks the onset of a fierce storm (*Phain.* 898–902), just as Theocritus uses its reappearance to mark the return of fair weather. Man's own foolishness is responsible for his trouble, but the blame is deflected from the sailors to the ships themselves (note esp. vv. 17–18); we may compare the familiar emphasis upon the *Argo*, rather than the Argonauts, as a crucial moment in cultural history.[38] Ships have minds and motives all their own.[39] The orderly repetitiveness of the heavens is evoked by matched participles linked by rhyme, δύνοντα καὶ οὐρανὸν εἰσανιόντα | ἄστρα (vv. 8–9),[40] and perhaps also by the absence of necessary enjambment in the opening verses, a style imitative of order and κόσμος;[41] against this is set against the randomness of natural violence (cf. v. 11) and the disorder of the broken ship (vv. 13–14) which results from the ignoring of divine signs. Whether this moralising slant may be identified as specifically 'Hellenistic' may be doubted – the idea that men bring trouble upon themselves by ignoring divine warnings is the subject of a famous complaint by Zeus at the very start of the *Odyssey* (*Od.* 1.32–43) – but it should at least be connected with a further aspect of the passage.

A clear difference between the two hymns is that Theocritus omits any explicit reference to prayers from the threatened sailors; contrast *h. Diosc.* 8–10.[42] In the *Homeric Hymn* there is a clear narrative causal link between the sailors' prayers and the 'appearance on swift wings' (vv. 12–13) of the Dioscuri who calm the wind and the waves.[43] In Theocritus, on the other hand, there are no prayers, the Dioscuri as such do not 'appear' – favourable constellations do instead (v. 21) – and the winds 'cease', rather than 'being ended' by the Dioscuri. Here too, however, there is no doubt whose hand is at work. It is important to note how this scene is recalled in the subsequent boxing-match, in which 'the son of Zeus' gets the better of the monstrous 'son of Poseidon' (vv. 95–7), thus replaying the victory over the storm at sea

---

[38] Cf. Hunter 1993.138.

[39] Cf. P. Hardie, 'Ships and ship-names in the *Aeneid*' in M. Whitby, P. Hardie, and M. Whitby (eds.), *Homo Viator. Classical Essays for John Bramble* (Bristol 1987) 163–71.

[40] Sens 1994.68–9 notes that the language of v. 8 is strongly evocative of Aratus (cf. *Phain.* 571, 617, 821). 　[41] The enjambment of vv. 8–9 thus marks closure of the opening sequence.

[42] Cf. F. Griffiths 1976.360.

[43] Their appearance in the *Hymn* is very likely as St Elmo's fire (note v. 13 ἀΐξαντες), *pace* T. Lorenz, 'Die Epiphanie der Dioskuren' in *Kotinos. Festschrift für Erika Simon* (Mainz 1992) 114–22, at pp. 115–16. Lorenz does, however, offer a useful collection of material on the (appropriately!) twin conception of the Dioscuri as St Elmo's fire appearing above the mast during a storm, and as the stars whose emergence marks the return of calm weather.

and establishing once again the rule of orderly civilisation (v. 134) which is disturbed as much by Amycus' lack of social grace as it is by the violence of the elements. The differences between the Theocritean and the 'Homeric' accounts therefore must not be exaggerated, but the silences in Theocritus – silences which exist only because of the *Homeric Hymn* – do indeed establish competing modes of explanation. On the one hand, salvation is 'manifestly' the work of the θεοὶ σωτῆρες, and we might say that vv. 17–18 convey the point of view of the (god-fearing) sailors themselves. On the other hand, the prominence given to stars as signs and the intransitive expression of vv. 19–20 suggest a 'natural' explanation in terms of what would today be called 'weather patterns'. Such a duality of outlook, which sets 'scientific' and 'mythic' explanations side by side, is not specifically 'Hellenistic', but is well paralleled in this period,[44] and may be thought to be in part the product of an increasingly scholastic mentality; if indeed Aratus is echoed in these verses, then Theocritus may well be acknowledging that poet's 'poeticisation' of science. Be that as it may, Theocritus' technique again reveals historical process – the apparently competing claims of a 'theological' and a 'scientific' mode of explanation mark the text in ways analogous to the rewriting of earlier texts which I have already discussed; these explanations do not so much compete, as reveal change over time.

TWO GODS AND TWO POETS

Duality lies at the centre of Idyll 22, the hymn to the twin gods. In proclaiming equality and duality, the opening verses also inscribe a problematic inequality into the poem, an inequality between Leda and 'aegis-bearing Zeus', and between Castor and 'Polydeuces, who is terrible to challenge in boxing, when once he has wrapped the ox-hide straps around his arms'.[45] As I have already noted, the story told in the third part of the hymn was the traditional validation for the fundamental difference between the twins, and the exploration of difference in sameness structures the whole poem. Vv. 23–6,

---

[44] For Aratus cf. Hunter 1995d; for Apollonius cf. Hunter 1993.80–1.

[45] Contrast the matched noun–epithet pairs of *h. Diosc.* 3. Commentators apparently overlook the verbal point of v. 3, χεῖρας ἐπιζεύξαντα μέσας βοέοισιν ἱμᾶσιν, evoking another kind of yoking; for the frequent connections in ancient poetry between bulls and boxers cf. *CQ* 39 (1989) 557–61. Sens (1994.72 n. 34) suggests rather that the verse evokes horse-taming (cf. *Il.* 23.324), a famous attribute of the Dioscuri.

ὦ ἄμφω θνητοῖσι βοηθόοι, ὦ φίλοι ἄμφω,
ἱππῆες κιθαρισταὶ ἀεθλητῆρες ἀοιδοί,
Κάστορος ἢ πρώτου Πολυδεύκεος ἄρξομ' ἀείδειν·
ἀμφοτέρους ὑμνέων Πολυδεύκεα πρῶτον ἀείσω.

O helpers both of mortals, beloved pair, horsemen and harpers,
athletes and singers, with Castor or first with Polydeuces shall I begin
my song? As I am to hymn both, I shall sing first of Polydeuces.

dramatise the boldness of the decision to hymn the twins individually
as well as collectively; having to make a choice between them
threatens the very equality instantiated in the dual forms. What has
seemed to many critics an awkward and rather clumsy poetic choice is
in fact what points us towards the very centre of the poem.

The narratives of Polydeuces and Castor play off against each
other in both content and form. Both tell of a duel and both duels are
indebted to the duels between Menelaos and Paris in *Iliad* 3 and
between Hector and Ajax in *Iliad* 7; the two Theocritean duels are
linked by verbal echo.[46] Even here, however, an important Iliadic
pattern is overturned. Whereas in the *Iliad* boxing is a 'sporting'
struggle between allies (cf. *Il.* 23) and armed duels are fought out
between enemies, in Idyll 22 it is φίλοι who use the weapons of war
against each other, and strangers who box. This is not, I think, merely
a witty conceit, but is part of the whole challenge to the inherited
hymnic, and indeed epic, tradition which the poem represents. The
internal poetic *agon* between the two duels echoes the wider *agon*,
made explicit in the final verses, between the poem as a whole and the
past poetic tradition. I shall return to this at the end, but here we may
note that just as the form of the whole poem differs radically from the
inherited body of hexameter hymns, so the two internal narratives are
more obviously contrasted than alike. In the Polydeuces narrative the
two principals exchange words in a remarkable stichomythia (vv.
53–75), which is framed by introductory and concluding formulae of
a kind familiar from epic, but is otherwise a complete surprise.[47] It is,
however, entirely apt for the display of the directly opposed values
which are at stake in the encounter with Amycus; such an opposition

---

[46] On all of this cf. Gow's commentary *passim*; Kurz 1982.104; Sens 1992. Sens makes an
interesting case for a closer dependence of the clash of Castor and Lynceus upon the duel of
Menelaos and Paris than had earlier been supposed; the most interesting parallel discussed
by him is *Iliad* 3.214 with v. 153 (on which cf. below p. 68) – Theocritus would then be writing
the kind of speech Menelaos made on the reported occasion when he went to Troy,
presumably urging the Trojans to give Helen up.

[47] Wilamowitz 1906.186 rightly associated the stichomythia with the bucolic tradition, cf.
Idylls 4, 5, 8, and 10. Cf. further Rossi 1971.85; Thomas 1995.

is absent from the clash between Castor and Lynceus, and is thus one of the many structural differences between the two sections. In the Lynceus narrative we are offered only one voice, a long speech by the doomed Lynceus. Finding this intolerable, Wilamowitz marked a lacuna after v. 170 and assigned vv. 171–80 to Castor (with the adoption of Λυγκεύς rather than Κάστωρ in v. 175). I shall return to this suggestion presently,[48] but here it is sufficient to note that Wilamowitz's intervention would produce a rhetorical *agon* as a preliminary to the ritualised martial *agon* to follow, just as the stichomythic form should be seen as a verbal analogue of the 'cut and thrust' of the boxing match to follow. Whether sameness or difference is more likely in this poem is perhaps a moot point.

A further contrast between the two narratives lies in the model texts presupposed by them. Whereas the Castor narrative seems predominantly indebted to the *Cypria* and to Pindar's Tenth Nemean and is written in a style which has seemed to many to be a pastiche of Iliadic battle narrative,[49] the story of Polydeuces and Amycus, while full of Homeric reminiscence, finds its closest relative in the corresponding scene of Apollonius' *Argonautica* (2.1–163). The relative chronology of the two texts, together with that of the corresponding Hylas narratives (Idyll 13 and *Arg.* 1.1153–1357), has been endlessly debated. The purely general considerations raised here – that Idyll 22 is a poem in which rewriting of prior texts is an important mode for the exploration of duality – might be thought to favour the priority of Apollonius; a full discussion of this question would take us far afield, but I wish to focus on the relationship between the two Theocritean narratives as a possible way of increasing our understanding of the account of Polydeuces and Amycus.

Whereas Apollonius places the meeting with Amycus and the Bebrycians inside the Propontis, Theocritus places it on the Black Sea coast after the *Argo* had successfully negotiated the Clashing Rocks. Doubtless, contemporary geographical writing could have been cited for both locations,[50] but what is important is that Idyll 22 (like *Argonautica* 2) presupposes the loss of Heracles to the expedition; its narrative time is subsequent to that of Idyll 13, which is explicitly set in the Propontis (vv. 30–1).[51] To this must be added the fact that the

---

[48] Cf. below pp. 70–2.   [49] Cf. below pp. 74–5.

[50] Cf. E. Delage, *La Géographie dans les Argonautiques d'Apollonios de Rhodes* (Bordeaux 1930) 117–22; Vian's edition, I 132–3.

[51] Sens 1994.72 makes the attractive suggestion that the *Argo* of Idyll 22 'negotiated the Rocks' in vv. 10–16 through verbal echoes of *Argonautica* 2.

striking similarities between the two Idylls are manifested in an almost[52]
complete avoidance of verbal repetition. With 13.22, ἅτις κυανεᾶν
οὐχ ἅψατο συνδρομάδων ναῦς, 'the ship which did not touch the
Kyaneai ['dark ones'] which clash together', compare 22.27–8 ἡ μὲν
ἄρα προφυγοῦσα πέτρας εἰς ἓν ξυνιούσας |'Αργώ, 'the *Argo* then had
escaped the rocks which come together in one'; in 22.29 the Argonauts
are θεῶν φίλα τέκνα, 'dear children of the gods', whereas in Idyll 13
they are θεῖος ἄωτος ἡρώων, 'divine flower of the heroes' (vv. 27–8);
in the two poems the similar 'bivouac' scenes[53] both use the 'one and
the many' motif, but use it in quite different ways (13.33, 22.30). The
loci amoeni in which Hylas and the Dioscuri find themselves are, of
course, generically similar, and yet they have almost nothing in
common:

τάχα δὲ κράναν ἐνόησεν
ἡμένωι ἐν χώρωι· περὶ δὲ θρύα πολλὰ πεφύκει,
κυάνεόν τε χελιδόνιον χλωρόν τ' ἀδίαντον
καὶ θάλλοντα σέλινα καὶ εἰλιτενὴς ἄγρωστις.
ὕδατι δ' ἐν μέσσωι Νύμφαι χορὸν ἀρτίζοντο,
Νύμφαι ἀκοίμητοι, δειναὶ θεαὶ ἀγροιώταις,
Εὐνίκα καὶ Μαλὶς ἔαρ θ' ὁρόωσα Νύχεια.

(13.39–45)

Soon in a low-lying place he spied a spring, round which grew rushes
thick, and dark celandine, green maiden-hair, and wild celery luxur-
iant, and creeping dog's-tooth. In the water Nymphs were arraying
the dance, the sleepless Nymphs, dread goddesses for countryfolk,
Eunica, and Malis, and Nycheia with Spring in her eyes.

Κάστωρ δ' αἰολόπωλος ὅ τ' οἰνωπὸς Πολυδεύκης
ἄμφω ἐρημάζεσκον ἀποπλαγχθέντες ἑταίρων,
παντοίην ἐν ὄρει θηεύμενοι ἄγριον ὕλην.
εὗρον δ' ἀέναον κρήνην ὑπὸ λισσάδι πέτρηι,
ὕδατι πεπληθυῖαν ἀκηράτωι· αἱ δ' ὑπένερθε
λάλλαι κρυστάλλωι ἠδ' ἀργύρωι ἰνδάλλοντο
ἐκ βυθοῦ· ὑψηλαὶ δὲ πεφύκεσαν ἀγχόθι πεῦκαι
λεῦκαί τε πλάτανοί τε καὶ ἀκρόκομοι κυπάρισσοι
ἄνθεά τ' εὐώδη, λασίαις φίλα ἔργα μελίσσαις,
ὅσσ' ἔαρος λήγοντος ἐπιβρύει ἂν λειμῶνας.

(22.34–43)

Together Castor of the swift steeds and wine-hued Polydeuces wan-
dered apart from their comrades and viewed the varied wild wood-
land on the hill. Beneath a smooth rock they found a perennial spring
brimming with clearest water, the pebbles in its depths showing like

---

[52] Cf. below p. 61.   [53] Cf., e.g., Köhnken 1965.34 n. 2.

crystal or like silver. Hard by tall pines were growing, poplars and planes and tufted cypresses, and fragrant flowers farmed gladly by the shaggy bees – all flowers that teem in the meadows as spring is on the wane.

The two poems, of course, have different poetic requirements: what is important in Idyll 13 is the mysterious darkness and fertile lushness which mark the *locus* as female space, whereas in Idyll 22 the remarkable variety of undestroyed nature is set against the solitary and imposing figure of Amycus. Theocritus could ring infinite changes upon the theme, and yet the avoidance of common elements remains noteworthy, when added to the other phenomena which I have catalogued. Finally, there is a case of sameness, rather than difference. Both 13.32 and 22.32 begin with the half-verse ἐκβάντες δ' ἐπὶ θῖνα, 'disembarking onto the shore'; opinions will no doubt differ as to how likely it is that such a half-verse could recur in precisely the same position in poems where verbal similarity is otherwise so scarce. It seems clear, however, that whatever the relationship between Theocritus and Apollonius, Idylls 13 and 22 are closely connected, and it may be worth entertaining the working hypothesis that 22 was composed after 13 and forms a kind of narrative completion of it. One of the techniques of that completion would be an elaborate verbal *uariatio* in the presentation of broadly similar scenes; the 'formula' in the thirty-second verse would then act as a formal marker of the relationship between the poems.

This can, of course, be no more than a hypothesis; it may, nevertheless, assist with other puzzling features of these poems. Whereas Apollonius provides Heracles with a task – cutting a new oar – while dinner is prepared and Hylas wanders away from the Argonauts, in Idyll 13 the great hero appears simply to be one of the group preparing camp while his beloved goes off (13.32–5). Whatever the chronological relation between Idyll 13 and *Argonautica* 1, there is no sign in Theocritus' poem of the Apollonian Heracles' expedition to get a new oar; there are, however, points of contact between this expedition and Idyll 22. The finding of a beautiful spring puts the Dioscuri on a par with Hylas, but the 'sight-seeing' stroll around a wooded mountainside which the sons of Zeus take instead of joining the group activities on the beach is strikingly like the task of Heracles, another υἱὸς Διός (*Arg.* 1.1188), who goes 'into a wood' to find a suitable tree.[54] Whereas, of course, Heracles destroys nature, the

---

[54] Cf. Sens 1995. Note εὖρον at the head of v. 37 corresponding to εὖρεν at *Arg.* 1.1190. ἀποπλαγχθέντες (v. 35) is curiously matched by ἀποπλάγξειεν in a later part of the same Apollonian episode (1.1220).

Dioscuri admire it. If we adopt the working hypothesis that there is a chronological priority of Apollonius over Theocritus and at least a narrative priority of Idyll 13 over Idyll 22, then it becomes clear that in Idyll 22 Theocritus was able to use material from the Apollonian narrative of Hylas which he had left untouched when composing his own Hylas narrative. One model text is thus distributed over two rewritings in a virtuoso manifestation of the central theme of Idyll 22.

There may yet be more. The Dioscuri come upon Amycus sitting in the *locus amoenus*. Not only, like the Apollonian Heracles in the Hylas episode,[55] does the poet characterise this figure with echoes of the Homeric Cyclops,[56] but like Heracles he is wearing a lion-skin (an attribute not otherwise associated with the Bebrycian king). It is tempting to believe that the Dioscuri here come face to face with their literary model, the Apollonian Heracles, lost to the expedition before the passage through the Rocks.[57] That this suggestion has not been made before is due in part perhaps to some kind of aesthetic revulsion at the description of Amycus: 'ugly', 'hideous', and 'monstrous' are some of the nicer things which recent critics have had to say about Theocritus' Amycus.[58] Clearly, the king *is* strikingly contrasted with the natural beauty of the spot; in particular, his muscles like the boulders in a winter torrent (vv. 49–50) are contrasted with the gleaming pebbles at the bottom of the spring (vv. 38–40). He is indeed δεινὸς ἰδεῖν, 'terrifying to behold', and ὑπέροπλος (v. 44) can denote both moral and physical excess,[59] but the modern critical reaction seems somewhat exaggerated, despite the echoes of the Cyclops. An important influence on this reaction has been the famous late Hellenistic statue of the 'Terme boxer', a bronze figure of an ageing and scarred fighter which many critics have mentioned in the context of the Theocritean Amycus or even identified as the Bebrycian king; σφυρήλατος οἷα κολοσσός, 'like a statue beaten out with a hammer' (v. 47), clearly invites us to think of works of art, but we should not be too hasty in our conclusions.[60] But for his battered ears,

---

[55] Cf., e.g., J. J. Clauss, *The Best of the Argonauts. The Redefinition of the Epic Hero in Book 1 of Apollonius's Argonautica* (Berkeley 1993) 186–9.   [56] Cf. n. 63 below.

[57] A stronger version of this thesis is obviously available: Amycus, the great *kolossos* of a man, represents 'epic' which here meets its match in the refined aesthetics of modern poetry, as represented by the young gods. I am not averse to the general direction of such a reading.

[58] Cf., e.g., Effe 1978.66; Zanker 1987.86; Hutchinson 1988.146; Kurz 1991.239.

[59] Apollonius makes Amycus ὑπεροπληέστατος ἀνδρῶν (*Arg.* 2.4), cf. M. Campbell, *Hermes* 102 (1974) 40–1.

[60] For the 'Terme boxer' cf. Pollitt 1986.145–7. P. L. Williams, 'Amykos and the Dioskouroi', *AJA* 49 (1945) 330–47, argued that the 'Terme boxer' and the 'Terme ruler' (Pollitt

Amycus bears an unmistakable resemblance to the great hero of the labours; even the ears, however, are paralleled in some late Hellenistic representations of Heracles,[61] who was both the greatest boxer of Greek legend and 'patron' of all boxers. If indeed Amycus is shaped to evoke the figure of Heracles, now lost to the Argonauts but a principal literary model and counterpoint to the Dioscuri, it becomes clear that ἀδηφάγος, 'glutton' (v. 115), refers not merely to the proverbial appetite of athletes, but also to one of the most familiar characteristics of Heracles himself. In Idylls 13 and 22, therefore, Theocritus has produced his own narrative to match the closing sequences of *Argonautica* 1 and the opening scene of Book 2.

This reconstruction seems to make sense of the poetic facts, but must, of course, remain at the level of hypothesis. Its value lies in its emphasis upon the relation between this poem and other texts, for not only is this what Theocritus stresses at the end of the poem[62] but it also addresses the literary technique most closely allied to the poem's central concern with 'duality'. As we have seen with Theocritus' use of the *Homeric Hymn to the Dioscuri* and as may be illustrated at great length from the corresponding texts of Theocritus and Apollonius, reworking and rewriting prior texts, indeed the whole process of literary allusion, establishes patterns of similarity and difference and explores what is at stake in those patterns; so too does this poem which threatens to drive a wedge between the indissoluble heavenly pair.

PLEADING WITH THE DIVINE

Nowhere is the structuring dualism of Idyll 22 more obvious than in the conduct of the two fights which it portrays. Whereas Polydeuces wins by cleverness and skill – as Odysseus outwitted Polyphemus – [63] no emphasis at all is given to such virtues in Castor's victory over Lynceus. Amycus is spared, whereas Lynceus is killed with grimly

---

1986.72–4) were actually Castor and Amycus from an original triptych which would have been completed by a statue of Polydeuces; Theocritus' poem would thus be drawing upon the original of these statues. More usually, however, the 'Terme ruler' is considered to be the figure of a Hellenistic prince; Smith 1988.84–5 does not consider Williams' thesis worthy of mention.

[61] Cf. *LIMC* s.v. Herakles, nos. 175, 189. Bronze statuettes of the seated hero are unmistakably like the 'Terme boxer' (cf. nos. 936, 938). The famous 'Heracles Epitrapezios' of Lysippos showed the hero 'seated on a rock covered with lionskin, looking up, holding cup in right hand, left hand resting on club' (*LIMC* IV.1, p. 774). [62] Cf. below p. 76.

[63] For Amycus as the Cyclops cf. Kurz 1982.88–9; my note on Ap. Rhod. *Arg.* 3.176–81; Laursen 1992.78–81; Hunter 1993.160.

physical precision (vv. 202–3). Modern criticism has tended to see this contrast in moral, as well as purely narratological, terms; as Hutchinson puts it: 'in the first story the dialogue sets Amycus very firmly in the wrong; in the second Lynceus' speech sets the Dioscuri at a moral disadvantage'.[64] So too, Polydeuces' behaviour has been seen as dictated by modern 'civilising' virtues, Castor's by an older set of 'heroic' *mores*.[65] It is certainly true that the story of the rape of the Leucippides evokes the 'lost' world of raiding and constant warfare familiar, for example, from the tales of Nestor in the *Iliad*, and that the 'civilised' virtues of Polydeuces are also on display in the parallel scene of Apollonius' *Argonautica*.[66] Moreover, Lynceus' attempt to win over the Dioscuri by appealing to the number of other available marriages (vv. 156–64) seems a clear evocation of the quarrel between Achilles and Agamemnon in the *Iliad*.[67] Such struggles over female captives – familiar not only from the *Iliad* but also from the opening chapters of Herodotus – act as markers of the distant beginnings of history and the historiographical process; their place in literary history marks them as 'early'. In reworking a story from the *Cypria* which told of events leading up to those of the *Iliad*, Theocritus takes us back even before the primary heroic epic. Although the Argonautic expedition too occurred a generation before the Trojan War, the Polydeuces narrative rewrites scenes from the 'later' *Odyssey* (especially the scenes of Polyphemos and the beggar Iros), and the stichomythic form of the exchange with Amycus marks it stylistically as a secondary development from 'epic' narrative. There is, therefore, more than a little truth in a critical approach which sees the contrast between the two fights as a difference between the 'new' and the 'old', instantiated through reworkings of, respectively, the *Odyssey* and the *Iliad*;[68] this is also, of course, in keeping with the dualising structures of the poem. As so often, however, the contrast is simultaneously obvious and subtly nuanced.

What version of the story of the rape of the Leucippides is presupposed in Idyll 22 must remain unclear. Like the Polydeuces

---

[64] Hutchinson 1988.164.

[65] Cf., e.g., C. Moulton, 'Theocritus and the Dioscuri', *GRBS* 14 (1973) 41–7, at p. 46. Sanchez-Wildberger 1955.16–17 sees a contrast between the Tyndarid Castor, 'der grausame, unnachsichtige Gegner . . . gegen den Feind, der im Recht ist', and Polydeuces, the son of Zeus, who is 'heldenhaft und edel'.   [66] Cf. Hunter 1993.28–9, 160.

[67] Cf., e.g., Zanker 1989.86–7; Zanker rightly rejects over-simple readings of the morality of the Lynceus narrative, but does not engage in detailed analysis.

[68] Cf., e.g., Kurz 1991.246.

narrative, it begins as though it were familiar – τὼ μὲν ἀναρπάξαντε κτλ. (v. 137) – which does not mean that we should assume that it *was* familiar.[69] I have argued above that the style of the opening of the Polydeuces narrative (ἡ μὲν ἄρα προφυγοῦσα πέτρας . . . , 'The *Argo*, then, had escaped the rocks . . .', v. 27) has, in part, a specific explanation in the relation between this poem and Idyll 13. Hellenistic narrative, however, also experiments not only with how the reader's knowledge can be exploited, but with how that knowledge can actually be constructed. A technique of elliptical narrative suggests that what we are hearing or reading follows a well-known story (which may, of course, also be true); such a technique invests the narrative with a surface 'authority', which is however meant to be understood for what it is, namely an internally generated 'authority' independent of the existence of external witnesses. In essence this technique is a literary imitation and extension of the indications in the Homeric text as to how a bard would begin a 'well-known story', such as we see when Demodocus sings as Odysseus has asked him:

ὣς φάθ', ὁ δ' ὁρμηθεὶς θεοῦ ἄρχετο, φαῖνε δ' ἀοιδήν,
ἔνθεν ἑλὼν ὡς οἱ μὲν ἐϋσσέλμων ἐπὶ νηῶν
βάντες ἀπέπλειον   (*Od.* 8.499–501)

So spoke Odysseus. The bard felt the prompting of the god and began his utterance of the lay, taking it up where the Argives had
boarded their well-benched ships and departed. (Trans. Shewring,
adapted)

Thus both the technique and the subject acquire a seal of hallowed antiquity; it would, however, be very naive to assume that all is as it seems. Callimachus' famous ἀμάρτυρον οὐδὲν ἀείδω, 'I sing nothing which is not attested by witnesses' (fr. 612), the original context of which is quite unknown, bears considerable responsibility for much modern confusion about the nature of Hellenistic narrative.

Theocritus' main sources for the narrative of the confrontation between the Dioscuri and the sons of Aphareus seem to have been the *Cypria* and Pindar, Nemean 10, a poem which itself exploited the archaic epic narrative. Gow's synthetic account of that archaic narrative is as follows: 'The Apharidae had taunted the Dioscuri with paying no bride-price for their brides, the Leucippides; whereon the Dioscuri stole the cattle of the Apharidae and gave them to

---

[69] The use of ἀναρπάζειν in fact might suggest that we are going to get the 'usual' story of the dispute over cattle, cf. *Il.* 5.556, Sens 1995.

Leucippus. In the ensuing fray Idas killed Castor (with whom Polydeuces subsequently shared his own immortality), Polydeuces killed Lynceus, and Zeus struck Idas with a thunderbolt.'[70] Theocritus' debt to Nemean 10 is most clearly marked in v. 212 in the conclusion to the Castor narrative:[71]

οὕτω Τυνδαρίδαις πολεμιζέμεν οὐκ ἐν ἐλαφρῶι.

Thus no light thing it is to war with the sons of Tyndareus.

This verse reworks the 'moral' of the corresponding Pindaric narrative:[72]

χαλεπὰ δ' ἔρις ἀνθρώ-
ποις ὁμιλεῖν κρεσσόνων.

(*Nemeans* 10.72)

For men to strive with their betters is a difficult struggle.

Such an intertextual marker, however, serves to draw attention most of all to the very great differences in the two narratives. Whereas in Theocritus the Apharidae are upset about the loss of their brides, in Pindar Idas is said to be angry 'concerning cattle' (v. 60); Theocritus uses this motif by making cattle part of the alleged bribe to Leucippus (v. 150). In Pindar, Castor is killed, but then raised again by Zeus after Polydeuces opts for an existence alternating between heaven and the Underworld; in Pindar, Polydeuces must pursue Idas and Lynceus, as his brother is already dead, whereas in Theocritus Castor is the pursuer (198ff.). The death of Lynceus is not dissimilar in the two poems (*Nemeans* 10.69–70; 22.201–2), although his killer is of course different.[73] Such variation is perhaps no more than we would expect in a Hellenistic reworking of archaic narrative, but in the light of what we have seen to be the concerns of this poem, the variation assumes unusual significance. Of particular importance is the fact that some, at least, of the Theocritean 'narrative' must be reconstructed from the speech of Lynceus. It is not to be assumed that apparent contradictions between the story as suggested by the narrative frame and that suggested by Lynceus' speech *are* merely apparent and that things would be sorted out if more of the mythographic tradition had

---

[70] Gow II 383. The relevant section of Proclus' summary of the *Cypria* is on p. 103 of Vol. v of the OCT Homer.   [71] Cf. above p. 54n . 32.

[72] Note also κεραυνόν in *Nem.* 10.71 with κεραυνῶι in 22.211, and κρεσσόνων in *Nem.* 10.72 may be picked up by the emphatic κρατέουσι . . . κρατέοντος in 22.213.

[73] In the Pindaric narrative, Lynceus is also burned up by the bolt which Zeus hurls at Idas (vv. 71–2); this might give particular point to συνέφλεξε in 22.211.

survived. Perhaps they would, but scholarly caution in this matter might also be a brake upon understanding. These apparent contradictions might in fact be the very features of the narrative upon which the poet wishes us to focus. To take a simple example: Lynceus' accusation that the Dioscuri bribed Leucippus to deprive them of their marriage has usually been accepted as 'the (unproblematic) truth'. It is in fact not very difficult to reconcile this accusation with a scenario in which the girls seem to be carried off unwillingly – perhaps Leucippus was bribed into conniving with the Dioscuri, while appearing to support the sons of Aphareus etc. – but once we remember, with Wilamowitz,[74] that Lynceus' statements are 'Insinuation des Rivalen' we may decide to look more closely at the rest of his speech to see if all is quite as it seems.[75]

Lynceus begins by remonstrating with the Dioscuri: δαιμόνιοι he calls them (v. 145), picking up Polydeuces' earlier question to Amycus (v. 62).[76] He speaks, of course, more truly than he knows, for the Dioscuri could indeed be viewed as δαιμόνιοι, divine beings who mediate between man and god and share characteristics of both (cf. Plato, *Symp.* 202d–e).[77] The very opening of Lynceus' speech is thus marked by an irony which reveals his ignorance and the depth of his misapprehension; such a marker will guide our reading of the rest of his speech. His opening question, 'Why do you wish to fight?', might seem rather odd, as the Dioscuri do not wish to fight – they want to keep the girls they have carried off – but it makes sense as a way of conveying the fact that Idas and Lynceus are determined not to give way without a struggle. The 'naked μάχαιραι' which Lynceus alleges the Dioscuri to be brandishing have been thought to be inconsistent with the later narrative (esp. vv. 185–91), and Gow ascribes this to carelessness by Theocritus. The inconsistency could in fact be explained away, or regarded as simple exaggeration, but it might also be a marker of the fact that we are listening to special pleading; too many critics have sought to re-create 'what really happened', without realising the dangers of such a reading strategy. There is no 'real scene' beyond the text; the selection of details (and of oddities) is, of

---

[74] Wilamowitz 1906.190. O. Könnecke, 'Zu Theokrit', *Phil.* 72 (1913) 373–91, p. 381, objects that Wilamowitz's description has no justification in the text, but what justification does it need?

[75] There is an excellent analysis of Lynceus' speech in Sens 1995. I have not thought it worthwhile to record all the places where we have reached similar conclusions, or our occasional disagreements. [76] For this polite exasperation cf. 16.22 (below p. 106).

[77] Strictly speaking, of course, the Dioscuri would be δαίμονες, rather than δαιμόνιοι, but the latter form is needed for the 'surface' layer of meaning.

course, not really a selection at all – this is all there is. The 'naked μάχαιραι' have an important rôle to play in marking the change in status of the sons of Aphareus from prospective bridegrooms to victims whose death is a kind of butchery,[78] and it is such thematic considerations which determine what has prominence in the poem. The accusation of bribery and corruption (vv. 149–51) is, moreover, delivered in a *cento* of Iliadic phrases,[79] and the familiarity of the phrasing suggests that we are listening to familiar, and indeed standard, charges: no accusation is more common in legal oratory than that one's opponent has offered and/or accepted bribes. Few scholars would devote much energy to worrying about whether such charges were 'true' when they occur in an Athenian legal speech; do very different standards apply here? The substantive poetic issue is rather that such charges, whether or not we are to take them seriously, occur in a hymn, not a legal speech; I shall return to this matter presently.[80]

No aspect of Lynceus' speech is stranger than his report in direct speech of the kind of speech he often made to the Dioscuri in the past, 'though I am a man of few words' (v. 153).[81] An initial reaction might be that this speech proves his claim to be false, for οὐ πολύμυθος ἐών looks like an epic way of saying 'unaccustomed as I am . . .', i.e. another standard oratorical ploy. Moreover, remembered direct speech within direct speech might portray the speaker as a 'reasonable' person who has tried persuasion before, but this form also in fact calls attention to our lack of control over the truth of the report. We have no way of knowing what value to place upon Lynceus' account of the past. It may be helpful to compare an earlier instance from Greek literature, namely Hecuba's account in Euripides' *Trojan Women* of how in the past she sought to persuade Helen to leave Troy:

> καίτοι σ' ἐνουθέτουν γε πολλὰ πολλάκις·
> ''Ὦ θύγατερ, ἔξελθ' · οἱ δ' ἐμοὶ παῖδες γάμους
> ἄλλους γαμοῦσι, σὲ δ' ἐπὶ ναῦς Ἀχαιικὰς
> πέμψω συνεκκλέψασα· καὶ παῦσον μάχης
> Ἕλληνας ἡμᾶς τ' ''· ἀλλὰ σοὶ τόδ' ἦν πικρόν.
> (Eur. *Tr.* 1015–19)

---

[78] Cf. Sens 1995.

[79] οὐ κατὰ κόσμον, ἄλλοισι κτεάτεσσιν, and βουσὶ καὶ ἡμιόνοισι are all found in the *Iliad* in these metrical positions.   [80] Cf. below p. 73.

[81] For the probable echo of the *Iliad* here cf. n. 46 above.

And yet often I urged you insistently: 'Daughter, be off; my sons will find other marriages, and I shall help you get away unnoticed to the Achaean ships. Put an end to the fighting for the Greeks and for us.' But this was not to your taste.

In the tragedy our reaction to Hecuba's words is complicated by our knowledge of the *Iliad*, in which Helen is quite unlike the character painted here and Hecuba does not say this kind of thing; she may, of course, have done so in other early epic now lost to us. In Idyll 22 we must rely largely upon the curious form of the speech, and the ironic markers with which it opens, to warn us of the possible dangers of too literal a reading. What Lynceus says is, moreover, not entirely unproblematic. He pleads that the Dioscuri would have little trouble in finding brides:

> ὡς ἀγαθοῖς πολέες βούλοιντό κε πενθεροὶ εἶναι,
> ὑμεῖς δ᾽ ἐν πάντεσσι διάκριτοι ἡρώεσσι,
> καὶ πατέρες καὶ ἄνωθεν ἅπαν πατρώιον αἷμα. (Vv. 162–4)

For many would wish to have good men (*agathoi*) as their sons-in-law, and you are pre-eminent among all heroes, you and your fathers, and all your paternal ancestors from of old.

Gow notes that 'Lynceus's reference to the πατρώιον αἷμα ['paternal ancestry'] is perhaps not very happy, for not only do he and his brother share it with the Dioscuri but so do the Leucippides', and Dover observes that 'this would be a patronising utterance if Lynkeus regarded Polydeukes as son of Zeus . . . and he must mean, "your father Tyndareos and Tyndareos's father"'. No doubt Lynceus, *qua* character in the narrative, is not trying to be patronising, but again the full depth of his misapprehension is revealed, and again he speaks more truly than he knows, for the ancestry of Polydeuces' father (at least) is, as every reader knows, a very distinguished one indeed. We may feel sorry for Lynceus, but his position is helpless. When he notes that there are countless other girls from whom to choose, and even appears to offer to help the Dioscuri catch another couple of hapless young ladies (v. 166), he completely misunderstands the nature of the divine: it is *these* girls whom the Dioscuri want, and therefore *these* whom they shall have. Just as soteriological divinities choose the moment to intervene, so their actions may appear to some mortals to be harsh and capricious. If the god so chooses, Amycus will be spared and Lynceus disembowelled. Appeal to ordinary ethical standards is beside the point. Taken together, the three scenes of Idyll 22 show three aspects of divine action – the saving intervention, the preservation of commonly accepted moral values, and the power which can seem inexplicable, particularly when it is exercised in a way which does not always seem 'fair'. To the modern, western tradition, these aspects of the divine may seem inconsistent; Theocritus' audience would, I think, have had little trouble in recognising that all three views of the divine were true and were demonstrated regularly in the affairs of men. We may compare the stories of Teiresias and Erysichthon, which are juxtaposed by Callimachus, and which similarly illustrate quite different aspects of divine action. Lynceus' regret that 'χάρις ['charm', 'grace'] did not attend my words' (v. 168) is well founded: not only was this reported speech unsuccessful, it seems to have been singularly ill-conceived.

If Wilamowitz's textual intervention were correct, then much of this analysis might require revision or more cautious expression. Castor might have answered Lynceus' charges in a way which would shed new light upon them. Wilamowitz's suggestion has now fallen somewhat out of favour,[82] and a recently published papyrus text of the second century AD (*PColon.* 212) offers at least no support to the idea;[83] nevertheless, the suggestion (as so often) proves a useful point of entry to various aspects of the text.

As, *pace* Wilamowitz and Gow, we have no way of knowing what is likely or unlikely in a Theocritean hymn, the case for Wilamowitz's proposal boils down to the fact that ὅμαιμος in v. 173 must mean 'brother', and 'Idas and my brother, the mighty Polydeuces' can only be said by Castor. If Lynceus is still speaking, then the less well attested Κάστωρ must be accepted in v. 175; corruption in either direction would be easy enough to explain. That ὅμαιμος *could* mean 'blood relation' rather than strictly 'brother' is, however, common ground among recent critics,[84] and it can at least be argued that Lynceus is more likely than Castor to refer to Polydeuces as 'mighty'; certainly, if Lynceus does speak v. 173, then it is in keeping with his earlier attempts at conciliatory

---

[82] Cf. White 1976; F. Griffiths 1976; Hutchinson 1988.164 n. 35; Kurz 1991; Laursen 1992. The earliest (printed) argument against it, of which I am aware, is Könnecke art. cit. (n. 74 above). It will be clear that I can hardly accept Könnecke's explanation for Castor's silence – Lynceus' charges are unanswerable!

[83] The bottoms of two adjacent columns offer vv. 130 and 190 respectively; the editor (M. Gronewald) calculates from this a height for the sheet of about 32 cm. It would be surprising if it was much longer, as it would have to be to accommodate many more than 60 verses.

[84] This is true whether we then read ἐμός or ἑός (Vossin). Kurz 1991.242 keeps ἐμός on the grounds that Idas is not really in our thoughts in this part of the hymn; this is not very happy.

flattery (vv. 163–4).[85] Moreover, Lynceus' delusion in regarding himself as related by blood to Polydeuces, whom we know to be the son of Zeus, would be of a piece with the other markers of his wretched situation. Of possible importance also is the speaker's reference to Castor and Lynceus as the younger of the pair of brothers (v. 176). Pausanias too makes Lynceus the younger of the two brothers (4.2.7), and the 'age difference' between the Dioscuri is a familiar element in the myth. At *Nemeans* 10.80–2 Zeus tells Polydeuces that Castor, the mortal twin, was conceived after him, and the idea appears again in a fragment of Epicharmus' comic version of the story of Amycus and Polydeuces; the speaker is presumably Castor:

Ἄμυκε, μὴ κύδαζέ μοι τὸν πρεσβύτερον ἀδελφέον
(Fr. 6 Kaibel)

Amycus, do not abuse my older brother.

It might seem 'natural' that the child of the immortal father should be conceived first, as Heracles the son of Zeus is usually said to have been conceived before Iphicles the son of Amphitryon,[86] but in such narratives 'age' as measured from birth is not always distinguished from 'age' measured by conception. Against the improbability (?) of Lynceus' knowing of the detailed conception of the Dioscuri – an argument which might seem to weigh in Wilamowitz's favour – must be placed the improbability of Castor appealing to this age distinction, as in Epicharmus' comedy. It is presumably funny for Castor proudly to describe his twin as his 'elder brother', but this might seem very out of place in Idyll 22. The ineptitude of the suggestion and the grim irony and pathos (vv. 177–80) which attend it seem to me to argue for Lynceus as the speaker; this, together with the other apparent awkwardnesses in the verses, suits a speaker already marked as unequal to the task.[87] The matter is finely balanced, and it is unlikely

---

[85] Cf. White 1976.405.

[86] Cf. Pherecydes, *FGrHist* 3 F13. In Plautus' *Amphitruo*, however, Hercules is conceived *after* Iphicles (vv. 481–5), and is thus *minor* (in one sense); the twins are, however, born together (v. 1138).

[87] A particular difficulty is the apparent contention that the survivors of the duel, of whom there will be three, will marry the girls, of whom there are two. We might have expected that the bridegrooms would be the winner of the duel and his brother, in which case ὧλλοι will mean 'the other party', i.e. the pair of brothers which includes the victor of the duel (cf. Laursen 1992.89 with n. 50, Sens 1995). White's solution (1976.406–7) that 'these girls' (vv. 179–80) mean the Leucippides and all the other girls 'I have recently mentioned' is unconvincing. Dover sees 'the compulsion of self-deception'.

that any argument will command universal assent. One further nuance is, however, worth mentioning here.

Lynceus (if indeed it is he) finishes by validating his proposal with a *gnome*:

> "ὀλίγωι τοι ἔοικε κακῶι μέγα νεῖκος ἀναιρεῖν."
> εἶπε, τὰ δ' οὐκ ἄρ' ἔμελλε θεὸς μεταμώνια θήσειν.
>
> (vv. 180–1)

'It is proper to end a great strife with a small ill'. So he spoke, and the god was not to make his words idle.

The phrasing of the narrator's comment is conventional, but in the context of the hymn we can hardly fail to ask 'Which god?'[88] In the event, the ὀλίγον κακόν is the death of both Lynceus and Idas, which from the point of view of the Dioscuri is indeed 'a small ill'; this savage irony seems to me to argue for Lynceus as the speaker of v. 180, for Lynceus seems much more likely than Castor to refer to the dispute as a 'great quarrel'. Both narratives in this hymn reveal that we bring disaster upon ourselves, and that we must bear the consequences of our own words. In a world where gods do not wear identifying badges, this can make life very difficult. Here again, the Hellenistic hymn appears to have built upon an idea already well developed in the archaic model texts.

One prominent narrative pattern in the *Homeric Hymns* to Aphrodite, Demeter, and Dionysus concerns a confrontation between mortals and the disguised god, or at least a god who is not recognised as such by the mortals; as the poet of *h. Dem.* puts it, 'gods are hard for mortals to recognise' (v. 111). Part of the 'didactic force' of these hymns, therefore, lies in the old truth (cf. Homer, *Od.* 17.485–7) that one should always behave as if gods were present, because 'you never can tell'. The two narratives of Idyll 22 are of this kind. Both Amycus and Lynceus fail to realise who it is they are dealing with: they do not recognise gods, or even 'half-gods', when they see them. Here then is an important element of continuity, or at least reconstruction, across the ages. There is also, however, a clear difference from the archaic hymns. In Idyll 22 the gods also do not know that they are gods. In the *Cypria* and in Pindar's Nemean 10, the story of the clash between the Dioscuri and the sons of Aphareus was, as we have seen, the crucial moment at which Zeus instituted the alternating pattern of life on Olympus and beneath the earth for the Dioscuri, for it was in

---

[88] Laursen 1992.89 observes 'The god must be Zeus...', but gives no reason for this assertion.

this clash that Castor was killed by Idas. If we read Idyll 22 with the assumption that the Dioscuri are believed and believe themselves to be the sons of Tyndareos and Leda, then the ironies of the text are seen to be quite different from the ironies of the archaic texts. We are assured in the opening verse that the twins are 'the sons of Zeus', but the other characters act in blind ignorance and thus make terrible mistakes.

There is also a more general point here about the nature of hymnic praise. The longer Homeric hymns present accounts of how a new god is accommodated within an existing order, how *timai* are shared out in what Jenny Clay has called 'the politics of Olympus'.[89] Hymns, therefore, reveal and celebrate the power of gods, as *timai*, 'honours paid', are the human response to the display of gods' powers, their *timai*, 'spheres of influence'; so too, Hesiod's *Theogony* sets out Zeus's distribution of divine powers and the Olympian dispensation to which man must accommodate himself as best he can. Power, particularly when it is power over us, is an uncomfortable poetic subject, because praise of the powerful can never be *simply* praise – it always contains a recognition of our vulnerability and an attempt to protect that vulnerability by 'buying off' the powerful with praise. It is well known that Hellenistic and Roman poetry was not shy of stories about gods which might bring 'discredit' upon those gods when viewed from the standpoint of human morality. Catullus 63, the story of Attis' regret at his self-castration while under the power of Cybele, is an obvious example. Already, of course, the *Homeric Hymn to Aphrodite* seems to offer an ambivalent presentation of the goddess honoured in that poem, and it remains true that Christian notions of a kind and just god still hover over too many discussions of Hellenistic religion; what is most important is that hymns articulate a relation of power, and Greeks as a whole never believed that such power was or even should be subject to the codes of human morality. The lessons which emerge from the punishment of the 'guiltless' Teiresias in Callimachus' *Hymn to Athena* are clear enough. It may well be that the Hellenistic period saw changes in the way that such power was 'thought about' and mediated to mortals – kingship and ruler cult are obviously very important here – but Theocritus' Castor remains no less 'worthy of praise' than is his Polydeuces; to deny Castor praise would be a very dangerous move indeed.

[89] J. S. Clay, *The Politics of Olympus: form and meaning in the major Homeric Hymns* (Princeton 1989).

THE SEAL OF THE POET

The verbal style of the martial descriptions within the Lynceus narrative is markedly different from that of the story of Amycus – one more pointed dualism – and poses a difficult critical problem. These verses are commonly referred to as 'an Iliadic pastiche', and a glance through LSJ or Gow's commentary will confirm the fact, if not the pejorative resonance, of the description. Most critics, moreover, find these verses broadly 'non-allusive', in that the understanding of them does not require detailed knowledge of *specific* Homeric scenes.[90] This view has recently been challenged with some success,[91] but at the very least it is clear that these verses have no real parallel within the Theocritean corpus: there are no rare glosses or *hapax legomena*, and no brief comparisons, let alone similes. Again, of course, we may plead our ignorance of the *Cypria*, but this will not sweep the problem away.

Explanations have ranged from an attempted reconstruction of the historical process of writing (Gow) to improbable accounts based upon supposed Alexandrian literary feuding. If, however, as many critics have thought, the battle-narrative is written with an eye on Apollonius – and this is at least not an absurd suggestion, in the light of Apollonius' apparent importance in the first part of the poem – it must be confessed that the 'parody' works by reducing its target to something quite other than what it is; the style of the passage is decidedly not 'much like that Apollonius might have used',[92] not even in the battle passages of that epic.[93] Whether, more broadly, Theocritus is mocking 'the pretensions of the latter-day Homeridae, even as he often does those of love poets'[94] is difficult to say in view of our ignorance of such contemporary poetry. What is, however, clear is that these verses have been declared 'pastiche', because they seem to be an uninventive[95] combination of ready-made elements; another

---

[90] For the distinction cf. Bing 1988.50–6.   [91] Cf. Sens 1992 (discussed above n. 46).

[92] Moulton art. cit. (n. 65) 45, approved by F. Griffiths 1976.362. Griffiths, like others before him, sees the invocation to the Muses at vv. 117–19 as a marker of Theocritus' debt to Apollonius, as such a relationship with the Muses is characteristic of the epic poet, but not elsewhere of Theocritus or Callimachus. If, however, 'Theocritus discomfits the Apollonian Muses by bringing them in at a most inopportune moment', it may be thought surprising that he chose to do this in the Polydeuces, rather than the Castor, narrative.

[93] For Apollonius' style cf. especially Fantuzzi 1988.7–46; on the battle-scenes Hunter 1993.41–5.

[94] F. Griffiths 1976.359.

[95] F. Griffiths 1976.358 notes, however, that Theocritus does not have Homeric precedent for a duel with swords. Whether it is as 'infelicitously' handled as Griffiths suggests remains a matter of opinion.

way of saying this is that these elements are familiar through use, and this appears to be directly relevant to what is said at the end of the poem. There Homer's activity is described as:

ὑμνήσας Πριάμοιο πόλιν καὶ νῆας Ἀχαιῶν
Ἰλιάδας τε μάχας Ἀχιλῆά τε πύργον ἀυτῆς
(22.219–20)

hymning the city of Priam and the ships of the Achaeans, the battles at Troy, and Achilles, a solid tower in warfare.

This brief catalogue of the subjects of the *Iliad* enacts the truth it conveys: these are familiar, 'ordinary' phrases precisely because of the fame, the *kleos*, which Homer has bestowed upon them; they have almost, as it were, 'passed into the language'.[96] So too the battle narrative can only be described as it has been, because Homer has made any other course impossible; that, at least, is the argument. Moreover, the choice of verb, 'hymning' (ὑμνήσας), can hardly be without significance, given the subject-matter and form of the poem. It is true that the verb has a very wide application, and no firm distinction was traditionally drawn between epic narrative and hexameter hymn – both were ἔπος – and 'epics' were often introduced by a hymn, as more narrowly defined; the purpose of both was praise and renown, ἔπαινος and κλέος. Nevertheless, in a passage in which Theocritus claims for himself some kind of equality with 'the Chian bard', he paradoxically accommodates Homer to his own poetic project, rather than vice versa.[97] Implicitly, he also requests for his verses the Homeric immortality which we have just seen instantiated in the description of the duel between Castor and Lynceus.

Two further problems in the *envoi* require comment. One is the apparent discrepancy between what Theocritus here seems to claim about the honour which Homer paid to the Dioscuri, and the minor rôle which they actually play in Homer; after all, the Dioscuri famously did not even go to Troy (cf. *Il.* 3.236–44). Two broad approaches to this apparent problem have been tried. Some have sought a literary explanation in Theocritus' demarcation of his difference from Homer; in doing what Homer actually failed to do,

---

[96] For similar techniques elsewhere cf. Hunter 1993.122, where Theocr. 16.48–9 is cited as an example; the context there is very similar to that of the end of Idyll 22.

[97] So too in Idyll 16 the activity of those whom we call 'archaic epic poets' is ὑμνεῖν (v. 50), not just because the context is the conferring of poetic immortality, but also because Theocritus wants to create an analogy between their activity and his own.

Theocritus asserts his own rival poetic stature.[98] That Theocritus' relation to the poetic heritage is involved here seems certain, and I shall return to this interpretation below. Others (most notably Dover) take ὑμῖν (218, 221) to refer not specifically to the Dioscuri, but to 'the gods and heroes of legend as a whole'.[99] Such an interpretation, which is not to be discounted simply because ἄνακτες (v. 218) is a familiar cult title of the Dioscuri, would make vv. 211–215a the closure to the immediate context, whereas vv. 215b–223 would then be a more generalised closure, applicable to the Dioscuri, but not exclusively so; θεοῖς (v. 223) may reasonably be extended to cover all of Hesiod's fourth age of heroes who are usually conceived as ἡμίθεοι (cf. *WD* 159–60).[100]

The other problem in the *envoi* is the meaning of the disjunction in v. 221. Are the 'Muses' own provisions' the style and model texts of the Lynceus narrative – i.e. the inherited poetic traditions of archaic and classical Greece – whereas Theocritus' own house, which we may assume to contain a more 'slender' store,[101] provides the modern novelties (and modern model texts) of the Amycus narrative? If so, the end of the poem reasserts the external *agon* of the poem, that is between Theocritus and inherited tradition, just as the opening sets out the structure of the internal *agon*, that is between the two encomiastic narratives. This internal *agon* is itself of course double: the narratives of the two twins play off against each other, and within each narrative each twin is matched with an opponent. The doubleness which is everywhere in this poem is here used to express the Hellenistic poet's familiar sense of the weight of tradition. Just as Polydeuces is not really imaginable without his brother, so Theocritus cannot really separate what is *his* from what the tradition offers; both make their contribution, and it is in that blending where we must look for the source of poetry.

---

[98] Cf. F. Griffiths 1976.363–5; Sens 1992.348 '[the Dioscuri become] major participants in a scene precisely parallel to the episode from which they are so strikingly absent in the *Iliad*'. The explanation of Laursen, 1992.92, that the honour paid to the Dioscuri consisted precisely in not including them, because 'the *Iliad* contains so much meaningless bloodshed that it was a benefit for [their] reputation that they did not partake in it', will not, I think, convince many.

[99] The objection of Sens, following Griffiths, that this 'excessively reduces the force of the final line of the poem' (1992.336 n. 3) ignores the very obvious concern with what it is that makes 'a god'. White 1976.407–8 again proposes a most improbable third alternative.

[100] μειλίγματα is quite compatible with this explanation, cf. above p. 54. So too in Idyll 17 Ptolemy is an ἀνήρ (vv. 3–4), but receives the same reward (i.e. ὕμνοι) as the immortals; from this, then, it is but a small step to seeing other similarities between the king and the gods. Cf. further below p. 81.   [101] Cf. Serrao 1971.49.

CHAPTER 3

Idyll 16: poet and patron

THE PTOLEMAIC PATTERN

Idyll 16, the *Charites or Hieron*, is an intriguing and difficult poem; at that point modern critical consensus dissolves. Together perhaps with Idyll 17 and Callimachus' *Hymn to Zeus*, it constitutes the most extensive and explicit Hellenistic meditation upon the relation between poet and patron, a relation which was crucial to much of the production of élite poetry in the third century. Not only, however, do the mode and generic models of the poem seem constantly to change, so too apparently does the stance of the poetic voice. What has caused most consternation to modern critics of Idyll 16 is precisely this apparent 'inconstancy' in a poem which, probably more than any other in the corpus, seems to demand knowledge of the date and circumstances of composition for its understanding. How can the poet's stance and circumstances apparently change in the course of a poem when, presumably, the external circumstances did not? Moreover, there has been an unfortunate critical tendency to assume that any 'real' poetic encomium would look like Idyll 17 (the *Encomium of Ptolemy*), a poem which indeed does have much in common with the *Charites*, and that the differences between the two poems are to be explained wholly by the difference in position of the two *laudandi*, rather than by differences of poetic form or by differences in the nature of the patronage relationship, as it is constructed in the two poems.

We know very little about the actual workings of Hellenistic poetic patronage, and certainly not enough to allow the assumption that there was really only a single model for such relationships, whether they be 'real' or poetically constructed. Part indeed of our critical problem has arisen simply through a poverty of terminology. 'Patron-age' must cover a multitude of possible relationships, differently nuanced

across a whole range of variables. Just as we must not assume that
Theocritus' relationship to Hiero was very like his relationship to
Ptolemy Philadelphus, so we must not assume that both Callimachus
and Theocritus, say, viewed Ptolemy as the 'same kind of patron' and
thus will have constructed their relationship with him in identical
ways. About Hiero's relations with poets we have virtually no evidence
beyond Idyll 16 itself. For Philadelphus, however, we are *relatively*
well supplied. The evidence is, broadly speaking, of three kinds: evidence
concerning the institutions of Ptolemaic patronage, principally the
Museum and the Royal Library,[1] a colourful anecdotal tradition
concerning the Ptolemies and their courtiers, and finally the poems
themselves. The second and third of these (at least) are themselves
inextricably involved in the construction and contesting of varying
models of patronage, and as such demand circumspect handling.

Modern accounts have in fact tended to build an edifice of royal
'control' upon the alleged fate of Sotades of Maroneia, whose mockery
of the 'incestuous' marriage of Philadelphus and Arsinoe II –

> εἰς οὐχ ὁσίην τρυμαλιὴν τὸ κέντρον ὠθεῖς[2]
> (Sotades fr. 1 Powell)

> you are pushing your prick[3] into an unholy hole

– is variously said to have led to execution by drowning or a long spell
in prison.[4] So it might well have done, and we also learn that Sotades
wrote a poem on Philadelphus' mistress Bilistiche;[5] but too much
should not be hung upon this single poet. Moreover, what we know of
Sotades adapts him to a familiar pattern of stories of early Hellenistic
'rebels' whose shared project is conceived as the deflation of the
pompous, the castigation of vice, and the dethroning of common
assumptions, and whose common weapon is 'outspokenness',
παρρησία;[6] if Diogenes the Cynic represents the more serious version
of the pattern, Sotades reflects a lighter and more literary mode. Thus
later antiquity regarded him as the 'inventor' of *kinaidologia*,[7] and it is

---

[1] The fundamental modern accounts remain Pfeiffer 1968.95–104 and Fraser 1972.1 305–35;
see also Weber 1993 *passim*.

[2] ὠθεῖς Plut. MSS: ὠθεῖ Ath. (C): ὠθει Ath. (AE). In the absence of context, a secure choice is
hardly possible.

[3] R. Pretagostini, *QUCC* 39 (1991) 111–14, suggests that τὸ κέντρον not only has the obvious
sexual sense, but also evokes the 'sceptre' of royal power, thus making the verse an indictment
of Philadelphus' administration.

[4] Cf. Ath. 14 620f–1b; Plut. *Mor.* 11a; M. Launey, 'L'exécution de Sotadès et l'expédition de
Patroklos dans la mer Egée (266 av. J.-C.)', *REA* 47 (1945) 33–45; R. Pretagostini, *Ricerche
sulla poesia alessandrina* (Rome 1984) 139–47.   [5] *Suda* σ 871.

[6] For Sotades' παρρησία cf. Ath. 14 620f.   [7] Cf. Strabo 14.1.41.

not improbable that he presented himself in some of his verses as a
kinaidos, that is a man whose enjoyment of the passive rôle in
homosexual intercourse represented an overturning of all the ordinary
assumptions of human conduct. So too, the nature of the 'Sotadean'
verse named after him, an ionic length allowing considerable variety
and freedom of substitution,[8] advertises its difference from the
regularity which is characteristic of Greek stichic rhythms; this verse
form is as 'unmanly' as the poet.[9] This 'rebellious' project is seen most
clearly in the rewriting of the *Iliad*, the 'manliest' poem of them all,
into Sotadeans.[10] Thus, the real or alleged fate of Sotades is a rather
insecure base for broad generalisations about Ptolemaic poetic
patronage.[11]

The relation between a poet and his (real or hoped-for) patron is a
relation of power and dependency, in which, however, the poet
himself has something to offer (namely *kleos*); that this relationship is
structurally analogous to that between man and god is clear, and so
the importance of the hymnic tradition in Hellenistic 'patronage
poetry' should not surprise us, as it is in hymns that man articulates
his relation with the gods.[12] In this chapter I wish to explore both this
reuse of the hymnic tradition and Theocritus' modelling of his
position as analogous to that of poets of earlier ages. Here Idyll 17
appears to offer a simpler model of the poet–patron relationship than
does Idyll 16. The *Encomium of Ptolemy* presents itself as a hymn in
traditional mould to a king who is both 'like' Zeus and Apollo, but
also 'like' an Achilles or Agamemnon.[13] In part, as we shall also find
in Idyll 16, this is done by extensive reworking of archaic texts,

---

[8] Cf. West 1982.144–5; M. Bettini, 'A proposito dei versi sotadei, greci e romani: con alcuni
capitoli di "analisi metrica lineare"' *MD* 9 (1982) 59–105.

[9] Cf. Demetrius, *On Style* 189 citing Sotades fr. 4a Powell.

[10] The apparent similarity of dactyls and ionics *a maiore* was obviously crucial to this enterprise.

[11] As it is also for Greek attitudes to 'brother–sister' marriage, though it has too often been used
in an attempt to shed light upon these; the account in Fraser 1972.1 117–18 seems
particularly exaggerated (Ar. *Clouds* 1371–2 is hardly good evidence for late fifth-century
Athenian attitudes to brother–sister marriage, let alone those of third-century Greeks living
in Egypt). For a more moderate assessment of Sotades' importance cf. Weber 1993.273.

[12] Cf. above p. 73.

[13] Cf., e.g., Meincke 1965.85–164 (much the fullest treatment of this poem); F. Griffiths
1979.71–82; A. E. Samuel, 'The Ptolemies and the ideology of kingship' in P. Green (ed.),
Hellenistic History and Culture (Berkeley 1993) 168–210. There is a helpful survey of the themes
of Ptolemaic poetic encomium in Weber 1993.212–43. Cairns' attempt (1972.100–20, and
cf. already Meincke 1965.88) to privilege a rhetorical tradition of prose encomium over the
hymnic tradition provides a helpful analysis of Theocritus' strategy in the deployment of
certain encomiastic *topoi*, but fails to give adequate weight to the fact that the later rhetorical
tradition is itself a descendant of the hymnic tradition; thus, for example, vv. 9–12 should be
illustrated not from Men. Rhet. 369.13–17 (Cairns 1972.106) but from the common
expression of hymnic *aporia*, out of which Menander's *topos* developed.

particularly the *Homeric Hymn to Apollo*, which is of central importance for the account of Ptolemy's birth on Cos to match that of Apollo on Delos, but whose opening – the reception of Apollo by Leto on Olympus – is already rewritten in Theocritus' account (17.17–33) of Soter and Heracles dining together on Olympus. This rewriting has thus both political and literary significance as a marker of the hymnic genre, but the 'likeness' of texts is also a manifestation of the poem's central strategy of praise. It is indeed 'likeness', the need to find the right category in which to place Ptolemy, that dominates the opening:

> ἐκ Διὸς ἀρχώμεσθα καὶ ἐς Δία λήγετε Μοῖσαι,
> ἀθανάτων τὸν ἄριστον, ἐπὴν †ἀείδωμεν ἀοιδαῖς†·[14]
> ἀνδρῶν δ᾽ αὖ Πτολεμαῖος ἐνὶ πρώτοισι λεγέσθω
> καὶ πύματος καὶ μέσσος· ὃ γὰρ προφερέστατος ἀνδρῶν.
> ἥρωες, τοὶ πρόσθεν ἀφ᾽ ἡμιθέων ἐγένοντο,
> ῥέξαντες καλὰ ἔργα σοφῶν ἐκύρησαν ἀοιδῶν·
> αὐτὰρ ἐγὼ Πτολεμαῖον ἐπιστάμενος καλὰ εἰπεῖν
> ὑμνήσαιμ᾽· ὕμνοι δὲ καὶ ἀθανάτων γέρας αὐτῶν.
> Ἴδαν ἐς πολύδενδρον ἀνὴρ ὑλατόμος ἐλθὼν
> παπταίνει, παρεόντος ἅδην, πόθεν ἄρξεται ἔργου.
> τί πρῶτον καταλέξω ἐπεὶ πάρα μυρία εἰπεῖν
> οἷσι θεοὶ τὸν ἄριστον ἐτίμησαν βασιλήων.
>
> (17.1–12)

From Zeus let us begin and, Muses, with Zeus let us end, the very best of immortals . . .; but of men let Ptolemy be named, first, last and in the midst, for he is the most outstanding of men.

The heroes who of old were sprung from demigods, when they had accomplished noble deeds, found skilled poets to honour them, but I who know how to praise must sing of Ptolemy; and songs are the prize even of the immortals themselves.

The woodcutter who comes to thickly-wooded Ida looks around to see where he should begin his task when there is so much material available. What shall I record first? Countless[15] to tell are the blessings with which the gods have honoured the best of kings.

---

[14] The reading here must be regarded as quite uncertain.

[15] This familiar hymnic *topos* has here particular point as Theocritus will be much concerned with 'counting' the riches of Egypt: cf. vv. 77–120 which are virtually framed by a reprise of the 'countless' motif and are replete with the language of plenty and excess; they make the point that Ptolemy's use of his 'countless' wealth is far more sensible than was that of the Atreidai. The numeration and cataloguing of vv. 82–94 suggest the practice of inventories, which are necessary in any complex kingdom, but are particularly richly documented in Pharaonic and Ptolemaic Egypt, cf. further below p. 89. This feature of the poem gives particular emphasis to μοῦνος in v. 121.

As Zeus is the 'best of immortals', Ptolemy is the 'best of kings'; by the end of the poem, however, we have seen that his father has an honoured place on Olympus, he himself is ἡμίθεος, 'demigod', and that the closest analogue to his marriage to his sister is Zeus's marriage to Hera. This king is thus *very* 'like' a god. The proem of Idyll 17, articulated around the central division marked by αὐτὰρ ἐγώ at the head of v. 7, plays upon questions of similarity and difference. How is Ptolemy the man different from Zeus the god? How are the 'heroes of old' like Ptolemy, and how (by implication) is Homer like Theocritus? The striking 'paratactic' comparison of vv. 9–12 draws our attention to this rhetoric of similarity.[16] Moreover, the whole proem is shaped by the evocation of a famous passage of Hesiod's *Theogony* (vv. 68–103) in which a very close relationship between Zeus, the Muses, (just) kings, and poets is established. This text, which is evoked time and again in Hellenistic encomium[17] and a further echo of which articulates the central division of Idyll 17 (vv. 73–6),[18] authorises for later poets this problem of the categorisation of kings, for the just king who 'decides ordinances with straight justice' (*Theog.* 85–6) is looked to by the citizens 'like a god' (*Theog.* 91); his actions upon the earth mirror those of Zeus in heaven (vv. 71–4, 84–87). Kings are 'Zeus-nurtured' (διοτρεφεῖς), 'from Zeus are kings', ἐκ δὲ Διὸς βασιλῆες (*Theog.* 96), a phrase which is literally stretched around the proem of Idyll 17 (ἐκ Διὸς . . . βασιλήων).[19] Apollonius too uses this same passage of the *Theogony* to describe King Alcinous going among his people to deliver judgement, and there are good reasons for believing that this character suggests the figure of Philadelphus (or perhaps Euergetes):[20]

---

[16] Cf. F. Griffiths 1979.72–3; Bernsdorff 1995.

[17] Cf., e.g., Bing 1988.76–83 on Call. *h.* 1. Note that the same Hesiodic verses (*Theog.* 81–2) may be reworked both about kings (17.74–5) and about poets (Call. fr. 1.37–8). We need not, however, assume any standard 'Alexandrian' view about Hesiod's own relations with βασιλῆες or the circumstances of performance of the *Theogony*; for some modern speculations cf. West's edition pp. 44–5.

[18] Alessandro Barchiesi points out that the Hesiodic model is thus treated just like the king it celebrates, i.e. it is used 'first, last (cf. v. 136), and in the middle'.

[19] On the probable echo of Aratus' *Phainomena* in v. 1 cf. M. Fantuzzi, ''Εκ Διὸς ἀρχώμεσθα, Arat. Phaen. 1 e Theocr. xvii 1' *MD* 5 (1980) 163–72. The Theocritean combination of Aratus and Hesiod is a notable example of the familiar technique of combining allusion to a literary model with allusion to that model's model.

[20] Cf. Hunter 1993.161–2, 1995c. It is, moreover, striking that the nearest Homeric parallel to these Hesiodic verses (*Od.* 7.69–84 about Arete) is also important for Theocritus' praise of Philadelphus and Arsinoe, cf. Hunter 1995c. On the figure of 'the good king' in the Hellenistic period there is much information and bibliography in F. Cairns, *Virgil's Augustan Epic* (Cambridge 1989) 10–28.

αὐτίκα δ' Ἀλκίνοος μετεβήσετο συνθεσίηισιν
ὃν νόον ἐξερέων κούρης ὕπερ· ἐν δ' ὅ γε χειρὶ
σκῆπτρον ἔχεν χρυσοῖο δικασπόλον, ὧι ὕπο λαοὶ
ἰθείας ἀνὰ ἄστυ διεκρίνοντο θέμιστας.

(*Arg.* 4.1176–9)

Without delay Alkinoos came out to reveal his decision about the girl in accordance with the agreement. In his hand he held the golden staff of legal authority with which he administered straight justice to the people in the city.

The Muses look with favour upon the Hesiodic king 'at his birth' (*Theog.* 82), and Theocritus' Muses enact these Hesiodic verses precisely by describing the birth of Philadelphus in his poetry (vv. 56–76); Callimachus offers a more elaborate reworking in which the unborn Apollo prophesies the birth of Philadelphus on Cos and is then himself born on Delos (*h.* 4.162–90, 249–74).[21]

Idyll 17 thus shows us the poet finding in Greek tradition various poetic models to which Ptolemy can be assimilated. In Idyll 16, however, the poet seeks various models for his own position, while that of the patron remains stable, rather distant, and much less well defined than in Idyll 17. The opening, which also recalls the *Theogony*, in which the Muses hymn the gods (vv. 11–21, 43–52), proclaims stability (αἰεὶ . . . αἰὲν . . . ἀείδοντι . . . ἀείδωμεν), but the poem seems to speak of change and decay, before finding in Hiero hope for a better future. Critics have usually found historical explanations for these differences between the poems: any encomiast, so the argument goes, would be hard pressed to find much to say about Hiero. Rather, the differences are to be explained by the fundamentally different nature of the two poems. This is not, of course, to say that the historical context of Idyll 16 is unimportant; rather, the wrong questions about it have too often been asked. It is with this that I begin.

THE PINDARIC PATTERN

The standard critical position on the date of Idyll 16 may be quoted from Gow's summary:

---

[21] The relative chronology of Callimachus and Theocritus has been much discussed, and the matter is further complicated by the question of the dating of Call. *h.* 1, cf. Meincke 1965.116–24; Weber 1993.213 n. 2; M. P. Funaioli, 'I fiumi e gli eroi', *Phil.* 137 (1993) 206–15. A literary argument for the priority of Callimachus is well put by Hutchinson 1988.198: '[if C. came first], Theocritus would then be adorning this poem to Ptolemy with allusions to one of his poets, and especially to passages involving Ptolemy'.

Hiero, then, rose to power at Syracuse in 275 BC or, less probably, in 269. All that can be gathered from T. is that at the date of the poem he is contemplating a campaign against the Carthaginians. The only known occasions when Hiero was so engaged are on his first rise to power, when according to Justin [23.4] he was made *dux aduersus Karthaginienses*, and as an ally of Rome in the First Punic War. It is possible that there were other ocasions of which we know nothing (for the history of Hiero's reign is fragmentary), and also possible that T., who may well not have been writing in Sicily, was not abreast of Sicilian affairs; but if we are to choose between the first and second of these two occasions there are good reasons for preferring the earlier. (II pp. 306–7)[22]

The supposed fighting against the Carthaginians in 275/4 is, however, very poorly attested,[23] and arguments – Gow's 'good reasons' – from Theocritus' silence about Hiero's family and past achievements and the apparent absence of the title βασιλεύς can be at best suggestive rather than conclusive.[24] Here arguments of a more literary character might prove helpful.

It is well understood that one strategy of Idyll 16 is to offer Hiero II the chance to enjoy the same relationship with Theocritus that Hiero I of Syracuse enjoyed with poets, particularly Pindar. The poem is replete with motifs from archaic praise poetry and, in particular, the poetry of Pindar.[25] The final invocation to the Graces (vv. 104–9) directly reworks Pindar's Olympian 14, a poem for a victor from Boeotian Orchomenos, the site of the most famous cult of the Graces:

Καφισίων ὑδάτων
λαχοῖσαι αἵτε ναίετε καλλίπωλον ἕδραν,
ὦ λιπαρᾶς ἀοίδιμοι βασίλειαι

---

[22] On the date of the poem see further Fantuzzi 1993b.155–6 (with bibliography).

[23] Cf. Hutchinson 1988.191. On the chronology of Hiero's early years see B. D. Hoyos, 'The rise of Hiero II: chronology and campaigns 275–264 BC', *Antichthon* 19 (1985) 32–56. Hoyos' reason for dating Idyll 16 to 275/4, 'for in Idyll 17 Theocritus has found patrons in Ptolemy II of Egypt and his queen Arsinoe', is nugatory. Because of its fundamentally encomiastic nature, Idyll 16 may have been written under Hiero's patronage rather than in pursuit of it (cf. R. Petroll, *Die Äußerungen Theokrits über seine Person und seine Dichtung* (diss. Hamburg 1965) 76–84; Cairns 1976.303), but we have nothing to go on except judgements of what is probable. A. Hardie, *Statius and the Silvae* (Liverpool 1983) 33, suggests that it was 'a competition piece, delivered at the Chariteisia Games at Orchomenos'.

[24] For such arguments cf. Meincke 1965.64; F. Griffiths 1979.12–14. Polybius tells us that Hiero acquired his rule 'through his own efforts' because fortune had given him 'neither wealth, nor reputation, nor anything else' (7.8.1).

[25] To the standard commentaries add, e.g., K. Kuiper, *Mnem.* 17 (1889) 384–6; E. B. Clapp, 'Two Pindaric poems of Theocritus', *CP* 8 (1913) 310–16; G. Perrotta, 'Teocrito imitatore di Pindaro', *SIFC* 4 (1925) 5–29. On echoes of Simonides in Idyll 16 cf. below pp. 97–109.

Χάριτες Ἐρχομενοῦ, παλαιγόνων Μινυᾶν ἐπίσκοποι,
κλῦτ', ἐπεὶ εὔχομαι· σὺν γὰρ ὑμῖν τά <τε> τερπνὰ καί
τὰ γλυκέ' ἄνεται πάντα βροτοῖς,
εἰ σοφός, εἰ καλός, εἴ τις ἀγλαὸς ἀνήρ.
οὐδὲ γὰρ θεοὶ σεμνᾶν Χαρίτων ἄτερ
κοιρανέοντι χορούς
    οὔτε δαῖτας· ἀλλὰ πάντων ταμίαι
ἔργων ἐν οὐρανῶι, χρυσότοξον θέμεναι πάρα
Πύθιον Ἀπόλλωνα θρόνους,
αἰέναον σέβοντι πατρὸς Ὀλυμπίοιο τιμάν.
                            (*Ol.* 14.1–12)

You who dwell by the waters of Kaphisos,
in the country where bright colts are bred,
ladies whose tuneful voices
haunt the lanes of glittering Orchomenos
and who guard the Minyans born of old,
hear me, Graces, for I pray:
if anything sweet or delightful
warms the heart of any mortal man,
whether he has beauty, or skill,
or the light of victory shining upon him,
it is your gift.
Even the gods depend on you
and would renounce
ordering the dance and feast
without your favour.
Of all that is done in heaven you have charge.
Seated beside Pythian Apollo,
god of the golden bow, your worship makes
the Olympian father's glory stream forever.
                            (Trans. Nisetich)

Whereas Pindar's Graces are associated with Apollo, Theocritus joins his Graces to Apollo's famous companions, the Muses; where Pindar has come with his *komos* (vv. 16–18), Theocritus waits at home for a sincerely intended invitation. Although Idyll 16 is a brilliant mosaic of Pindaric reminiscence, it is above all Pythian 1 which is the central Pindaric text for understanding this poem. Pindar's prayer for peace and his closing advice to Hiero are the key passages in this regard:

Ζεῦ τέλει', αἰεὶ δὲ τοιαύταν Ἀμένα παρ' ὕδωρ
αἶσαν ἀστοῖς καὶ βασιλεῦσιν διακρί-
    νειν ἔτυμον λόγον ἀνθρώπων.
σύν τοι τίν κεν ἁγητὴρ ἀνήρ,
υἱῶι τ' ἐπιτελλόμενος, δᾶμον γεραί-

ρων τράποι σύμφωνον ἐς ἡσυχίαν.
λίσσομαι νεῦσον, Κρονίων, ἥμερον
ὄφρα κατ' οἶκον ὁ Φοίνιξ ὁ Τυρσα-
νῶν τ' ἀλαλατὸς ἔχῃ, ναυ-
σίστονον ὕβριν ἰδὼν τὰν πρὸ Κύμας,
οἷα Συρακοσίων ἀρχῶι δαμασθέντες πάθον,
ὠκυπόρων ἀπὸ ναῶν ὅ σφιν ἐν πόντωι βάλεθ' ἁλικίαν,
Ἑλλάδ' ἐξέλκων βαρείας δουλίας.

(Pyth. 1.67–75)

May fortune such as they enjoy
   fall also to the kings and citizens of Aitna
      in the true report of men – through you, Zeus,
      their prince may follow his father,
         revering the people, leading them
      in the harmonies of peace.
      But I beseech you, son of Kronos,
   keep the Phoinikian at home,
stifle the battle-shout
               of the Tyrsanoi –
let them rue
     their pride at Kuma
        that burst into wailing for their fleet.
Such was the anguish the Syracusan king
inflicted on them, when he hurled their youth
from the swift ships into the waves, saving Hellas
from the iron yoke of slavery.

(Trans. Nisetich)

εἴ τι καὶ φλαῦρον παραιθύσσει, μέγα τοι φέρεται
πὰρ σέθεν. πολλῶν ταμίας ἐσσί· πολλοὶ
μάρτυρες ἀμφοτέροις πιστοί.
εὐανθεῖ δ' ἐν ὀργᾶι παρμένων,
εἴπερ τι φιλεῖς ἀκοὰν ἀδεῖαν αἰ-
εἰ κλύειν, μὴ κάμνε λίαν δαπάναις·
ἐξίει δ' ὥσπερ κυβερνάτας ἀνήρ
ἱστίον ἀνεμόεν. μὴ δολωθῆις,
ὦ φίλε, κέρδεσιν ἐντραπέ-
λοις· ὀπιθόμβροτον αὔχημα δόξας
οἷον ἀποιχομένων ἀνδρῶν δίαιταν μάννει
καὶ λογίοις καὶ ἀοιδοῖς. οὐ φθίνει Κροί-
σου φιλόφρων ἀρετά.

τὸν δὲ ταύρωι χαλκέωι καυτῆρα νηλέα νόον
ἐχθρὰ Φάλαριν κατέχει παντᾶι φάτις,
οὐδέ νιν φόρμιγγες ὑπωρόφιαι κοινανίαν

μαλθακὰν παίδων ὀάροισι δέκονται.
τὸ δὲ παθεῖν εὖ πρῶτον ἀέθλων·
 εὖ δ' ἀκούειν δευτέρα μοῖρ' · ἀμφοτέροισι δ' ἀνήρ
ὃς ἂν ἐγκύρσηι καὶ ἕληι, στέφανον ὕψιστον δέδεκται.

(Pyth. 1.87–100)

Even a trivial spark will start a blaze
  if it fall from you
    who are steward of many, and many
    will be your witnesses, for good or ill.
      But if indeed you yearn to hear
      your name forever sounded
      in the tones of praise,
    abide in these high spirits,
go on being lavish.
Unfurl your sails.
Don't be deceived
  by cunning thrift:
    glory follows a man,
  glory alone, when he is dead, reveals
  his manner of life to the lords
  of song and story.
Kroisos' mild-minded ways
perish not, but in all lands hateful speech
oppresses Phalaris, pitiless burner of men
in the brazen bull.
No lyres in hall
welcome him to the soft embraces of boys' voices.
Success is the first of prizes.
To be well spoken of is second.
But he who finds them both and keeps them
  wins the highest crown.   (Trans. Nisetich)

To the first passage corresponds Theocritus' prayer for peace (vv.
82–97) which concludes with a very close reworking of Pindar
(ἀλαλατός – βοά); to the second corresponds both the attack on the
hoarding of wealth and the pervasive theme of the posthumous *kleos*
which poetry, and poetry alone, can confer.[26] This prominent echo of
Pindaric references to the naval victories of Hiero I suggests that we
do not have to suppose that Hiero II was actually about to engage in
fighting when Idyll 16 was performed.[27] It is the very echoes of Pindar

---

[26] The fact that Theocritus is reworking an earlier passage gives particular point to ὡς πάρος in
  v. 14, which has a metaliterary, as well as a purely chronological, reference.

[27] So rightly, though for different reasons, J. Vahlen, 'Über Theokrits Hiero', *SBA* 1884.823–42
  = *Gesammelte philologische Schriften* II (Berlin 1923) 202–25, at pp. 218–22.

and the memory of what the first Hiero did to them which explain, and indeed motivate, the trembling of 'the Phoenicians' in Theocritus (vv. 76–7).[28] Moreover, the fighting between Syracuse and the Carthaginians was of such long standing that it might be thought that Theocritus' sentiments need not be tied to a particular engagement. Nevertheless, such a literary echo, together with the repeated ἤδη νῦν ... ἤδη (vv. 76–8), would indeed well suit the coming to power of a new king, προτέροις ἴσος ἡρώεσσι (v. 80): as soon as the new king appears, the Carthaginians are faced with the prospect of renewed defeat. More importantly, Pythian 1 is a foundation poem in which Hiero's military victories are linked with his foundation of the city of Aitna to be ruled over by his son Deinomenes; it is a poem of beginnings which look to the future. It is thus tempting to connect its reworking in Idyll 16 with another beginning, the coming to power of a new Hiero, to be celebrated by a new Pindar.

Behind Pindar's contrast between the *hubris* of the Phoenicians and the longed-for Syracusan 'harmonies of peace' lies Hesiod's contrast between the peace and prosperity of the 'just city' and the disasters which await those who practise *hubris*:

οἳ δὲ δίκας ξείνοισι καὶ ἐνδήμοισι διδοῦσιν
ἰθείας καὶ μή τι παρεκβαίνουσι δικαίου,
τοῖσι τέθηλε πόλις, λαοὶ δ' ἀνθεῦσιν ἐν αὐτῆι·
εἰρήνη δ' ἀνὰ γῆν κουροτρόφος, οὐδέ ποτ' αὐτοῖς
ἀργαλέον πόλεμον τεκμαίρεται εὐρύοπα Ζεύς·
οὐδέ ποτ' ἰθυδίκηισι μετ' ἀνδράσι λιμὸς ὀπηδεῖ
οὐδ' ἄτη, θαλίηις δὲ μεμηλότα ἔργα νέμονται.
τοῖσι φέρει μὲν γαῖα πολὺν βίον, οὔρεσι δὲ δρῦς
ἄκρη μέν τε φέρει βαλάνους, μέσση δὲ μελίσσας·
εἰροπόκοι δ' ὄιες μαλλοῖς καταβεβρίθασι·
τίκτουσιν δὲ γυναῖκες ἐοικότα τέκνα γονεῦσι·
θάλλουσιν δ' ἀγαθοῖσι διαμπερές· οὐδ' ἐπὶ νηῶν
νίσονται, καρπὸν δὲ φέρει ζείδωρος ἄρουρα.
οἷς δ' ὕβρις τε μέμηλε κακὴ καὶ σχέτλια ἔργα,
τοῖς δὲ δίκην Κρονίδης τεκμαίρεται εὐρύοπα Ζεύς.
πολλάκι καὶ ξύμπασα πόλις κακοῦ ἀνδρὸς ἀπηύρα,
ὅστις ἀλιτραίνηι καὶ ἀτάσθαλα μηχανάαται.
τοῖσιν δ' οὐρανόθεν μέγ' ἐπήγαγε πῆμα Κρονίων,
λιμὸν ὁμοῦ καὶ λοιμόν, ἀποφθινύθουσι δὲ λαοί·
οὐδὲ γυναῖκες τίκτουσιν, μινύθουσι δὲ οἶκοι

---

[28] Note the scholion on v. 76: 'the Phoenicians constantly made war on the Syracusans, as Pindar too says'.

Ζηνὸς φραδμοσύνηισιν 'Ολυμπίου· ἄλλοτε δ' αὖτε
ἢ τῶν γε στρατὸν εὐρὺν ἀπώλεσεν ἢ ὅ γε τεῖχος
ἢ νέας ἐν πόντωι Κρονίδης ἀποτείνυται αὐτῶν.

(*WD* 225–47)

Those who give straight judgements to strangers and citizens alike
and do not go beyond the bounds of what is just, their city flourishes
and the people prosper in it. There is peace which nurtures children
through their land, and broad-seeing Zeus does not devise grim warfare for them. Straight-judging men suffer neither famine nor disaster,
and in prosperity they tend their fields. The land bears them a rich
harvest, and on the mountains the tops of the oaks bear acorns while
bees nest in the middle of the trunks. Their woolly sheep are laden
with fleeces, and their wives bear children which resemble their parents. They flourish constantly with good things, and never travel on
ships, because the rich earth bears them its fruit. But upon those who
practise evil *hubris* and deeds of wickedness broad-seeing Zeus, the son
of Kronos, devises punishment. Often indeed a whole city suffers for
an evil man who commits wrong and lays reckless plans. Upon them
the son of Kronos brings great disaster down from heaven, famine
and plague together; the men perish, and the women do not bear
children, and the houses waste away through the plans of Olympian
Zeus. At other times the son of Kronos destroys their great army or
their fortifications, or shatters their ships on the sea.

The peaceful vision of 16.82–97 is clearly a 'bucolic' rewriting of this
Hesiodic passage, and its juxtaposition to a wish for Hiero's fame in
poetry (vv. 98–100) makes clear that, if achieved, the paradisiacal
peace will be a direct result of Hiero's rule. Here Theocritus takes the
idea, familiar in many cultures,[29] that the prosperity of the land
depends upon the ruler (cf., e.g., the opening of Sophocles' *Oedipus
Tyrannus*) and reshapes it as a wish for the future. Moreover, the
Hesiodic mode of this rewriting allows Theocritus to give full weight,
not merely to the (just) ruler, but also to his city, which forms,
together with him, an indivisible whole:

εἷς μὲν ἐγώ, πολλοὺς δὲ Διὸς φιλέοντι καὶ ἄλλους
θυγατέρες, τοῖς πᾶσι μέλοι Σικελὴν 'Αρέθοισαν
ὑμνεῖν σὺν λαοῖσι καὶ αἰχμητὴν 'Ιέρωνα.

(16.101–3)

I am but one; the daughters of Zeus love also many others, and may
they all wish to hymn Sicilian Arethusa together with her people and
the warrior Hiero.

---

[29] Cf. West on Hes. *WD* 225–47.

This combination of two Hesiodic ideas – the specially favoured king of the *Theogony* and the prosperous and just city of *Works and Days* – informs also the praise of Philadelphus in Idyll 17, for Egypt is depicted as a land of plentiful riches and a peace which is safeguarded by a 'good king' (vv. 77–105).[30] It is in this case the royal family itself which best exemplifies the Hesiodic truth[31] that, in a place of justice, children resemble their parents (vv. 55–7 and, by negative inference, v. 44). Moreover, these Hesiodic ideas have particular relevance in Idyll 17, as the Ptolemies themselves freely advertised the superabundant riches of their kingdom both to their Greek and to their Egyptian subjects.[32] Thus, for example, a contemporary hieroglyphic text (unfortunately broken) celebrates Philadelphus in terms strikingly similar to those of Idyll 17:[33]

> . . . good things, all good things abound in his reign
> . . . his granaries reach to heaven . . .
> . . . his soldiers outnumber the sands . . .
> . . . all the sanctuaries celebrate
> . . . seized the shield
> . . . by his power, broken in the face of his spear
> . . . all over their bodies
> . . . to make sacred offering to the gods

Just as elsewhere Alexandrian encomium has found in the Greek poetic tradition a language which can encompass the particular situation of the new rulers of Egypt, so in Idyll 17 Theocritus does not merely 'combine' the Greek poetic tradition with a native language of praise, but finds in the former the authorising pattern of the latter.

The new Pindar of Idyll 16 speaks with a very Hellenistic voice. The combination of mime,[34] comedy,[35] children's song,[36] hymn, and encomium is a brilliant and challenging experiment. Whatever else the poem may be, it has the wit and charm which Greek literary

---

[30] Cf. R. Merkelbach, 'Das Königtum der Ptolemäer und die hellenistischen Dichter' in N. Hinske (ed.), *Alexandrien* (Mainz 1981) 27–35, at pp. 31–2.

[31] Gow's note on 17.43–4 well exemplifies this familiar *topos*.

[32] Cf. above n. 15, and below p. 117 for this motif in Idyll 15.

[33] Cf. S. Sauneron, 'Un document Egyptien relatif à la divinisation de la reine Arsinoé II', *BIFAO* 60 (1960) 83–109, at p. 87. The text printed is my translation of Sauneron's French translation; I have not thought it worthwhile to signal the many uncertainties of interpretation. For an Egyptian parallel for some related *topoi* in Callimachus' *Hymn to Zeus* cf. H. Reinsch-Werner, *Callimachus Hesiodicus* (Berlin 1976) 53 n. 1.

[34] On the mimic element of the poem cf. especially the discussion of Fantuzzi 1993b.155–64.

[35] In vv. 5–21 we are presumably to imagine that the poet is at home musing to himself; the situation is reminiscent of Strepsiades' opening monologue in Aristophanes' *Clouds*.

[36] Cf. Merkelbach 1952.

critics would probably call χάρις or χάριτες; Theocritus has thus inscribed our response to his poem within the poem itself.[37] In the first book of the *Aitia* Callimachus prays to the Graces to wipe their hands upon his elegies 'so that they may last for many a year' (fr. 7.13–14), and Pfeiffer's note on that passage rightly refers to Pindar, *Nemeans* 4.6–8:

> ῥῆμα δ' ἐργμάτων χρονιώτερον βιοτεύει,
> ὅ τι κε σὺν Χαρίτων τύχαι
> γλῶσσα φρενὸς ἐξέλοι βαθείας.

> For the word lives longer than the deed,
> whenever the voice
> brings it from the depths of the mind
> blessed by the Graces' favour.
>
> (Trans. Nisetich)

So too the concluding τί γὰρ Χαρίτων ἀγαπητόν | ἀνθρώποις ἀπάνευθεν;, 'for what do men have without the Graces which is worth cherishing?', has a poetic, programmatic reference, as well as a broad application to life as a whole.[38] Already in the *Theogony* the Graces live next to the Muses (*Theog.* 64).

Not only does Theocritus here combine many different poetic traditions, but he also offers Hiero at least three models or paradigms for the power of the poet: not only Pindar, but also Homer (cf. vv. 48–57, 73–5) and Simonides (cf. vv. 34–47). I begin with Homer.

THEOCRITUS AND HOMER

Homer is not merely in Idyll 16 as an explicit paradigm for the poet who is able to confer immortal fame, but it is also clear that, throughout the Theocritean corpus, Homer, as the starting-point for all hexametric poetry, is the name against which the later poet marks out his poetic space. From the *ekphrasis* of the cup in Idyll 1, which offers an alternative world to that of the Homeric shield of Achilles, to the poet's direct comparison of himself to Homer at the end of Idyll 22,[39] it is Homeric epic against which Theocritus constantly measures himself.[40] Nor perhaps did this go unremarked in later antiquity. The bucolic *Lament*

---

[37] On literary *charis* see esp. Demetrius, *On Style* 128–9.
[38] For ἀγαπητός in this context cf. *amabile* at Lucretius 1.23, and for such stylistic invocations cf. also my note on Ap. Rhod. *Arg.* 3.1. [39] Cf. above pp. 74–6.
[40] The matter has often been discussed, but particularly helpful are J. Van Sickle, 'Theocritus and the development of the conception of bucolic genre', *Ramus* 5 (1976) 18–44, and Halperin 1983 *passim*.

for Bion contains an elaborate paralleling of Homer and Bion (vv. 70–84) which clearly depends upon a sense of rivalry between Homer and poetry in the style of Theocritus. The epigram which Artemidorus attached to his edition of Theocritean verse in the first century BC may pehaps allude to an analogy between Homer and Theocritus:

> Βουκολικαὶ Μοῖσαι σποράδες ποκά, νῦν δ' ἅμα πᾶσαι
> ἐντὶ μιᾶς μάνδρας, ἐντὶ μιᾶς ἀγέλας.
>
> (*Anth. Pal.* 9.205 = Epigram [xxvi] Gow)

> The Bucolic Muses were once scattered, but are now all united in one fold, in one flock.

Although the principal conceit of this epigram is that the poems are treated like a flock of sheep or goats, it is tempting to believe that Artemidorus was conscious of an epigram of uncertain date celebrating the Athenian tyrant Peisistratus (*Anth. Pal.* 11.442);[41] vv. 3–4 of that epigram refer to the alleged 'Peisistratid recension' of Homer:

> τὸν μέγαν ἐν βουλαῖς Πεισίστρατον ὃς τὸν Ὅμηρον
> ἤθροισα σποράδην τὸ πρὶν ἀειδόμενον.

> [I am] Peisistratos, great in council, who gathered Homer together; previously he had been sung in scattered parts.

Although a 'collected edition' of individual poems is a quite different undertaking from the task which the tyrant is imagined to have performed – presumably the 'compilation' of two monumental epics from separate and 'scattered' sections – the similarity of wording is suggestive, if far from conclusive: the 'history' of the Theocritean corpus would thus be made to resemble that of his great epic forerunner.[42] Another anonymous epigram, presumably originally prefixed or appended to a collection of Theocritus' poems, has also been interpreted as setting Theocritus off against Homer:

> ἄλλος ὁ Χῖος, ἐγὼ δὲ Θεόκριτος ὃς τάδ' ἔγραψα
> εἷς ἀπὸ τῶν πολλῶν εἰμὶ Συρακοσίων,
> υἱὸς Πραξαγόραο περικλειτᾶς τε Φιλίννας·
> Μοῦσαν δ' ὀθνείαν οὔτιν' ἐφελκυσάμαν.
>
> (*Anth. Pal.* 9.434 = *Epigram* [xxvii] Gow)

---

[41] This is Anon. xxxiv in *FGE*, pp. 338–9. On this epigram cf. especially Van Sickle art. cit., although his discussion goes in a very different direction from mine. A connection between this epigram and the epigram on Peisistratus was first suggested by J. Kohl, 'Die homerische Frage der Chorizonten', *Neue Jahrbücher* 47 (1921) 198–214, at p. 204; it is rejected by A. Skiadas, *Homer im griechischen Epigramm* (Athens 1965) 169.

[42] σποράδην is in fact a common adverb in late texts dealing with the collection and 'editing' of literature: this naturally weakens the case for a strong connection between the two epigrams.

The Chian is another, but I, Theocritus, the author of these works, am a Syracusan, one among many, the son of Praxagoras and renowned Philinna, and I have taken to myself no alien muse.

As Theocritus himself refers to Homer as 'the Chian poet' (7.47, 22.218) and v. 2 of the epigram is indebted to *Id.* 16.101, the poem in which Theocritus exploits Homer as a paradigm for his own position, this epigram has been taken to distinguish Theocritus from the greatest writer of hexameters in a different 'genre', namely Homer.[43] If so, it would be noteworthy that the epigram stresses the humorous, 'popular' elements in Theocritus' poetry: he is just one of 'the many Syracusans',[44] his presumably obscure mother is humorously called 'renowned', an epithet which Theocritus applies only to Berenice in the extant poems (17.34),[45] and the colourful expression of the final verse most probably refers to the Syracusan traditions of mime (Sophron) and comedy (Epicharmus, celebrated by Theocritus in Epigram XVIII). Nevertheless, it seems more probable that the epigram was originally intended to distinguish between Theocritus and Theocritus of Chios, a minor wit of the late fourth century, whose sayings were collected and 'published';[46] the epigram will thus play with the familiar problem of confusion between homonymous authors. We may, however, suspect that, whatever its original meaning, an epigram contrasting Theocritus with 'the Chian' reinforced antiquity's sense of the relationship of 'bucolic' and 'epic' hexameters, and there is indeed some slight evidence that the epigram was understood as referring to Homer in later antiquity.[47] Be that as it may, we can see that Virgil's positioning of his *Eclogues* against epic poetry is not to be viewed merely in terms of his allegiance to a 'Callimachean' aesthetic, but responds also to perceived phenomena in Theocritus' poems.

The scholarly activity visible in these epigrams may seem a long way from the self-presentation of the poet and his *charites* in Idyll 16, but the two are in fact linked. The poet's *charites* are, as Reinhold Merkelbach has most fully explained,[48] fashioned like a band of

---

[43] For this interpretation cf. Wilamowitz 1906.125–6, followed, e.g., by Halperin 1983.251 and J. Farrell, *Vergil's Georgics and the Traditions of Ancient Epic* (New York/Oxford 1991) 43–4.

[44] I have wondered whether there is some play with πολλῶν . . . Συρακοσίων suggesting the large numbers which end with -κοσιοι.

[45] If the epithet does not have the humorous nuance which I have suggested, then it presumably must be explained from the standard rhetoric of epitaphs, cf. G. Kaibel (ed.), *Epigrammata Graeca ex lapidibus conlecta* (Berlin 1878), nos. 405 and 685.

[46] So Gow; see the discussion of Gutzwiller 1995.   [47] *Vita Homeri* VI Allen, cf. Gow II 549.

[48] Merkelbach 1952. Cf. also Dover 218, and W. D. Furley, 'Apollo humbled: Phoenix' Koronisma in its Hellenistic literary setting', *MD* 33 (1994) 9–31, especially pp. 20–1 on Theocritus 16.

children going from house to house; such bands would sing songs requesting food or other gifts and wishing good upon the house which provided (cf. 16.82–100) and harm upon that which did not (cf. the American 'trick or treat'). The archaic iambist Hipponax seems to have presented himself as a 'begging poet' with motifs taken from such songs, but Theocritus' position in vv. 5–12 appears rather to resemble a 'Fagin' figure who sends the children out on their rounds and either enjoys the fruits of their labours or suffers (as they do) when they return empty-handed; the position of a Pindar or a Simonides who sends his song out 'across the sea' to the victor is thus here rewritten in a much more homely mode. The poet himself is not presented as a child, but as someone whose quest for patronage is conducted through children. In vv. 68–70, however, the image may have changed somewhat:

δίζημαι δ' ὅτινι θνατῶν κεχαρισμένος ἔλθω
σὺν Μοίσαις· χαλεπαὶ γὰρ ὁδοὶ τελέθουσιν ἀοιδοῖς
κουράων ἀπάνευθε Διὸς μέγα βουλεύοντος.

I am seeking to whom of mortals I may come as a welcome guest together with the Muses; for hard are the ways for poets without the daughters of great-counselling Zeus.

Although these verses do not necessarily imply that the poet himself is 'on the road' – for the 'path' of song is a familiar enough metaphor – there is here a suggestion that the poet and his Muses are now travelling in search of a welcome.[49] The apparent change from the Graces to the Muses has long been prepared (cf. vv. 29, 58) and is here mediated by κεχαρισμένος which suggests that the poet will have *both* the Muses and the Graces with him, as indeed he promises to have when he answers the patron's call (vv. 106–9).[50]

There is here an interesting analogue with the 'Herodotean' *Life of Homer*, a text apparently dating from the imperial period but probably going back to sources of the pre-Hellenistic age.[51] Like most *Lives* of Homer, this text presents the poet as a wanderer who survived by reciting his verses in return for food and shelter (cf. Theocritus in Idyll 16). Thus, for example, at one point we find the poet outside a shoemaker's house seeking admittance with the following verses:

[49] Cf. perhaps Diogenes wandering about 'looking for a man' (Diog. Laert. 6.41); χαλεπαί in v. 69 perhaps evokes Hesiod's 'hard road' towards virtue (*WD* 289–92).
[50] Unsurprisingly, the Muses are also present on the poetic journey of Idyll 7 (cf. v. 12).
[51] Text: Vol. v of Allen's OCT of Homer, pp. 192–218. For the date and sources of the text cf. the brief remarks of Lesky, *RE* Suppl. 11.687–8. For the *Eiresione* cited below see also O. Schönberger, *Griechische Heischelieder* (Meisenheim am Glan 1980) 17–42.

αἰδεῖσθε ξενίων κεχρημένον ἠδὲ δόμοιο
οἳ πόλιν αἰπεινὴν Κύμην ἐριώπιδα κούρην
ναίετε κτλ.   (*Vit. Hom.* 101–3, p. 197 Allen)

You who dwell in the steep city, Kyme, the fair-faced maid, show
respect to one who needs hospitality and shelter . . .

On another occasion the blind poet is on Samos and we find him
going to the wealthiest (εὐδαιμονέσταται) houses, guided by some
local children; the verses ascribed to him, the so-called *Eiresione*
('Harvest Garland'), are the text of a traditional 'begging' performance.
The song begins as follows:

δῶμα προσετραπόμεσθ' ἀνδρὸς μέγα δυναμένοιο,
ὃς μέγα μὲν δύναται, μέγα δὲ βρέμει, ὄλβιος αἰεί.
αὐταὶ ἀνακλίνεσθε θύραι· πλοῦτος γὰρ ἔσεισι
πολλός, σὺν πλούτωι δὲ καὶ εὐφροσύνη τεθαλυῖα,
εἰρήνη τ' ἀγαθή.   (*Vit. Hom.* 467–71, p. 214 Allen)

We have come to the house of a very powerful man, who holds great
power, who thunders loudly, for ever blessed. Doors, open up! Great
wealth will enter, and with wealth will come joy and prosperity, and
the blessings of peace.

Theocritus too waits to be invited and, if my interpretation of vv.
68–70 is correct, he too is a 'wandering poet'; like Homer, he holds
out the prospect of peace, and instead of prosperity he offers
something of far greater value, eternal *kleos*. That vv. 5–21 and 68–70
use the model of the begging Homer thus seems to me very likely;
certainly, the dismissive 'Homer is enough for all' (v. 20) gains point if
Theocritus is precisely presenting himself in these verses as a new
Homer. 'Homer' and a band of children offer two models for a
'begging' which is not shameful and which it would be foolish to
refuse; the behaviour of the good host stands in the catalogue of duties
next to the honouring of poets (vv. 28–9) because the latter is in some
senses a special case of the former.

If the poem begins with the poet associated with children, it ends,
not merely with an evocation of Pindar's Graces (above p. 83–4), but
also with an apparent echo of a famous ode of Euripides on old age:

καλλείψω δ' οὐδ' ὔμμε· τί γὰρ Χαρίτων ἀγαπητόν
ἀνθρώποις ἀπάνευθεν; ἀεὶ Χαρίτεσσιν ἅμ' εἴην.
(16.108–9)

Nor will I leave you behind, for without the Graces what do men have which should be cherished? May I always live with the Graces.

In the second stasimon of Euripides' *Heracles Furens* the chorus of old men lament their old age – a burden compared to Sicilian Etna – and pray for a life of continual song with the Muses. Both the regret and the prayer serve as devices of praise for the *arete* of the young hero Heracles:

οὐ παύσομαι τὰς Χάριτας
ταῖς Μούσαισιν συγκαταμει-
    γνύς, ἡδίσταν συζυγίαν.
μὴ ζῴην μετ' ἀμουσίας,
αἰεὶ δ' ἐν στεφάνοισιν εἴην·
ἔτι τοι γέρων ἀοιδὸς
κελαδῶ Μναμοσύναν,
ἔτι τὰν Ἡρακλέους
καλλίνικον ἀείδω
παρά τε Βρόμιον οἰνοδόταν
παρά τε χέλυος ἑπτατόνου
μολπὰν καὶ Λίβυν αὐλόν.
οὔπω καταπαύσομεν
Μούσας αἵ μ' ἐχόρευσαν.
            (Eur. *HF* 673–86)

I shall not cease from mingling the Graces with the Muses, sweetest of unions. May I not live without the Muses, but may I wear garlands for ever. An aged poet, I glorify Mnemosyne still, and still I sing of the triumph of Heracles, when Bromios brings wine and the seven-stringed lyre and the Libyan flute sound. Never shall I abandon the Muses who have set me dancing.

As in Theocritus 16, 'the *laudandus* in Euripides . . . is one to whom considerations of wealth are largely irrelevant',[52] although it is the concern for wealth which has displaced special honour for 'good men' (vv. 669–71).[53] The rôle of the Muses in celebrating Heracles is very comparable to that of the Graces in Idyll 16; Theocritus' closing declaration might perhaps be summarised on the model of Euripides' chorus as μὴ ζῴην μετ' ἀχαριστίας.[54] Between the poles of childhood

---

[52] H. Parry, *AJP* 86 (1965) 366. The whole of Parry's discussion is a valuable account of the epinician motifs in this ode.

[53] The reference to 'rolling time' in those verses uses a familiar epinician motif, as does the parallel reference in 16.71–2; whereas, however, a Pindar will normally apply the motif to the great deeds of the patron, i.e. 'only future time will give a clear indication of virtue' *uel sim.*, Theocritus applies the motif to his hopes of gaining a patron.

[54] Note also Pind. *Pyth.* 9.89–90, Χαρίτων κελαδεννᾶν | μή με λίποι καθαρὸν φέγγος.

and old age, the eternal rôle of the poet, its constancy marked by the repeated ἀεί which frames the poem (vv. 1, 109), emerges as always the same and always renewed.[55]

The echo of the *Heracles* ode is also important for the Sicilian patron. Any potential patron might have welcomed even an implicit comparison to the youthful civiliser of Greece, particularly after Alexander's powerful exploitation of the figure of this hero. It is hardly surprising that Hiero used the image of Heracles on his silver coins,[56] and there is no good evidence that he particularly sought to associate himself with the great hero. Nevertheless, Heracles' reception on Olympus was 'the mythic archetype for every victor's "requital"',[57] and this paradigm hardly required elaborate evocation or defence. Pindar celebrates the great hero in Nemean 1, a poem whose importance for Theocritus we have already noted in connection with Idyll 24.[58] In that poem, written for a Syracusan victor and celebrating that city (vv. 1–4, cf. *Id.* 16.102), Pindar presents himself in a now familiar rôle:

> ἔσταν δ' ἐπ' αὐλείαις θύραις
> ἀνδρὸς φιλοξείνου καλὰ μελπόμενος,
> ἔνθα μοι ἁρμόδιον
> δεῖπνον κεκόσμηται, θαμὰ δ' ἀλλοδαπῶν
> οὐκ ἀπείρατοι δόμοι
> ἐντί·   (*Nem.* 1.19–23)

At the courtyard doors of a liberal host, I stand
  singing his noble deeds
    here, where a brilliant banquet has been laid out for me.
    Indeed, this house has often been
    no stranger to guests from abroad.   (Trans. Nisetich)

In a passage which strikingly foreshadows Idyll 16, Pindar notes the proper use of wealth:

> οὐκ ἔραμαι πολὺν ἐν
> μεγάρωι πλοῦτον κατακρύψαις ἔχειν,
> ἀλλ' ἐόντων εὖ τε παθεῖν καὶ ἀκοῦ-
> σαι φίλοις ἐξαρκέων.   (*Nem.* 1.31–2)

---

[55] It is at least noteworthy in this context that Callimachus also seems to use this ode of the *Heracles* when adopting the voice of an old man in his 'Reply to the Telchines' (fr. 1), cf. R. Pfeiffer, *Hermes* 63 (1928) 328–30, Gutzwiller 1983.237–8.
[56] Cf. W. Giesecke, *Sicilia Numismatica* (Leipzig 1923) 123.
[57] L. Kurke, *The Traffic in Praise* (Cornell 1991) 113.   [58] Cf. above pp. 12–13.

I love not to keep great wealth buried deep in hall,
but to make good use of what I own
   and be of good repute
     among my friends.   (Trans. Nisetich)

The model for this good report among men, and thus by implication the divine paradigm for the Syracusan victor, is Heracles, whose life of struggle is rewarded with eternal peace, *hesychia*, and marriage to Hebe ('Youth'), celebrated with feasting on Olympus (vv. 69–72). If Hiero too was νέος, Theocritus' encomiastic strategy of literary evocation will have been particularly pointed.

It is indeed the choral lyric of the early classical period which offers Theocritus the closest parallel for the relationship which he claims to want with a patron. A key element of such a relationship, as constructed in the poems of Pindar, is *charis*.[59] *Charis* is the hallmark both of the 'charm' of the poet's offering and of the power that he can bestow upon his patron; this reciprocity is not unlike, and indeed closely connected to, that between the long-lasting *kleos* of the patron which the poet confers and the long-lasting *kleos* of the poet himself. Poet and patron need each other, and are in much the same boat; that at least is the theory. Moreover, in the patronage relationship as it is most commonly figured in Pindar, poet and patron are, if not actually on an equal footing, at least both bound in the networks and obligations of *philia* and *xenia*, and both obey and instantiate the values and norms of aristocratic society. A central strategy of Idyll 16 is to play off this 'theory of equality' against the more mundane realities of power and dependence; the figure of Simonides is the main vehicle for this strategy.

THEOCRITUS AND SIMONIDES

By the third century Simonides had become the subject of a large anecdotal tradition; the two main themes of these anecdotes are his wisdom and his love of money.[60] Callimachus (fr. 222) cited a phrase of Pindar, ἐργάτις . . . μοῦσα, 'the Muse for hire', and referred it to Simonides;[61] Chamaileon (late fourth, early third century) wrote an

---

[59] On *charis* in Pindar cf. esp. H. Gundert, *Pindar und sein Dichterberuf* (Frankfurt 1935) 30–76; Kurke op. cit. (n. 57) *passim*; B. Maclachlan, *The Age of Grace. Charis in Early Greek Poetry* (Princeton 1993) 87–123; more briefly, and with further bibliography, Goldhill 1991.132–4. For the development in this idea over time cf. the survey in G. Tarditi, 'Le Muse e le Chariti tra fede del poeta ed *ethos poietikon*', *Aevum Antiquum* 2 (1989) 19–45.

[60] For texts and discussion cf. Wilamowitz, *Sappho und Simonides* (Berlin 1913) 140–2, 148–9; J. M. Bell, 'Κίμβιξ καὶ σοφός: Simonides in the anecdotal tradition', *QUCC* 28 (1978) 29–86.

On Simonides (frr. 33–5 Wehrli[2]), and a papyrus of the first half of the third century preserves a collection of alleged witticisms of Simonides on the subject of monetary expenditure (*PHibeh* 17). At a relatively early date Simonides had been identified as the 'inventor' of poetry as a purely commercial enterprise, the first poet to be available for monetary hire to anyone who could afford him. Why Simonides was singled out for this rôle may be the subject of literary and sociological conjecture – we presumably have to do with the transition from an exchange based on hospitality and *philia* to a more purely financial arrangement –[62] but the undoubted fact of Simonides' reputation is what is important for Idyll 16. A rather neglected witness here is the *Hiero* of Xenophon, in which a conversation between Hiero and Simonides reflects aspects both of the familiar 'wise man – tyrant' dialogue and of the pattern of Socratic writings.[63] The Xenophontic dialogue may help us to understand how Theocritus uses the figure of Simonides.

The second part of the *Hiero* (Chapters 8–11) is devoted to Simonides telling the tyrant how he can gain most *charis* from his rule; these chapters are a recipe for an enlightened despotism, of a kind familiar elsewhere in Xenophon's writings. When viewed from the perspective of Idyll 16, the emphasis upon *charites* in these chapters is striking. One of the ways in which the ruler can gain *charis* is by leaving to others unpleasant tasks, such as the administration of corrective punishment, while devoting himself to such things as offering and awarding prizes for civic competitions (including poetic competitions) and helpful suggestions as to how the state might be

---

[61] Cf. Pind. *Isthm.* 2.6. As Fuhrer 1992.214 n. 806 rightly notes, it is not strictly necessary to assume that Callimachus believed that the Pindaric phrase referred to Simonides; he could have made the connection himself, and been followed in this by the Pindaric scholiasts. The image of the phrase in Callimachus is of the Muse as a prostitute with the poet as her *pornoboskos* (cf. LSJ s.v. τρέφω II 2); this idea is developed from Pindar's description of 'silvered-faced' songs for sale (*Isthm.* 2.7–8). Two further points are also worthy of note. Pindar expresses his contrast between 'then' and 'now' in terms of a contrast between 'love songs' for boys and songs as female prostitutes; in view of Callimachus' paederastic persona, it is tempting to believe that he took up this aspect of the Pindaric passage as well. Secondly, we may note here a further link (cf. fr. 1 Pfeiffer) between Callimachus' programmatic language and the language of the literary contest in Ar. *Frogs* (cf. *Frogs* 944 ἀνέτρεφον; 1305–8 the prostitute Muse, though interpretation there is disputed, cf. Dover *ad loc.*).

[62] Cf., e.g., B. Gentili, *Poetry and its Public in Ancient Greece* (trans. T. Cole, Baltimore/London 1988) 151–4.

[63] For an overview and bibliography cf. V. J. Gray, 'Xenophon's *Hiero* and the meeting of the wise man and tyrant in Greek literature', *CQ* 36 (1986) 115–23. For the various attempts to locate the historical context of the *Hiero* cf. M. Sordi, 'Lo Ierone di Senofonte, Dionigi I e Filisto', *Athenaeum* 58 (1980) 3–13.

better run. Nor should Hiero worry about the cost, even to his own private resources (9.11, 11.1–15); just so did Pindar advise the same ruler, μὴ κάμνε λίαν δαπάναις, 'do not trouble too much about expense' (*Pyth.* 1.90). In particular, Hiero should support horse-training in his city so that there should be the greatest possible number of Syracusan victors at the various pan-Hellenic games (11.5–6). In this way Hiero will win not only *philia* (cf. Theocr. 16.66) but even *eros* (11.11); the way to enrich himself is to enrich his *philoi*, to surpass them in benefaction (εὖ ποιῶν, cf. Theocr. 16.25–6). The end that Hiero will thus achieve, the κάλλιστον καὶ μακαριώτατον κτῆμα, is a mixture of happy prosperity and the goodwill of men, 'for even in prosperity you will not be the object of envy (*phthonos*)' (11.15); just so does Pindar conclude his advice to Hiero:

> τὸ δὲ παθεῖν εὖ πρῶτον ἀέθλων·
>   εὖ δ' ἀκούειν δευτέρα μοῖρ' · ἀμφοτέροισι δ' ἀνήρ
> ὃς ἂν ἐγκύρσηι καὶ ἕληι, στέφανον ὕψιστον δέδεκται.
>
> (Pyth. 1.99–100)

Success is the first of prizes.
                To be well spoken of is second.
But he who finds them both and keeps them
wins the highest crown.   (Trans. Nisetich)

The shared motifs of Pythian 1 and Xenophon's *Hiero* have an easy generic explanation in the fact that in both texts 'a wise man offers political advice to a ruler', and Xenophon may of course actually be drawing upon lyric poetry (perhaps Pindar and Simonides) in these chapters. Xenophon has never enjoyed a wide reputation as an ironic writer,[64] but we ought at least to entertain the possibility that part of the point of the second part of the *Hiero* is that Simonides cunningly disguises his famous φιλαργυρία behind the improving language of civic administration. Who after all is more *philos* than the poet? Will not a series of glorious chariot victories require poets to celebrate them? Simonides tells Hiero that, if he takes the poet's advice, 'all men will hymn (ὑμνοῖεν ἄν) his virtue' (11.8); who better to do this than a poet famous for hymns and epinicians? If such a reading does illuminate one aspect of Xenophon's *Hiero*, then we see a text from the early fourth century negotiating the problems posed by the 'theory of patronage' when it is confronted by the realities of economic power.

---

[64] Gray art. cit. sees the Simonides of the first part of the *Hiero* as (Socratically) ironic, but does not consider the closing chapters in this light.

Xenophon's Simonides uses the language of public service to present a case for generous patronage; Theocritus cloaks himself in the poetic tradition and uses Simonides as one of his main weapons.

Simonides is not merely used as a prime exemplum in the body of Idyll 16 (vv. 34–47), for it has been recognised at least since the composition of the Theocritean scholia that the shape of the whole poem exploits a famous anecdote about that poet. The anecdote survives in various versions, but the point is clearest in that of Stobaeus 3.10.38:

When someone asked Simonides to write an encomium and said that he would have his thanks (χάρις) but he would not give him any money, Simonides said, 'I have two chests, one for thanks (χάριτες) and one for money. When I need to use them and open them up, the one for thanks is always empty, it's the other one which is useful'.

Theocritus clearly uses χάριτες in a somewhat different way, and he has one chest rather than two, but the link between anecdote and poem is not to be denied. In the anecdote *charis* is what the mean patron offers the poet, in Idyll 16 the poet sends his χάριτες to mean patrons, and so on. Simonides, the very type of the 'avaricious' (φιλοκερδής) poet, is used to decry the 'avariciousness' and 'miserliness' (φιλοκερδεία) of patrons (vv. 15, 63).[65] Moreover, Theocritus appears to have combined this anecdote with another one about the same poet.[66] Aristotle (*Rhet.* 2.1391a8–12) reports that when Hiero's wife asked Simonides whether it was better to be rich or wise, he replied 'rich, because I see the wise hanging around the doors of the rich (ἐπὶ ταῖς τῶν πλουσίων θύραις διατρίβοντας)'.[67] This tone of ironic self-deprecation is taken over into Idyll 16, where, however, it is the poems, not the poet himself, which hang around at the doors seeking admission. It is perhaps relevant that διατρίβειν παρά became a standard way of describing 'royal service' in the early Hellenistic period, and is also found of poets enjoying royal patronage.[68] To 'hang around at the doors' is different from this

---

[65] φιλοκερδεία seems to be used by Theocritus with the reciprocal sense which is most familiar from φιλαργυρία, cf. W. Ludwig, *Phil.* 105 (1961) 57–8. Vv. 16–17 make plain that the potential patrons are *both* miserly and avaricious. [66] Cf. Gentili op. cit. (n. 62) 174.

[67] Pl. *Rep.* 6 489b6–c2 refers to the same anecdote, but not necessarily to Simonides, as this is a 'floating' anecdote found elsewhere associated with Antisthenes and Aristippos, cf. Bell art. cit. (n. 60) 44–6. It is, however, not improbable that Plato is thinking of Simonides as ὁ τοῦτο κομψευσάμενος, given that poet's rôle elsewhere in Plato (so, e.g., Adam *ad loc.*).

[68] Cf. G. Herman, 'The "friends" of the early Hellenistic rulers: servants or officials?', *Talanta* 12/13 (1980/1) 103–49. Poets: *Vitae Arati* III and IV Martin.

semi-official use of the verb, but Theocritus clearly has in mind both the realities of the patronage situation and the kind of language which Pindar used of his relationship with his patron in Nemean 1 (vv. 19–20, cited above).

The anecdotal tradition also helps to explain the terms in which Theocritus describes Simonides:

> εἰ μὴ θεῖος[69] ἀοιδὸς ὁ Κήιος αἰόλα φωνέων
> βάρβιτον ἐς πολύχορδον ἐν ἀνδράσι θῆκ' ὀνομαστούς
> ὁπλοτέροις· (16.44–6)

had not a bard inspired, the man of Ceos, tuned his varied lays to the lyre of many strings and made [his patrons] famous among the men of later days

This passage – like so much of the poem that we can no longer identify –[70] seems to contain echoes of Simonides' own verse,[71] and it is possible that αἰόλα φωνέων βάρβιτον ἐς πολύχορδον is indebted to a self-description by the poet.[72] Be that as it may, the actual detail of the description is important. The *barbitos* makes its only appearance here in major Hellenistic poetry outside the *Anthology*. In the archaic and classical periods this type of lyre was associated particularly, though not exclusively, with the eastern Aegean and, above all, with Anacreon; Pindar (fr. 125 S–M) ascribed its invention to Terpander of Lesbos, the seventh-century poet around whose name clustered many musical innovations.[73] It gradually disappears from artistic representations during the late classical period,[74] and thus its appearance in Idyll 16 is itself a piece of 'musical archaeology'.[75] Gow and others have been inclined to dismiss the usage as a mere synonym for the more usual *kithara*,[76] and it is certainly true that poets do not always preserve nice terminological distinctions; nevertheless, the present passage seems distinctive enough to call for an explanation. Out of context αἰόλα φωνέων and πολύχορδον would most naturally suggest a virtuoso instrumentalist like the famous Timotheus whose *Persai*

---

[69] Cf. below p. 107 n. 90.
[70] In particular, the grim pessimism of vv. 30–41 may be importantly indebted to Simonides' *Threnoi*; suggestive is *PMG* 522, 'all things come to grim Charybdis; proud virtues (*aretai*) and wealth'. [71] Cf. Parsons 1992.10–12.
[72] αἰόλον φων[apparently began an archaic lyric poem by an unknown poet, cf. *SLG* s286 col. iii.5.
[73] Cf. in brief West 1992.329–30; Maas–Snyder 1989.39–40; Seaford on Eur. *Cycl.* 40. For the association with Anacreon cf. *Anth. Pal.* 7.25.10 (=*HE* 3333), 7.29.4 (=*HE* 273).
[74] Cf. Maas–Snyder 1989.170.
[75] For a discussion of such phenomena in Hellenistic poetry cf. below Chapter 5.
[76] Cf., e.g., A. Barker, *Greek Musical Writings I: The musician and his art* (Cambridge 1984) 264 n. 19.

nome survives (*PMG* 791): both αἰόλα[77] and πολυ – suggest the
poikilia of 'the new music', whose novelty lay largely in its emphasis
upon rapid changes and instrumental 'runs', and πολυχορδία frequently
appears in descriptions of this flamboyant style.[78] Instruments with
more than the standard seven strings are in fact a familiar feature of
this virtuoso music, but the abstract noun need not refer literally to
the number of the strings. A famous kitharist of the first half of the
fourth century, Stratonikos of Athens, was considered to be the
'inventor' of purely instrumental πολυχορδία,[79] and it is at least
curious that the anecdotal tradition made him, like Simonides, a
master of witty sayings; Ephorus in fact explicitly compared him to
the Cean poet.[80] Theocritus' description thus figures Simonides as a
professional musician and poet of the 'modern' type, and although
the *barbitos* belongs in reality to a different milieu, it reinforces the
distinction between Simonides and earlier, 'non-professional' poets
such as Homer. Just as Stratonikos was said to have been the first to
take pupils in harmonics, so Simonides' professionalism is at the heart
of his rôle in Idyll 16. For his virtuoso performances he, like the horses
(vv. 46–7), received τιμή. This equivocation with τιμή as both 'pay'
and 'honour' will come to be seen as crucial to Theocritus' strategy in
this poem.

The difference between Simonides and earlier poets is forced into
relief by the repeated pattern of εἰ μή clauses which articulate the
argument (vv. 44, 50, 57). The earlier poets 'hymned' (v. 50) and
'benefited' (v. 57) the subjects of their songs, without receiving benefit
themselves, but Simonides' performances were of a quite different
kind. The *barbitos* itself is, as we have seen, part of that difference,
because the word does not appear in Homer, whose bards use the
phorminx. It is possible that we are to envisage Simonides playing an
instrument with more strings than the Homeric *phorminx*, hence
πολύχορδος, either because it was believed that the latter had had
only four strings[81] or because Simonides himself used an instrument

---

[77] For this epithet cf. Telestes, *PMG* 806 (admittedly corrupt); *Anth. Pal.* 9.584.3 (concerning
    'Eunomus', a virtuoso kitharist) αἰόλον ἐν κιθάραι νόμον ἔκρεκον.
[78] Cf. E. K. Borthwick, *CQ* 17 (1967) 146–7; Maas–Snyder 1989.169–70; below pp. 145–9.
[79] Phainias *apud* Ath. 8 352c (= fr. 32 Wehrli²), cf. Maas–Snyder 1989.168–9, '. . . probably
    means that Stratonikos made use of frequent changes from one harmonia to another,
    presumably by retuning, not by literally introducing more strings to the instrument'. On
    Stratonikos see also A. S. F. Gow, *Machon* (Cambridge 1965) 80–1; West 1992.368.
[80] *FGrHist* 70 F2.
[81] Whether or not the lyre did increase in historical times from four strings to seven is debated by
    modern experts, but seems certainly to have been believed in antiquity, cf. Maas–Snyder
    1989 *passim*; M. L. West, *AJP* 112 (1991) 274–5; id. 1992.52–3.

with more than seven.[82] Be that as it may, by travelling through musical time and across styles, no less than by encompassing both childhood and old age (cf. above pp. 94–6), Theocritus makes clear that we all need poets.

To return to the 'theory' of the equality of poet and patron, it will be clear that this 'theory' has been pushed to its limit in a representation of patrons as mean and avaricious (vv. 16–21), just as poets are seen to be grasping beggars. This illuminates the choice of Simonides' rather undistinguished Thessalian patrons, a choice which has bothered some critics.[83] It is not simply that their lack of distinction means that they really do owe any *kleos* they may have to Simonides, but their anecdotal reputation for meanness to the poet turns them into analogues of that poet; in antiquity, no less than today, meanness and avarice often travelled together.[84] This novel expression of the equality of poet and patron – an equality which also helps to explain the insistence of the opening verses upon the shared status of singer and sung as βροτοί – provides one of the keys to vv. 58–70, the hinge passage which leads into the encomium of Hiero:

ἐκ Μοισᾶν ἀγαθὸν κλέος ἔρχεται ἀνθρώποισι,
χρήματα δὲ ζώοντες ἀμαλδύνουσι θανόντων.
ἀλλ' ἴσος γὰρ ὁ μόχθος ἐπ' ἠιόνι κύματα μετρεῖν   60
ὅσσ' ἄνεμος χέρσονδε μετὰ γλαυκᾶς ἁλὸς ὠθεῖ,
ἢ ὕδατι νίζειν θολερὸν διαειδέι πλίνθον,
καὶ φιλοκερδείηι βεβλαμμένον ἄνδρα παρελθεῖν.
χαιρέτω ὅστις τοῖος, ἀνήριθμος δέ οἱ εἴη
ἄργυρος, αἰεὶ δὲ πλεόνων ἔχοι ἵμερος αὐτόν·
αὐτὰρ ἐγὼ τιμήν τε καὶ ἀνθρώπων φιλότητα
πολλῶν ἡμιόνων τε καὶ ἵππων πρόσθεν ἑλοίμαν.
δίζημαι δ' ὅτινι θνατῶν κεχαρισμένος ἔλθω
σὺν Μοίσαις· χαλεπαὶ γὰρ ὁδοὶ τελέθουσιν ἀοιδοῖς
κουράων ἀπάνευθε Διὸς μέγα βουλεύοντος.   70

From the Muses comes good report to men, but the possessions of the dead are wasted by the living. Yet no less toil it is to compute the waves upon the beach when wind and grey sea roll them landward,

---

[82] Late sources, in fact, include Simonides in the list of musicians who added strings to the lyre, in his case the eighth, cf. Pliny, *HN* 7.204.

[83] Cf., e.g., N. Austin, 'Idyll 16: Theocritus and Simonides', *TAPA* 98 (1967) 1–21, at pp. 8–9. J. H. Molyneux, *Simonides. A Historical Study* (Wauconda, Ill. 1992) 117–45 (written before the publication of the new elegiacs), discusses Simonides' Thessalian patrons, but little emerges except their obscurity and our ignorance. There is perhaps particular point in referring to the Aleuadai, whose friendly relations with the Persians were well known in history (*RE* 1.1373), through echoes of Simonides' poem on the Greek dead at Plataea.

[84] Cf. above n. 65.

or in clear water to cleanse a brick of clay, than to persuade a man
maimed by covetousness. Farewell to such as he; and countless silver
may he have, and with desire of more be ever possessed. But I would
choose honour (*time*) and the friendship of men before many mules
and horses. And I am seeking to whom of mortals I may come as a
welcome guest in company of the Muses; for hard are the ways to
minstrels that go unaccompanied by the daughters of the great coun-
sellor Zeus.

The first six verses recapitulate what has gone before and the
difficulties of the poet's position. In v. 59 Theocritus seems to bring
forward a new argument for spending your money (on poets) now,
namely that your heirs will waste it after your death.[85] ἀλλά in v. 60
then marks a turning-point. The poet realises the hopelessness of his
task,[86] and therefore resolves to find a patron to whom he may go with
charis and who will need him because he will have done heroic deeds
(vv. 73–5). Here, almost implicitly, Theocritus creates a link between
the meanness of patrons and their failure to do great deeds. Although
vv. 14–15, 'no more, as before, are men eager to win praise for
glorious deeds, but are overcome (νενίκηνται) by gain', leave open the
possibility that great deeds are still being done, the verb suggests the
misery of defeat and hints that current patrons are not only
tight-fisted, they are also unsuccessful warriors. Hiero will change
both parts of that.

In vv. 66–7 the poem seems again to set off in a new direction:

---

[85] For this *topos* cf. Nisbet and Hubbard on Hor. *Carm.* 2.14.25; it is noteworthy that it occurs at
Hor. *Carm.* 4.7.19–20 together with what may be a memory of Theocr. 16.24. The idea may
have already been hinted at in vv. 40–1, unless those verses are to be taken as part of the
apodosis, i.e. 'they would have derived no pleasure . . . and would have lain unknown . . . had
not . . .' Gow does not consider this possibility, and Dover's view is unclear; Vahlen art. cit.
(n. 27) 208 explicitly denies that v. 40 belongs with the 'hypothetische Gedankenverhältnis',
but his translation perhaps betrays some unease, 'aber der Reichtum nützt ihnen nichts'; that
vv. 40–1 are part of the conditional complex is assumed (without comment) by, e.g.,
Gutzwiller 1983.227.

[86] παρελθεῖν (v. 63) is difficult. The scholiast glosses this verb as ἀπατῆσαι καὶ ἀφελεῖν τι, and
this is followed by Horstmann 1976.129–30; with this reading the verb would be an
amusingly 'honest' description of the poet's aim – almost a dramatic aside taking us back to
the mode of vv. 5–21. Gow and Dover take the sense to be 'persuade' with reference to the
arguments of vv. 58–9; cf. Vahlen art. cit. (n. 27) 211 'bekehren'. The interpretation of the
scholiast may gain support from the positioning of φιλοκερδείηι before the caesura, an order
which invites us to construe it with the infinitive and thus refer it to the poet rather than with
βεβλαμμένον of the patron, i.e. 'by cunning avarice to "get past" a man who has been
damaged'? Note too Hesiod, *Theog.* 613 where παρελθεῖν in the sense 'deceive' follows closely
on the thought that one's heirs waste one's property (vv. 606–7). I have also considered the
possibility that, in a rather compressed use, the sense might be 'enter (as client-poet) [the
house of a] man damaged . . .'

αὐτὰρ ἐγὼ τιμήν τε καὶ ἀνθρώπων φιλότητα
πολλῶν ἡμιόνων τε καὶ ἵππων πρόσθεν ἑλοίμαν.

But I would choose honour (*time*) and the friendship of men before
many mules and horses.

These verses have caused some critical trouble because, although the
ideal expressed in them is very close to expressed Pindaric ideals,[87]
they do not seem to fit squarely with Theocritus' approach to Hiero. I
quote from Dover's note on the passage: 'If Theokritos is thinking of
himself *as poet*, his wish is a little out of place in a poem which is
basically a request for money; but he seems, at least in part, to be
putting himself into the position of the rich man (who might acquire
honour and friends if only he would spend his money) while in part
remaining a poet content that the rich should be rich (Pindar's
patrons were notably rich in "mules and horses") so long as he is loved
and honoured for his poetry.'[88] Clearly this has an important element
of truth. The patron wishes for *time* (cf. v. 46), and *philia* is a prized
aristocratic possession which the poet can offer not merely by
spreading word of the patron's *euxenia*, but by coming κεχαρισμένος
(*both* 'welcome' and 'free of charge', *gratis*) and presenting himself as a
philos. The patron should prefer such things to the hoarding of
possessions (note πολλῶν in v. 67 picking up vv. 34 and 36). These
verses, however, apply equally well to a poet who wants *time* and *philia*
in the sense prescribed by the 'theory of patronage'. Just as χάριτες
can be both 'poems' and the 'favour' or 'pay' which those poems
bring, so, as well as 'honour', *time* can also mean 'pay' or 'public
office', and Theocritus clearly exploits this double sense here, a
double sense which perfectly catches the doubleness of the patronage
relationship, both its 'theory' and its reality. The rejection of 'many
mules and horses' is not merely a sarcastic reference to a patron's
possessions, but it looks back specifically to Simonides and his
Thessalian patrons. A well-known anecdote about Simonides'
willingness to praise mules for a raised fee must lie behind the sarcasm
here.[89] Again, then, it is the figure of Simonides who functions as both
a positive and a negative exemplum for both patron and poet.

This double sense of τιμή accurately reflects, of course, the gradual
shift which was necessary in the relations between poets and patrons

---

[87] Cf. Meincke 1965.58 citing Pind. *Nem.* 1.31ff., 8.37ff.
[88] For this interpretation cf. further Schwinge 1986.53; F. Griffiths 1979.33.
[89] Cf. Arist. *Rhet.* 3 1405b23 = *PMG* 515.

brought about both by increased specialisation and professionalism and by the spread of a monetary economy. The theme first enters the poem as the poet moves from the mean responses of potential patrons to a passage of good advice:

ἀλλ' εὐθὺς μυθεῖται· "ἀπωτέρω ἢ γόνυ κνάμα·
αὐτῶι μοί τι γένοιτο." "θεοὶ τιμῶσιν ἀοιδούς."
"τίς δέ κεν ἄλλου ἀκούσαι; ἅλις πάντεσσιν Ὅμηρος." 20
"οὗτος ἀοιδῶν λῶιστος, ὃς ἐξ ἐμεῦ οἴσεται οὐδέν."
δαιμόνιοι, τί δὲ κέρδος ὁ μυρίος ἔνδοθι χρυσός
κείμενος; οὐχ ἅδε πλούτου φρονέουσιν ὄνασις,
ἀλλὰ τὸ μὲν ψυχᾶι, τὸ δέ πού τινι δοῦναι ἀοιδῶν·
πολλοὺς δ' εὖ ἔρξαι πηῶν, πολλοὺς δὲ καὶ ἄλλων 25
ἀνθρώπων, αἰεὶ δὲ θεοῖς ἐπιβώμια ῥέζειν,
μηδὲ ξεινοδόκον κακὸν ἔμμεναι ἀλλὰ τραπέζηι
μειλίξαντ' ἀποπέμψαι ἐπὴν ἐθέλωντι νέεσθαι,
Μοισάων δὲ μάλιστα τίειν ἱεροὺς ὑποφήτας,
ὄφρα καὶ εἰν Ἀίδαο κεκρυμμένος ἐσθλὸς ἀκούσηις, 30
μηδ' ἀκλεὴς μύρηαι ἐπὶ ψυχροῦ Ἀχέροντος

25 δ' εὖ codd: εὖ Kreussler

But immediately [the potential patron] says: 'The shin is further than the knee; I only hope for something myself.' 'Gods honour poets.' 'Who would listen to another? Homer is enough for all.' 'The best poet will be the one who gets nothing from me.' My friends, what profit to you is the vast hoard of gold lying within? Men of sense see that this is not the benefit of being rich, but rather to indulge oneself, and perhaps give something to some poet, to do well by many of one's relations, always to sacrifice to the gods, not to be a bad host, but to entertain with a generous table and send [guests] on their way when they wish to leave, and above all to honour the sacred interpreters of the Muses, so that, even when you are concealed in Hades, you may enjoy a fair reputation and not weep forgotten [*lit.* 'without *kleos*'] on the banks of the cold Acheron . . .

This difficult passage moves from the language of honouring (v. 19), to that of giving (v. 24), and then back again to honouring (v. 29). In this transition is revealed the 'truth' behind the language of the patronage relationship, which can be represented as a euphemistic sham. Mean patrons seek to 'buy off' poets by using the 'moral' sense of τιμᾶν (v. 19), whereas what poets really want is a more solid kind of 'honour'; here too Simonides can be seen in retrospect to play an important role. The dismissive 'gods honour poets' evokes a famous story (*PMG* 510) of how Scopas once paid Simonides only half the agreed price for a poem in his honour because too much of the poem was devoted to praises of the Dioscuri; the twin gods, so said Scopas, should be asked for the rest. Simonides did indeed get paid when the Dioscuri saved his life in a disaster in which Scopas was killed. Thus the attitude of the mean patron in v. 19 is a dangerous one, which any sensible patron will resist. The ringing declaration of v. 29, 'but most of all pay honour to (τίειν) the holy interpreters of the Muses', both shows *why* poets deserve honour – because they confer immortality and stand close to the divine, an idea picked up in the description of Simonides in v. 44 as θεῖος ἀοιδός -[90] and suggests an alternative interpretation, 'put the highest (monetary) value upon the holy interpreters of the Muses'.[91] This secondary sense which both wording and context evoke is also reinforced by the sequencing of vv. 24–9 which, in an almost priamel-like form, suggests that, whatever else a rich man may do, it is *only* by 'paying' particular attention to poets that there is a guarantee of a reward. This latter point is also made by the repeated language of 'benefit' – if you are wise, you will see that the 'benefit' (ὄνασις) of wealth (v. 23) consists in being 'benefited' (ὤνασαν) by poets.[92] To be useful, your gold should not 'lie (hidden) inside' (vv. 22–3), but should be used to ensure that you yourself have a good reputation when 'hidden in Hades' (v. 30). An apparently very similar passage in Idyll 17, which moves these general reflections to the level of the particular by actually predicating them of Ptolemy, avoids this play with the language of patronage:

οὐ μὰν ἀχρεῖός γε δόμωι ἐνὶ πίονι χρυσός
μυρμάκων ἅτε πλοῦτος ἀεὶ κέχυται μογεόντων·
ἀλλὰ πολὺν μὲν ἔχοντι θεῶν ἐρικυδέες οἶκοι,
αἰὲν ἀπαρχομένοιο σὺν ἄλλοισιν γεράεσσι,

---

[90] θεῖος seems to me much more pointed than the other ancient reading δεινός; for the arguments cf. Gow *ad loc.* and (*contra*) Gallavotti 1986.13. That θεῖος ἀοιδὸς ὁ Κήιος teases us with its similarity to θεῖος ἀοιδὸς ὁ Χῖος (cf., e.g., 22.218, Ar. *Frogs* 1034) supports the reading within the specific concerns of Idyll 16. In a passage very probably indebted to this one, Horace notes that heroes who lived before Agamemnon are forgotten *carent quia uate sacro* (*Carm.* 4.9.28); this passage does not, of course, guarantee the Theocritean text (and *potentium | uatum* at *Carm.* 4.8.26–7 could be invoked to defend the other reading).

[91] A. Wifstrand, 'Zu Theokrits Charites' in *Miscellanea di studi alessandrini in memoria di Augusto Rostagni* (Turin 1963) 308–10, suggests strong punctuation after v. 28 and taking μάλιστα closely with ὄφρα: 'man muss ... ein guter Gastwirt sein; die Dichter aber soll man vor allem aus *dem* Grunde ehren, damit man auch nach dem Tode ...' Although he is correct that Gow's paraphrase of the passage rather fudges the issue (cf. further below), his account of vv. 29–30 is very hard to believe. Coming after a succession of recommended modes of behaviour, μάλιστα τίειν is most naturally seen as the climax of that sequence.

[92] Cf., e.g., Wilamowitz 1906.57–8.

πολλὸν δ' ἰφθίμοισι δεδώρηται βασιλεῦσι,
πολλὸν δὲ πτολίεσσι, πολὺν δ' ἀγαθοῖσιν ἑταίροις.
οὐδὲ Διωνύσου τις ἀνὴρ ἱερούς κατ' ἀγῶνας
ἵκετ' ἐπιστάμενος λιγυρὰν ἀναμέλψαι ἀοιδάν,
ὧι οὐ δωτίναν ἀντάξιον ὤπασε τέχνας.
Μουσάων δ' ὑποφῆται ἀείδοντι Πτολεμαῖον
ἀντ' εὐεργεσίης. τί δὲ κάλλιον ἀνδρί κεν εἴη
ὀλβίωι ἢ κλέος ἐσθλὸν ἐν ἀνθρώποισιν ἀρέσθαι;
τοῦτο καὶ 'Ατρεΐδαισι μένει· τὰ δὲ μυρία τῆνα
ὅσσα μέγαν Πριάμοιο δόμον κτεάτισσαν ἑλόντες
ἀέρι παι κέκρυπται, ὅθεν πάλιν οὐκέτι νόστος.
                                                    (17.106–20)

Yet not useless in that rich house lie the piles of gold like the riches of
the ever-toiling ants. Much the glorious temples of the gods receive,
for firstfruits ever, and many another gift he sends them; much has he
given to mighty kings, to cities, and to his trusty comrades. And
never comes there for the sacred contests of Dionysus one skilled to
raise his clear-voiced song but he receives the gift his art deserves, and
those mouthpieces of the Muses sing of Ptolemy for his benefactions.
And for a prosperous man what finer aim is there than to win him
goodly fame on earth? That is abiding even for the House of Atreus,
while the countless treasure won when they took the great halls of
Priam lies hidden somewhere in that darkness whence there is no return.

In Idyll 17 Theocritus presents a relatively straightforward picture:
Ptolemy 'honours' only his divine parents and the gods, and to all
other men he 'gives' from the abundance of his wealth. In Idyll 16,
however, the situation is rather more nuanced.

The sequence of thought in the passage of Idyll 16 (vv. 22–33)
which I have been considering has been much discussed. The
apparent redundancy of 'poets' (v. 24) and 'holy prophets of the
Muses' (v. 29) has aroused great suspicion and ἀοιδῶν has often been
emended away.[93] That this word above all could have mistakenly
displaced another in this poem is easy to believe,[94] but the coyness of
πού τινι would seem to suit 'poets' far better than, say, 'friends'.[95]
Wilamowitz and Gow thus adopt the solution of deleting the first δέ in
v. 25, thereby making vv. 25–33 a new set of recommendations to the
potential patron, rather than a continuation of the list begun in v. 24.

[93] Fritzsche's note lists seven proposed emendations. The most obvious and probably the best is
Meineke's ἑταίρων (cf. 17.111).
[94] There is not only ἀοιδοῖς and ἀοιδούς at verse-end in vv. 1 and 19, but also ἄλλων
immediately below in v. 25.
[95] Cf., e.g., Vahlen art. cit. (n. 27) 207n.; Wilamowitz 1906.57–8; Meincke 1965.49.

Decision is not easy, but the apparent redundancy of vocabulary seems less difficult than the enforced break between v. 24 and v. 25. The poet's strategy is, in any case, clear. His general 'complaints' about contemporary meanness are, of course, aimed for the ears of Hiero, and he uses the privileged cover afforded by the apparently frank voice of mime and children's song to expose the realities of poetic patronage much more explicitly and at greater length than we find in the previous tradition. The complexities and nudging suggestiveness of this extraordinary poem merely echo the social and linguistic codes in which the patronage game is played.

CHAPTER 4

Idyll 15: imitations of mortality

THEOCRITUS AND COMEDY

Despite the ever increasing gap in the Hellenistic age between élite and 'popular' culture, a frequent strategy of high poetry was the incorporation and reworking of elements from this 'popular' culture into new, literary modes. Crucial to the effect of such reworkings was the audience's knowledge of these 'popular' origins; the clothing of literary art was thus designed to reveal as much as to conceal. Thus it is, for example, that a major formative element in Herodas' *Mimiamboi* is the kind of popular mime performances which survive on some tattered papyri, and much of the particular flavour of these poems comes from the juxtaposition of quite diverse traditions and very different social levels. The distinction between élite and popular culture is perhaps at its most fragile with writers such as Menander, whose very great popularity throughout the Greek-speaking world was accompanied by the interest and admiration of learned men.[1] So, too, the fifth-century Syracusan traditions of comedy (Epicharmus) and mime (Sophron) attracted 'learned' attention as early as the fourth century (Plato and Aristotle),[2] and by the third were very much the subject of élite interest. As the scholars of the Alexandrian Library collected, catalogued, and canonised, all forms of written 'literature' were slowly appropriated to élite concerns; if, as has often been suggested, the very notion of 'literature' really has meaning only with the institution of the Library, then intensive study of 'pre-literary' texts, which were often the product of social conditions radically different from those now prevailing and for which an 'élite–popular'

---

[1] For Menander and Hellenistic poetry see R. F. Thomas, 'New Comedy, Callimachus, and Roman Poetry', *HSCP* 83 (1979) 179–206 (although Thomas does not, to my mind, establish his case for Callimachus' aesthetic distaste for the genre), and A. Henrichs in A. W. Bulloch *et al.* (eds.), *Images and Ideologies. Self-definition in the Hellenistic World* (Berkeley 1993) 180–7.

[2] Cf. Körte, *RE* 3A.1100–1.

distinction would be entirely inappropriate, both changed the meaning of those texts and helped to erect the barriers.

Theocritus is no less involved in these traditions than are his contemporaries. As a Syracusan, he may well have had a particular patriotic interest in the mimic tradition, whose importance we see in Idylls 2 and 15 (cf. below). Attic Comedy too, however, was clearly of interest to him, as the 'shopping epigrams' of Asclepiades (xxv, xxvi G–P) prove also for that poet, and we have seen good reasons for thinking that Theocritus followed Asclepiades in more than one respect.[3] It is above all in Idyll 14, the conversation of Aischinas and Thyonichus, that the influence of comedy is visible. This poem is often classed with the 'Theocritean mimes', and it may indeed be tempting to see in Idylls 14 and 15 respective reworkings of Sophron's 'mimes for men' and 'mimes for women'.[4] Moreover, nice distinctions between comedy and mime may well be misleading in tracing Hellenistic literary affiliation. Thus, for example, the familiar characters of 'the bawd' (Herodas 1 etc.) and 'the komast'[5] are mime figures with very close analogues in comedy, and the two 'genres' overlap at many points;[6] mime troupes seem indeed to have used comic scenarios remoulded to their own modes. Nevertheless, the strictly comic affiliations of Idyll 14 seem clear. Its subject – a narrative of unhappy love followed by advice to go off to serve with Ptolemy as a mercenary – has no real parallel in the mime tradition, but the links with Attic comedy are strong. The poem begins with Thyonichus' enquiry and subsequent teasing:

ΑΙ. χαίρειν πολλὰ τὸν ἄνδρα Θυώνιχον. ΘΥ. ἄλλα τοιαῦτα
Αἰσχίναι. ὡς χρόνιος. ΑΙ. χρόνιος. ΘΥ. τί δέ τοι τὸ μέλημα;
ΑΙ. πράσσομες οὐχ ὡς λῶιστα, Θυώνιχε. ΘΥ. ταῦτ' ἄρα λεπτός,
χὠ μύσταξ πολὺς οὗτος, ἀυσταλέοι δὲ κίκιννοι.
τοιοῦτος πρώαν τις ἀφίκετο Πυθαγορικτάς,
ὠχρὸς κἀνυπόδητος· Ἀθαναῖος δ' ἔφατ' ἦμεν.
ΑΙ. ἤρατο μὰν καὶ τῆνος; ΘΥ. ἐμὶν δοκεῖ, ὀπτῶ ἀλεύρω.
ΑΙ. παίσδεις, ὠγάθ', ἔχων· ἐμὲ δ' ἁ χαρίεσσα Κυνίσκα
ὑβρίσδει· λασῶ δὲ μανείς ποκα, θρὶξ ἀνὰ μέσσον.

(14.1–9)

AISCH. A very good day to you, Thyonichus.

THY. And to you, Aischinas; it's been a long time.

---

[3] Cf. above pp. 19–22. For the comic predecessors of Asclepiades' 'shopping epigrams' cf. Hunter 1983a.210.　[4] Cf. F. Griffiths 1979.84, 120.　[5] Cf. above p. 8.
[6] For discussion and bibliography cf. Hunter 1995b.

AISCH. A long time indeed.

THY. What's bothering you?

AISCH. Things aren't too good with me, Thyonichus.

THY. That would explain why you're thin, and why you've got the large moustache and these unkempt locks. You remind me of some Pythagorist who turned up the other day, pale and barefoot. He said he was an Athenian.

AISCH. Was he too in love?

THY. I think so – with loaves of bread.

AISCH. Have your joke, my friend. But the lovely Kynisca is torturing me; I'll go crazy before I know it –I'm very close to it already.

This scenario, in which one character teases another about his lovesickness, is familiar from a number of genres,[7] and occurs again in Idyll 10,[8] but seems in fact to be particularly associated with comedy. Thus Menander's *Heros* begins with a conversation between two slaves, Getas and Daos, in which Getas asks Daos why he is groaning and tearing out his hair, and when he learns that Daos has fallen in love, he extracts the full story from his friend, but not without some gentle humour (made explicit in Daos' question at v. 39, 'Are you laughing at me?', cf. 14.8 above). So too the opening exchange between the slaves Toxilus and Sagaristio in Plautus' *Persa* contains a very close parallel to Idyll 14:

> SAG. satin tu usque ualuisti? TOX. hau probe.
> SAG. ergo edepol palles. TOX. saucius factus sum in Veneris proelio.
> sagitta Cupido cor meum transfixit.   (Plautus, *Persa* 25–7)

> SAG. How have you been keeping?
> TOX. Not very well.
> SAG. That would explain this pale colour!
> TOX. I have received a wound in Venus' battle: Cupid has transfixed my heart with an arrow.

By themselves these parallels are no more than suggestive, but the cumulative case for comic influence is a strong one. Pale and greedy Pythagoreans are a constant source of humour in the fragments of fourth-century Attic comedy,[9] and it is perhaps not fanciful to suggest that the (alleged) Athenian origin of the Pythagorean of Idyll 14 not merely points to a source for this character in Athenian 'literature', but also offers an acknowledgement of the generic debts of the poem as a whole.[10] At the other end of the poem, Aischinas' decision to seek

---

[7] Cf. Cairns 1972.169–75.   [8] Cf. below pp. 125–7.   [9] Cf. Gow on v. 5.

[10] For such metaliterary notes at the beginning of a poem cf. below p. 151 n. 38.

a cure for lovesickness with overseas mercenary service is also a motif familiar from comedy (Plautus, *Mercator*; Moschion's charade in Menander's *Samia* etc.). Aischinas' narrative of the symposium[11] finds echoes throughout Greek literature, but again Middle and New Comedy provide a rich body of parallel narratives (in part, of course, because of Athenaeus' particular interests),[12] and the theme of drunken violence (cf. vv. 29–38) is particularly common in comedy, although not of course restricted to it.[13] The grim consequences of violent jealousy were explored by Menander in the *Perikeiromene* ('the girl whose hair was hacked'), and perhaps also in the *Rhapizomene* ('the girl who was slapped').[14]

If the principal debt of Idyll 14 is to comedy, the literary texture of the poem nevertheless runs deep. Twice in Aischinas' narrative Homeric comparisons are evoked. The description of Kynisca bursting into tears when being teased clearly reworks Achilles' question to the weeping Patroclus:

ἁ δὲ Κυνίσκα

ἔκλαεν ἐξαπίνας θαλερώτερον ἢ παρὰ ματρὶ
παρθένος ἑξαετὴς κόλπω ἐπιθυμήσασα.

(14.31–3)

But Kynisca suddenly burst into tears – more than a six-year old girl who wants her mother's lap.

τίπτε δεδάκρυσαι, Πατρόκλεες, ἠύτε κούρη
νηπίη, ἥ θ' ἅμα μητρὶ θέουσ' ἀνελέσθαι ἀνώγει,
εἰανοῦ ἁπτομένη, καί τ' ἐσσυμένην κατερύκει,
δακρυόεσσα δέ μιν ποτιδέρκεται, ὄφρ' ἀνέληται.

(*Iliad* 16.7–10)

Why are you crying, Patroclus, like a little girl who runs beside her mother and asks to be picked up, pulling at her dress and keeping her back though she is in a hurry, and looking at her through her tears until her mother picks her up?

There is sarcasm in Aischinas' bitterness here: presumably a *parthenos* was the last thing that Kynisca was, at least in the fervid memory of a scorned lover. So too, Aischinas' description of Kynisca's hurried

---

[11] For various aspects of this narrative cf. Burton 1992.

[12] For these comic narratives cf. E. Fraenkel, *De media et nova comoedia quaestiones selectae* (diss. Göttingen 1912) 9–32.   [13] Cf. Hunter 1983a.186–9.

[14] Cf. further McKeown's introduction to Ovid, *Amores* 1.7; of his examples from Roman comedy, Plaut. *Bacch.* 859–60 and *Truc.* 926–7 also show a jealous *soldier* threatening violence.

departure evokes Achilles' words again, this time his account to the embassy in *Iliad* 9 of his wearisome life:[15]

> μάστακα δοῖσα τέκνοισιν ὑπωροφίοισι χελιδών
> ἄψορρον ταχινὰ πέτεται βίον ἄλλον ἀγείρειν·
> ὠκυτέρα μαλακᾶς ἀπὸ δίφρακος ἔπτετο τήνα
> ἰθὺ δι' ἀμφιθύρω καὶ δικλίδος, ἆι πόδες ἆγον.
>
> (14.39–42)

The swallow gives a morsel to its young in their nest in the eaves and then is off again swiftly to find more food; more quickly than this did she fly from her soft seat, straight through the porch and the house-door, wherever her feet took her.

> ὡς δ' ὄρνις ἀπτῆσι νεοσσοῖσι προφέρῃσι
> μάστακ', ἐπεί κε λάβῃσι, κακῶς δ' ἄρα οἱ πέλει αὐτῆι,
> ὡς καὶ ἐγὼ πολλὰς μὲν ἀύπνους νύκτας ἴαυον,
> ἤματα δ' αἱματόεντα διέπρησσον πολεμίζων,
> ἀνδράσι μαρνάμενος ὀάρων ἕνεκα σφετεράων.
>
> (*Iliad* 9.323–7)

Like a bird that gives every morsel it finds to its chicks which cannot fly, and herself goes without, so I too have spent many sleepless nights, and passed my days in the blood of war, fighting with men for the sake of their wives.

At one level, of course, these evocations of the Homeric Achilles, another 'soldier' who lost his beloved girl, are purely humorous, not unlike the mythological comparisons in Ovid, *Amores* 1.7 in which the poet has messed up his girl's hair; they point to the contrast between the grandeur of the setting and emotions of the *Iliad* and the ordinariness of what is described in Idyll 14. The effect is somewhat similar to that of the thick Homeric and Sapphic texture of Idyll 2, although Aischinas seems a much more simple, less manipulative narrator than Simaitha. On the other hand, these Homeric echoes, within a hexameter poem, serve to place the Idyll within a tradition, by emphasising the distance between the text and its model. In a poem which speaks of the place of the soldier in a contemporary world, the evocation of the *Iliad* makes clear what has changed.

The reference to and praise of Ptolemy with which the poem ends suddenly contextualises the conversation within a 'real' world:[16]

---

[15] For the form of this 'paratactic simile' cf. Bernsdorff 1995, who sees it as emphasising the speed of movement of which the text speaks.

[16] On this encomium cf. Burton 1992; Weber 1993.206–9.

εὐγνώμων, φιλόμουσος, ἐρωτικός, εἰς ἄκρον ἁδύς,
εἰδὼς τὸν φιλέοντα, τὸν οὐ φιλέοντ᾽ ἔτι μᾶλλον,
πολλοῖς πολλὰ διδούς, αἰτεύμενος οὐκ ἀνανεύων,
οἷα χρὴ βασιλῆ᾽· αἰτεῖν δὲ δεῖ οὐκ ἐπὶ παντί,
Αἰσχίνα.   (14.61–5)

Kindly, cultured, knows about love, as pleasant as could be; he
knows who his friends are, and even better who are not; he is generous to many, doesn't refuse when asked, as you would expect from a
king; you mustn't however ask on every occasion, Aischinas.

This encomium seeks consciously to avoid the stylised rhetoric of
praise, seen clearly in Idyll 17, a rhetoric which marks that encomium
as belonging to a literary discourse divorced from 'everyday speech'.
By comparison, the asyndetic list of Idyll 14 seeks, at one level, to
assimilate Ptolemy to 'everyday' experience, to adapt him to the
milieu of the poem. Ptolemy's virtues become traditional Greek
aristocratic virtues, such as, for example, those praised throughout
the corpus of Theognis: he is just the kind of 'man's man' who would
be a sympathetic paymaster for 'a free man' (v. 59), a description
which here carries, as often, moral as well as juridical meaning. At
another level, however, the verses conspire against any such simple
'realism'. An individual Greek mercenary would doubtless wish to
know that the king he served was 'a good chap' who was well supplied
with money, but, as many critics have observed, the praises suit the
patron of a poet at least as well as the employer of a soldier;
Thyonichus seems to hold out the prospect that Aischinas will be able
to establish some personal connection with Ptolemy, but paying for
mercenaries is not what was traditionally understood as 'generosity'.[17]
Theocritus wants us to feel the rupture in the poem here, and to hear
now his voice rather than that of Thyonichus. The echo of the martial
poetry of Tyrtaeus (fr. 10.31–2 West) in Thyonichus' mouth:

ὥστ᾽ εἴ τοι κατὰ δεξιὸν ὦμον ἀρέσκει
λῶπος ἄκρον περονᾶσθαι, ἐπ᾽ ἀμφοτέροις δὲ βεβακώς
τολμασεῖς ἐπιόντα μένειν θρασὺν ἀσπιδιώταν,
ἇι τάχος εἰς Αἴγυπτον.   (14.65–8)

So if you fancy fastening your cloak over your right shoulder and you
have the courage to stand firm on both feet to meet the charge of a
bold shield-bearer, be off to Egypt with all speed.

---

[17] On the Ptolemies' heavy dependence upon mercenaries from outside Egypt cf. G. T. Griffith,
The Mercenaries of the Hellenistic World (Cambridge 1935) 108–41.

reinforced as it is by the Homeric ἀσπιδιώτας, 'shield-bearer' (cf. *Iliad* 2.554, 16.167), does not merely pick up, and gently mock, the Homeric echoes in Aischinas' words,[18] it also opens again the gap between the subject of the poem and the style in which that is described. Our knowledge of the traditions of the hexameter is used to set at risk the 'believable fiction' of the poem. Idyll 14, therefore, explores in a Theocritean mode the implications of treating comedy as an 'imitation of life'. What kind of imitation can literature in fact offer? Idyll 15, the dramatised visit to Arsinoe's Adonis festival by Gorgo and Praxinoa, two women of Syracusan origin resident in Alexandria, raises these questions more insistently and in different ways throughout the poem. It is with this poem that the rest of this chapter will be concerned.

MIME AND *MIMESIS*

When Praxinoa and Gorgo finally succeed in entering the palace, their attention is first caught by the tapestries (τὰ ποικίλα)[19] with their lifelike figures (τἀκριβέα γράμματα, ἔτυμα, ἔμψυχ᾽ οὐκ ἐνυφαντά, 'accurate, true, alive not woven'): σοφόν τι χρῆμ᾽ ἄνθρωπος ('what a clever thing is man!') exclaims Praxinoa, before moving to describe a representation of Adonis with his first beard just showing. After a brief interruption, Gorgo draws attention to 'the Argive woman's daughter', a 'very clever singer', and bound to sing something καλόν; the song itself describes Aphrodite and the young Adonis in a marvellous tableau representing their 'marriage', and Gorgo responds with admiration: σοφώτατον ἁ θήλεια κτλ. This brief summary makes clear the obvious analogies between the two palace artefacts, the tapestries and the hymn, but those analogies allow more than one inference. It may be that we are simply supposed to understand that Gorgo and Praxinoa would respond with such admiration to anything beyond the normal sphere of their experience, and the point lies not in fact in any similarity of the song to the tapestries but precisely in their difference which we, but not the women, can appreciate; Gorgo and Praxinoa have only one register for admiration and use it across widely different categories. Whereas the women emphasise the 'reality', the 'lifelikeness', of the woven figures, the hymn seems rather concerned to point the 'unreality', the fabulousness, of what it

---

[18] Tyrtaeus may also be appropriate if, as many critics have thought, we are to imagine that the poem is set in the Peloponnese.   [19] Cf. Gow on v. 78 for this interpretation.

describes – πάντεσσι καλοῖς (111) . . . ὅσα (112) . . . ὅσσα (115) . . . παντοῖα (116) . . . ὅσσα (117) . . . πάντα (118). This superabundance of good things which defy cataloguing may reflect a deliberate stress by Ptolemy and Arsinoe on the incredible riches of Egypt, a motif seen also in Idyll 17 and in the standard representations of Arsinoe with a cornucopia 'full with all the good fruits of the season' (Ath. 11 497b-c).[20] Moreover, this plenty creates a pointed contrast between the mundane and necessarily frugal lives of Praxinoa and Gorgo (cf. vv. 18–20, 35–7) and the over-full lushness of the palace, a contrast which runs parallel to that between the sensuality of the Adonis cult and the 'lovelessness' of the marriages in which the women find themselves.[21] There is also here a more literary dimension. The analogies direct our attention to the relationship of the two 'artefacts', particularly as the designs on the tapestries (vv. 81–6) and the tableau described by the singer are pointedly similar.

The 'realism' of the tapestries is based on a comparison with actual experience – they are ἔμψυχα; so also the hymn appeals to, and our response to it must be conditioned by, our experience of such poems (and such tableaux)[22] in 'real life'. Our sense of familiarity with 'generic *topoi*' is in fact analogous to our sense of the familiarity and variety of 'ordinary experience'. The effect of this is that the literary mime itself inscribes possible models of its own reception in the text. It does not require a long survey of the history of discussions of 'mimetic realism' to realise how closely the reactions of the women foreshadow familiar modes of critical response. We might not naturally choose Gorgo and Praxinoa as models for ourselves, and their reactions might seem 'unsophisticated', but the poem forces us to consider the basis and validity of our own critical judgements.[23] This is made

---

[20] Cf. D. B. Thompson, *Ptolemaic Oinochoai and Portraits in Faience* (Oxford 1973) 32–3; on Idyll 17 cf. above p. 89. For τρυφή as a Ptolemaic ideal cf. also J. Tondriau, *REA* 50 (1948) 49–54; H. Heinen, *Ktema* 3 (1978) 188–92; Weber 1993.70. τρυφή is, of course, a double-edged motif, particularly for moralising writers (cf. Phylarchos, *FGrHist* 81 F40, on the ἄκαιρος τρυφή of Philadelphus), and we must be wary of lessening the differences between earlier and later Ptolemies; nevertheless, the picture which emerges from the poetry written under Philadelphus is pretty consistent, and cf. Ath. 5 203b-c.

[21] The most enlightening discussion of this is F. Griffiths 1981 who explores the difference and interplay between the erotic 'ideology' of Adonis (best described by J.-P. Vernant, *Myth and Society in Ancient Greece* (London 1980) 130–67) and the existence led by the women; cf. also Goldhill 1994. 216–23 and (with a rather different nuance) J. Whitehorne, 'Women's work in Theocritus, Idyll 15', *Hermes* 123 (1995) 76–81. Griffiths p. 257 well observes that 'the self-encumbering fecundity of housewives is complemented by Ptolemy's and Arsinoe's childless sibling union, whose generativity sustains and enriches the whole society'.

[22] Cf. Gow II p. 266 'the details of Arsinoe's tableau are presumably drawn from life'. For the 'historicity' of Arsinoe's festival cf. below n. 75. [23] Cf. Goldhill 1994.216–23.

particularly sharp by the fact that the women claim to be Syracusans (v. 90) and they have apparently moved from that city to Alexandria. In as much as we may claim to know anything about Theocritus, he too appears to have been a Syracusan who certainly worked, if not also lived, at Alexandria. Gorgo and Praxinoa, who describe the scene for us and thus act the rôle of the informing poet, are fashioned as a comically distorted image of 'the actual poet'; their visit to the palace may be seen as a rendering of Theocritus' 'coming' to the royal palace in Alexandria and his gaining of 'admittance' (i.e. royal patronage), whereas his *charites* in Idyll 16, like many of the pressing crowd in Idyll 15, failed to gain entry through the doors of the great.[24] As embodiments of the poetic voice, Gorgo and Praxinoa guide us as we are usually guided by the poet; we cannot simply ignore their voice. The fact that a related strategy seems to be at work in Herodas' fourth Mimiamb[25] might suggest that this concern with its own reception is a genuine and persistent feature of a 'genre' which was only too conscious of the fact that it was not really a part of 'literature'. It is a genre constantly looking over its shoulder to see 'how it is going down'; its lowness is of a very knowing kind.

Even if Theophrastus was not responsible for the definition of μῖμος as μίμησις βίου τά τε συγκεχωρημένα καὶ ἀσυγχώρητα περιέχων, 'an imitation of life encompassing both the permitted and the illicit' (Diomedes XXIV.3.16–17 Koster),[26] there was without doubt already in the third century a clear link between mime and '*mimesis* of life'; the women's reactions to the tapestries, as we have seen, provide one model for the reception of the poem in which they appear. If, however, there is anything in the report of the *Hypothesis* in the scholia that Theocritus 'modelled' (παρέπλασε) his poem on Sophron's 'The Women at the Isthmian Festival',[27] then we can see that this *mimos* is a *mimesis* in another sense too. There are two important aspects of this literary debt. One is that, just as Gorgo and Praxinoa have moved from Syracuse to Alexandria, so has the mime. Even if Praxinoa's proud assertion 'we are Corinthians by descent' (v. 91)

---

[24] Such verses as 61–2, 'Is it easy to get in then?', and 65, 'Look, Praxinoa, what a crowd there is around the doors', lend themselves easily to such a satirical reading. For a related reading of Idyll 14 cf. Burton 1992.240–2. The relation between poets and the 'houses' (real and metaphorical) of the great is a recurrent motif of Roman poetry (cf. now the overview in P. White, *Promised Verse* (Harvard 1993)), and here too there is a Greek background which should not be ignored.   [25] Cf. Hunter 1995b.

[26] For discussion and bibliography cf. H. Reich, *Der Mimus* (Berlin 1903) 263–74; R. Janko, *Aristotle and Comedy* (London 1984) 48–9; Zanker 1987.144–5.

[27] Gow II p. 265 enjoins caution in ascribing much except 'the general idea' to Sophron.

does not amusingly glance at Sophron's mime, and it is a pure (if attractive) speculation that Sophron too represented Syracusan women present at a Corinthian festival,[28] Gorgo's arrival at her friend's house, not unlike the arrival of 'the bawd' in Herodas 1,[29] marks the arrival in Alexandria of a new literary form, embodied in the amusing shapes of Gorgo and Praxinoa and in a rough hexametric technique which may seek to imitate in verse the half-way house of Sophron's rhythmical mimes.[30] With their admission to the palace, the Syracusan mime tradition has reached the Alexandrian court. Such conscious self-reference, which may be described as a kind of literary history written into the poem, is hardly surprising in any product of Alexandrian poetry, but again we may wish to see a mode which is peculiarly adapted to the mime. Secondly, we can see that it is the literary mime of Herodas and Theocritus which foreshadows, in the implicit poetics of poetry itself, the connection between two senses of *mimesis* which we find in later poetic theory;[31] these senses are the *mimesis* familiar from Aristotle's *Poetics*, that is the transference of the inherent mimetic qualities of human beings to a criterion for (particularly dramatic) poetry as imitative of the actions of men, and *mimesis* as the imitation of literary models. The literary mime interweaves these two senses in such a way as to explore the relation between them. Thus, for example, Gorgo's praise of the tapestries, λεπτὰ καὶ ὡς χαρίεντα, 'how fine they are and how lovely' (v. 79), echoes the account of Circe's weaving at *Od.* 10. 222–3 to dramatise the artifice, the *mimesis*, of the 'naturalism' of this mime.

Rather more complex perhaps is the episode which separates the admiration of the tapestries from the Adonis-song. A nameless man asks the women to be quiet because their 'broad vowels' (as well as their ceaseless chatter) are driving him to distraction. 'Unless', as Dover notes, 'there has been interference with the transmitted text on a large scale', the man too speaks in Doric.[32] If we take this little scene

---

[28] Cf. Legrand 1898.132.

[29] I have discussed this in 'The presentation of Herodas' *Mimiamboi*', *Antichthon* 27 (1993) 31–44; cf. also C. Miralles, 'La poetica di Eroda', *Aevum Antiquum* 5 (1992) 89–113.

[30] For the versification of Idyll 15 cf. Fantuzzi 1995 and n. 59 below. For Sophron cf. E. Norden, *Die antike Kunstprosa* (Leipzig 1898) 1 46–8.

[31] Cf. D. A. Russell, 'De imitatione' in D. West and T. Woodman (eds.), *Creative Imitation and Latin Literature* (Cambridge 1979) 1–16.

[32] For what it is worth, the transmission of these verses is fairly unanimous. What the man says *could* be rewritten in *koine* without damage to the metre, although the corruption of *ἐκκναίσουσι to ἐκκναισεῦντι would be hard to credit.

at face value, then either, as Gow puts it, 'we are plainly invited to
suppose that [despite the dialect of the text] he is not a Dorian', or we
must suppose that Syracusan Doric was thought to sound particularly
broad in comparison with other Dorian accents or dialects.[33] It seems
to be generally true for Theocritus that 'stylistic variation inside the
same idyll does not depend on breaks in the convention of the dialect
but on differences of vocabulary, theme, and feelings,'[34] but the second
explanation can hardly be ruled out; what for the man is an unbearably
grating sound, is for Praxinoa pure and original Doric (vv. 90–3).
Dialectal questions have, of course, a peculiar significance in a 'genre'
which advertises its connections with 'life'; to call attention to the
apparent gap between the speech presupposed by what is actually
said and the text itself is again to dramatise the tension between literary
artifice and the appeal to mimetic realism which lies at the heart of
the literary mime of Herodas and Theocritus. As all the characters of
the poem figure in a 'Syracusan mime' they will speak appropriately
(cf. below), but what they say and how they say it dramatises the
presuppositions of this awkward 'genre'. The effect is somewhat
analogous to the layers of meaning in the encomium of Ptolemy at the
end of Idyll 14. It is therefore worth considering the nature of the
linguistic *mimesis* of Idyll 15 at a little greater length.[35]

   The language of Idyll 15 is characterised by an absence of marked
'Homerisms' and poeticisms and a metrical 'roughness' which aligns
this poem most closely with Idyll 11, the song of the lovesick
Cyclops.[36] These poems have something else in common also – their
principal characters are Syracusans, a fact which is noted explicitly in
the course of the poems (11.7, 15.90). As Theocritus himself came
from Syracuse, it would be unsurprising if the Syracusan dialect had
had some influence on the Doric of his poems; that Idyll 15 was indeed
composed in the Syracusan dialect was argued by Victor Magnien,[37]
but without conspicuous success, which was in any case hardly to be
expected, given the dialectal mess presented by our papyri and
manuscripts and the fact that the majority of dialectal alternatives are
metrically equivalent. Nevertheless, it is in Idylls 11 and 15, if
anywhere, that we might be tempted to seek specifically Syracusan
features. Two facts make the case of Idyll 15 particularly interesting.
One is the fact already considered that the poem itself makes the

---

[33] On the ancient conception of Doric and its local versions cf. Cassio 1993.
[34] Fabiano 1971.522.   [35] For the detailed argument for what follows cf. Hunter 1995a.
[36] Cf. Di Benedetto 1956.53.   [37] Magnien 1920.

dialect of the characters an important issue (vv. 80–95), and the other is that, in this same passage, much the earliest witness to the text, *PHamburg* 201 of the first century AD, preserves a rare dialect form which had been totally lost to the tradition:

ΠΡ. πότνι' Ἀθαναία, ποῖαί ψ' ἐπόνασαν ἔριθοι,   80
  ποῖοι ζωογράφοι τἀκριβέα γράμματ' ἔγραψαν.
  ὡς ἔτυμ' ἐστάκαντι καὶ ὡς ἔτυμ' ἀνδινεῦντι,
  ἔμψυχ', οὐκ ἐνυφαντά. σοφόν τι χρῆμ' ἄνθρωπος.
  αὐτὸς δ' ὡς θαητὸς ἐπ' ἀργυρέας κατάκειται
  κλισμῷ, πρᾶτον ἴουλον ἀπὸ κροτάφων καταβάλλων,   85
  ὁ τριφίλητος Ἄδωνις, ὁ κἠν Ἀχέροντι φιληθείς.
ΞΕΝ. παύσασθ', ὦ δύστανοι, ἀνάνυτα κωτίλλοισαι,
  τρυγόνες· ἐκκναισεῦντι πλατειάσδοισαι ἄπαντα.
ΠΡ. μᾶ, πόθεν ὤνθρωπος; τί δὲ τίν, εἰ κωτίλαι εἰμές;
  πασάμενος ἐπίτασσε· Συρακοσίαις ἐπιτάσσεις.   90
  ὡς εἰδῇις καὶ τοῦτο, Κορίνθιαι εἰμὲς ἄνωθεν,
  ὡς καὶ ὁ Βελλεροφῶν. Πελοποννασιστὶ λαλεῦμες,
  δωρίσδειν δ' ἔξεστι, δοκῶ, τοῖς Δωριέεσσι.
                             (15.80–93)

80 ψεφονασαν PHamb.: σφ' ἐπόνασαν PAnt.,
codd.   82 ἀν- PHamb.,   PAnt. : ἐν-
codd.   88 πλατιάζοισαι   PAnt.   93
]ρισδ[POxy. 1618 (5th cent. AD) :   ]ιν PAnt. :
δωρίσδεν codd. *teste Gallavotti*[38]

PRAXINOA Lady Athena, what workers they must have been that made them, and what artists that drew the lines so true! The figures stand and turn so naturally they're alive not woven. What a clever thing is man! And look at him; how marvellous he is, lying in his silver chair with the first down spreading from the temples, thrice-loved Adonis, loved even in death.

STRANGER My good women, do stop that ceaseless chattering – perfect turtle-doves, they'll bore one to death with all their broad vowels.

PRAXINOA Gracious, where does this gentleman come from? And what business is it of yours if we do chatter? Give orders where you're master. It's Syracusans you're ordering about, and let me tell you we're Corinthians by descent like Bellerophon. We talk Peloponnesian, and I suppose Dorians may talk Dorian.

ψε (v. 80) is a third-person plural pronoun whose appearance in Sophron (fr. 94 Kaibel) caused the later grammatical tradition to regard it as a Syracusan form;[39] it occurs, however, also at 4.3, a poem

---

[38] Gallavotti's report of the papyrus readings here is erroneous.
[39] Cf. Gow on 4.3; Gallavotti 1986.10.

set in southern Italy, is attested on Crete,[40] and may therefore have had wider currency than we can now tell. Nevertheless, its disappearance from the text of the poem seems a very good reason to seek other 'Syracusan features' in the speech of the women.

There are, however, also good reasons for caution. Although the main features of the language of the Corinthian colonies are well understood, our knowledge of the Syracusan variant is very scanty indeed, and is far too reliant upon the vagaries of manuscript traditions. As we have already seen, attestations for 'Syracusan dialect' in the grammatical tradition very often mean no more than that a word was used by Epicharmus or Sophron, and we can hardly doubt that Theocritus' Alexandrian readers were interested in the possible difference between an 'echo' of one of these Syracusan poets and a genuine feature of (archaising or contemporary) Syracusan speech. Secondly, analogies from other literary traditions (both ancient and modern), such as the presentation of non-Attic dialects in the comedies of Aristophanes, suggest that *mimesis* of speech-forms – particularly for the purposes of humour or some other marked effect – is unlikely to be linguistically 'accurate' or consistent; it is 'difference' which is important for the reception of the represented speech. Moreover, we should not underestimate the difficulty of 'accurate representation' of the sound of 'other' dialects in the absence of agreed graphic conventions. Finally, in an Alexandrian context, we can hardly rule out the possibility that Theocritus envisaged a differentiated response within his audience to the language that Praxinoa and Gorgo speak, according to the familiarity of that audience with Syracusan Doric.

In as much as our manuscripts permit it, detailed examination of the language of Idyll 15 reveals few examples of features for which a good case for marked 'Syracusanness' can be made.[41] Our ignorance, and the great vitality and variety of the Doric dialects in the third century, imposes too many barriers. There has, moreover, been a natural critical tendency to seek specifically Syracusan forms which distinguish this poem from the other Doric poems of Theocritus, as though it was certain that the original context for the reception of this poem was within a corpus of Theocritean poems ('a poetry book'). If this was indeed the case, then we would hope to be able to identify a pattern of difference to which significance could be attached.[42] If, however, we treat Idyll 15 on its own, a rather different picture emerges. The language of Praxinoa and Gorgo is marked by its difference from

---

[40] Cf. Buck 1955.§§87, 119.5.   [41] Cf. Hunter 1995a.   [42] Cf. above p. 31.

the ordinary language of hexameter poetry, whether Ionic or Doric, a difference which consists in the absence of the most familiar features of poetic style. To this extent it lays a claim to a kind of 'mimetic realism' which associates it with the language of everyday discourse. On the other hand, it appears (as far as we can tell) to make no attempt to reproduce to any great extent the special and the individual in the speech of Syracusan women living in Alexandria. In a loose analogy, one might say that the pan-Doric features of their language correspond to the generic features of the literary *mimesis* (women visiting, *ekphrasis* of art etc.), so that both the form and the language illustrate the poem's concern with the tension between the 'artificial' and the 'real'. The language of the poem, no less than the characters and the 'plot', gestures towards 'the realistic' but determinedly refuses to embrace it. By seeing Idyll 15 solely within the Theocritean corpus, the nature of the mimetic effect sought by Theocritus has been obscured in modern criticism. When Praxinoa and Gorgo use Doric forms, at one level the effect remains 'mimetically analogous' to Syracusan speech, even when those forms were either not specifically Syracusan or in fact not actually in use in Syracuse. If no other Theocritean poem had survived, there would be much less critical disagreement about the linguistic *mimesis* of the poem. On the other hand, the generalised nature of the language ironically distances the poem from its own claim to represent reality.

ADONIS AND THE PTOLEMIES

In turning now to the Adonis-song, we must bear in mind this complex mimetic texture in which it is set. It too advertises its claim to be a 'real performance', the song of 'the Argive woman's daughter', and indeed critics have seen here a reference to a specific contemporary performer.[43] Moreover, just as critical discussion of Gorgo and Praxinoa has usually assumed (without argument) that they are characters at whom we are supposed to laugh, so the standard critical approach to the Adonis-song has been a move from its alleged 'mediocrity'[44] to an explanation for this in terms of general or specific

---

[43] Cf. Gow *ad loc.*

[44] 'A farrago of conventional writing . . . so long, so tedious, and so dull' (W. C. Hembold, *CP* 46(1951)17); 'a mediocre piece. It begins well enough, but its insistence on the riches and splendour of the display is not devoid of vulgarity, and the catalogue of heroes who do not share Adonis's privileges is clumsy and perfunctory' (A. S. F. Gow, *JHS* 58 (1938) 202); 'polished but uninteresting verses . . . Theocritus does not seem to be absorbed in the subject' (Fraser 1972.1 673).

parody. Dover's observation puts the conventional view well: 'I should have expected Theokritos to take the opportunity of showing how well he could write a hymn, not the opportunity of showing how badly most people wrote them; but this expectation founders on the hymn we have before us.'[45] Occasional voices of praise for the passage are heard,[46] but on the whole it has suffered from the same distaste that some modern scholars profess to feel for the 'mass entertainment' which Arsinoe provided. Even F. T. Griffiths, in an excellent discussion of Idyll 15,[47] cannot escape from this perspective: 'The rococo flamboyance of the festival epitomises bad taste, and therefore Theocritus can share a laugh with his patron by memorializing the masses' susceptibility to such vulgarity in his own impeccably refined verse.' 'Bad taste' and 'vulgarity' are, however, very dangerous critical weapons. It is, of course, possible that Philadelphus regarded with aesthetic contempt his own lavish pavilion and procession which survive for us in the account of Kallixeinos (Ath. 5 196a–203b),[48] but there is no evidence for such a hypothesis (and it is hard to imagine what form such evidence could take).

'Deliberately bad' poetry can be notoriously difficult to detect. If the charge of being 'deliberately mediocre' is to be upheld against this song, then it can only be done so within generic boundaries. When Theocritus rewrites a *Homeric Hymn*, as he does in the opening twenty-six verses of Idyll 22, or an archaic maiden-song, as in Idyll 18, he does so in a recognisably appropriate style, producing in each case a version of a particular type of poem. It is true that the framing narrative of Idyll 15 seems to move in a world beneath the cultural level of these other two poems, but 'parody' may here be the wrong

---

[45] Dover p. 210.

[46] Cf. Zanker 1987.12–18; Hutchinson 1988.152; H. Beckby, *Die griechischen Bukoliker* (Meisenheim am Glan 1975) 454 'das feierliche und dichterisch hochstehende Lied der Sängerin'; F.-J. Simon, Τὰ κύλλ' ἀείδειν. *Interpretationen zu den Mimiamben des Herodas* (Frankfurt 1991) 39 considers that the song 'behält . . . einen schönen Schein', but then goes on to admit that a number of passages give him cause for critical concern.

[47] F. Griffiths 1981; my quotation comes from p. 256. An earlier version of Griffiths' reading of Idyll 15 may be found in F. Griffiths 1979.116–28; p. 128 offers a sensitive appreciation of the Adonis-song.

[48] Cf. E. E. Rice, *The Grand Procession of Ptolemy Philadelphus* (Oxford 1983). That the funeral car of Alexander as described by Diodorus (18.26.3–27.5) is stylistically of a piece both with Philadelphus' procession and with the bower of Adonis as described by Theocritus is not to be forgotten; note Diodorus' stress on the thousands of spectators attracted by the car, 'unable to get enough of the pleasure of viewing' (18.28.1, cf. Ap. Rhod. *Arg.* 4.428–9). It is obviously very tempting to move from these similarities to generalisations about a 'Ptolemaic' style of representation, as well as of literary *ekphrasis*; cf. in general H. von Hesberg, 'Temporäre Bilder oder die Grenzen der Kunst', *JDAI* 104 (1989) 61–82.

category. It is always easy for those of intellectual pretension to laugh at 'popular' songs or poems written in fact with no parodic intention, and we have already noted that Idyll 15 itself is explicitly concerned with standards of aesthetic judgement. The Theocritean corpus offers very few cases in fact where we might seem to be on firm ground. One such may be Boukaios' little love-song (τι κόρας φιλικὸν μέλος) in Idyll 10 (vv. 24–37):

Μοῖσαι Πιερίδες, συναείσατε τὰν ῥαδινάν μοι
παῖδ᾽· ὧν γάρ χ᾽ ἄψησθε, θεαί, καλὰ πάντα ποεῖτε.
Βομβύκα χαρίεσσα, Σύραν καλέοντί τυ πάντες,
ἰσχνάν, ἁλιόκαυστον, ἐγὼ δὲ μόνος μελίχλωρον.
καὶ τὸ ἴον μέλαν ἐστί, καὶ ἁ γραπτὰ ὑάκινθος·
ἀλλ᾽ ἔμπας ἐν τοῖς στεφάνοις τὰ πρᾶτα λέγονται.
ἁ αἲξ τὰν κύτισον, ὁ λύκος τὰν αἶγα διώκει,
ἁ γέρανος τὤροτρον· ἐγὼ δ᾽ ἐπὶ τὶν μεμάνημαι.
αἴθε μοι ἧς ὅσσα Κροῖσόν ποκα φαντὶ πεπᾶσθαι·
χρύσεοι ἀμφότεροί κ᾽ ἀνεκείμεθα τᾶι Ἀφροδίται
τώς αὐλώς μὲν ἔχοισα καὶ ἢ ῥόδον ἢ τύγε μᾶλον,
σχῆμα δ᾽ ἐγὼ καὶ καινὰς ἐπ᾽ ἀμφοτέροισιν ἀμύκλας.
Βομβύκα χαρίεσσ᾽, οἱ μὲν πόδες ἀστράγαλοί τευς,
ἁ φωνὰ δὲ τρύχνος· τὸν μὰν τρόπον οὐκ ἔχω εἰπεῖν.

Pierian Muses, hymn with me the slender maiden, for all things that you touch you make fair.

Charming Bombyca, all call thee the Syrian, lean and sun-scorched, and I alone, honey-hued.

Dark is the violet and the lettered hyacinth, yet in garlands these are accounted first.

Goat follows after the moon-clover, wolf after goat, crane after plough, and I for you am crazy.

Would I had such wealth as Croesus, in the tales, once owned. Then should we both stand in gold as offerings to Aphrodite –

You with your pipes, and a rosebud or an apple, and I with raiment new and new shoes of Amyclae on either foot.

Charming Bombyca, like knuckle-bones your feet, and your voice a poppy, and your ways – they pass my power to tell.

The generic affiliations of such a poem are with popular song, and the structuring into seven couplets is clearly intended to suggest the 'folksy' feel of popular song;[49] we may compare the song of the goatherd at *Id.* 3.6–23 (six three-line 'stanzas'[50] with the whole

---

[49] Cf. Wilamowitz 1906.142–4; Gow II p. 16; R. Pretagostini, *Aevum Antiquum* 5 (1992) 82–4.
[50] Alternatively, three couplets followed by four three-line stanzas; in either case, the effect is much the same.

framed by vocative addresses to Amaryllis)[51] or the little love-songs in the final scenes of Aristophanes' *Ecclesiazousai*. 'Popular song' often, of course, apes the language of more formal verse, but Boukaios' opening invocation to the Muses seems incongruously grand. Μοῖσαι Πιερίδες, 'Pierian Muses', is almost a quotation of the opening of Hesiod's *Works and Days* (Μοῦσαι Πιερίηθεν, 'Muses from Pieria').[52] Hesiod is just the right model for this agricultural worker, and he is echoed again, perhaps more appropriately, in Milon's work-song which follows; moreover, the distorted echo of a Hesiodic phrase replays at the textual level the mental distraction which has turned Boukaios from hard work to what Hesiod warns against most vehemently, the attractions of the female. The hymnal style of the opening verse, however,[53] causes the enjambed παῖδα to come, if not as a surprise, at least with more than a tinge of bathos, particularly as 'slender' refers to a girl whom Milon has just characterised as a praying-mantis (v. 18). Whether or not the Muses answer Boukaios' call presumably depends upon our judgement of the κάλλος of the subsequent poem (cf. v. 25); here, however, there are two poets, Theocritus and Boukaios, and we may judge the same song differently, according as we view it as the work of one or the other.

In vv. 26–7 Boukaios employs the familiar lover's stratagem of euphemism, but it is not a lover's normal procedure to make the stratagem explicit, and with such emphasis as the exemplum of black flowers does;[54] the effect of such naïveté upon the beloved Bombyca may well be imagined, even if we take the verses as a way of saying 'I am the only chance you've got, as everyone else thinks you ugly.' The imperfect sequencing of vv. 30–1 (perhaps 'corrected' by Virgil at *Ecl.* 2.63–5), and the slight shift in the sense of διώκει between v. 30 and v. 31, are not themselves necessarily meant to be seen as inept; διώκειν, however, is common in the sense 'pursue with amorous intent' (Sappho fr. 1 etc.) and in the context of a love-song 'pursue with the intention of eating' suggests a conceit which has failed incongruously. The wish of vv. 32–5, 'a wish of hopelessly maudlin

---

[51] Unlike Boukaios, the goatherd finds two different adjectives for the beloved, χαρίεσσα and φίλα.

[52] Μοῦσαι Πιερίδες in fact begins a hexameter at *Aspis* 206.

[53] Cf. the Epidaurian hymn cited by the commentators *ad loc*. After ῥαδινάν we perhaps expect a reference to Aphrodite, cf. 17.37, Sappho fr. 102.2 Voigt etc.

[54] I suspect that vv. 28–9 contain some kind of word-play signalled by γραπτά: τὸ μέλαν is 'ink' and although the simple λέγω is not used for 'read' (LSJ s.v. III 13), the hint of 'are read' is not difficult to feel in the verb; the 'lettered hyacinth' is literally 'read'.

sentimentality, ending in bathos',[55] is meant, I think, to evoke the happy couple's marriage; Boukaios imagines a statue of Bombyca and himself dressed up in new clothes for their wedding. The fulfilment of such a wish may seem inconceivably remote. Commentators have noted the ambiguities of the closing half-verse which presumably means (for Boukaios) 'your character is so wonderful it defeats my powers of description', but could mean (for us) 'I don't know what your character is' or 'I can't put your character into verse (because I am not a very good poet)'.

What is clear from this example is that the potential for double reading, in which one reading destroys the effect of another, may act as a weapon of parodic incongruity; this is perhaps more familiar from the song of the Cyclops in Idyll 11, in which the double reading is based upon ignorance and knowledge of the *Odyssey*. So too, stylistic variation which serves no obvious poetic purpose (from the point of view of the singer) can produce a similar effect. Generic expectation is here particularly important, because generic familiarity generates a framework in which not everything needs to be said. Thus, a love-song is a kind of encomium. To praise in such a way as to reveal the faults of what you praise is, by ancient and modern standards, to fail in praise. Boukaios' song is thus a masterly text, but a poor love-song; the two different judgements reflect its two poets. Whether or not the Adonis-song is susceptible to similar analysis remains to be seen.

Gorgo introduces the song of the Argive woman's daughter as ὁ Ἄδωνις (v. 96), presumably 'the Adonis-song (which is a regular part of the festival)'; it is commonly, and rightly, described in modern literature as 'a hymn'. The opening and closing of the poem are indeed hymnic, as can be seen by a comparison not only with extant cult hymns but also with the hymns of Callimachus; encomium of Aphrodite and Adonis is precisely what we would expect to find in a hymn to them. On the other hand, there is almost no poetry extant[56] with which we may compare the Adonis-song, for Bion's *Lament for Adonis* is entirely different in both form and occasion. The singer's foreshadowing of lamentation for Adonis on the following day after the formal farewell of v. 131, a lamentation actually prefigured in the

---

[55] Hopkinson 1988.169.

[56] The one fragment of Praxilla's 'Hymn to Adonis' in lyric dactyls (*PMG* 747) is a lament by the god himself; whatever the tone and interpretation of that fragment, it is interesting to find a female poet writing on such a subject.

consolatio of the Catalogue of Heroes,[57] both calls attention to how this song is not what we might expect an Adonis-song to be and evokes the full compass of the festival; 'on a literal reading', as Cairns observes, 'the singer is giving in lines 136–44 an advance monodic performance of what the chorus will sing next day'.[58] Any such poem at a real festival is likely to have been an astrophic lyric song, composed in the traditional vocabulary and syntax of lyric; the fact that the metre of the Adonis-song is distinguished from the 'mimic' part of Idyll 15 by its rather greater conformity to the norms of Theocritus' 'epicising' poems[59] perhaps points to such a mimetic effect. Moreover, the description of the tableau at vv. 112–22 uses the simple cumulative syntax and avoidance of subordination which are a frequent mark of such astrophic lyric or verses which emulate this mode.[60] The opening eighteen verses of the song (vv. 100–17) fall easily into three sextets, the welcome to the gods (vv. 100–5), Aphrodite and the royal house (vv. 106–11), and the luxuries which surround Adonis (vv. 112–17),[61] and such a pattern should probably be seen as imitative of the rough correspondence between sense unit and rhythmical period which is regular in such lyric verse. Confirmation for this pattern may be sought in v. 123 which, if the pattern were to continue, should be end-stopped, but which in fact breaks the pattern, thereby gaining increased emotional emphasis;[62] the interlaced word-order and alliteration in the simile of vv. 121–2 mediate the transition to this exclamation. Whether, however, the hypostasised 'model' was in lyrics or hexameters,[63] there is clearly another reason why the song is hard to parallel.

The central part of the song is devoted to encomium of Berenice and Arsinoe and to the *ekphrasis* of the Adonis tableau.[64] This

---

[57] Cf. below pp. 135–7.   [58] Cairns 1992.14.

[59] Cf. P. Maas, *Greek Metre* (Oxford 1962) 94; Fantuzzi 1995 ; S. R. Slings, *ZPE* 98 (1993) 32. Cf. in general R. Stark, *Maia* 15 (1963) 375–7, and for the division of the corpus into different styles cf. above pp. 29–31.

[60] For this style in 'dithyrambic' passages of comedy cf. Hunter 1983a.166–7 (citing Aristotle).

[61] Cf. Gow on v. 118 for the punctuation there. For an attempt at a more elaborate structuring of the song into couplets cf. O. Ribbeck, *RhM* 17 (1862) 571–2. Gallavotti's structuring after two initial sextets (100–5 and 106–11) is 112–14, 115–18, 119–22, 123–6 etc.; complete critical agreement in such a matter is hardly possible.

[62] The varying prosody of ὤ in the verse may also mark 'mounting excitement'.

[63] In view of Adonis' eastern connections, the lyric hexameters addressed to the Great Mother in the *fragmentum dubium* of Menander's *Theophoroumene* (Sandbach, OCT p. 146) may be worthy of note in this context.

[64] The pictorialism of this tableau is studied by F. Manakidou, 'Bemerkungen über die Beziehung zwischen Dichtung und bildender Kunst: Bions Klage um Adonis und Theokrits 15. Idyll', *Prometheus* 20 (1994) 104–18.

ekphrasis may perhaps be seen as an equivalent to the sung description of cultic performance or sacrifice imagined as occurring simultaneously with the song; such passages are a not uncommon feature of celebratory hymns. On the other hand, the song has no narrative as such; the *muthos* of the royal house and the *ekphrasis* of the tableau have replaced any narrative of, presumably, the story of Aphrodite and Adonis. The content of the song is, of course, dictated by the design of Idyll 15, not by what was normally sung at real Adonis festivals. The singer takes over the rôle of Gorgo and Praxinoa in describing for us what we could not otherwise see, and the interplay between her voice and theirs is a crucial element in the whole. Thus, for example, the exclamation of vv. 123–4 (ὢ ἔβενος, ὢ χρυσός, ὢ ἐκ λευκῶ ἐλέφαντος | αἰετοί κτλ.) is the 'lyric' equivalent of the women's reactions at vv. 78–86, just as both Praxinoa and the singer focus upon Adonis' young beard (vv. 85, 130). It is, therefore, probably not too hazardous to guess that we would have to look for a very long time to find anything comparable in a 'real' festival song.[65]

Certain details of the Adonis-song have been dismissed as banal or conventional, without a proper appreciation of their rôle in such a hymn. Thus, for example, ἀενάω (v. 102) may indeed be a conventional epithet of hexameter poetry,[66] but it is important that Adonis has returned from what for everyone else is permanent exile in the land of the dead; μηνὶ δυωδεκάτωι (v. 103) is not just a circumlocution, but makes the point that the women have waited and counted the months until Adonis' return: this is an annual celebration and in its regularity, pointed by the counting off of the months, lies its glory and the comfort it brings; the repetition of Ὧραι (vv. 103–4) is an example of a familiar feature of Theocritean style[67] but here, together with the apparent glossing of μαλακαὶ πόδας by βάρδισται, enacts the meaning conveyed – the longed-for Hours seem to come slowly, but they do so surely and repetitively.[68] Of particular interest are vv. 128–30:

---

[65] Cf. F. Griffiths 1979. 26 '[the Adonis song] creates its own setting as real hymns would never have had to do'.

[66] This is suggested by its appearance in epigraphic poetry, cf. *CEG* 2.822 and 865. For an association with the Underworld commentators note σκῶρ ἀείνων at Ar. *Frogs* 146.

[67] Cf., e.g., Dover xlv–xlviii.

[68] C. H. White, 'Theocritus' "Adonis Song"', *MPhL* 4 (1981) 191–206, pp. 194–7, who argues that Theocritus' festival is set in spring. The Athenian Adonia were celebrated in the middle of summer ('the Dog Days').

τὸν[69] μὲν Κύπρις ἔχει, τὰν δ' ὁ ῥοδόπαχυς Ἄδωνις.
ὀκτωκαιδεκετὴς ἢ ἐννεακαίδεχ' ὁ γαμβρός·
οὐ κεντεῖ τὸ φίλημ' · ἔτι οἱ περὶ χείλεα πυρρά.

Kypris embraces him, and the rosy-armed Adonis holds her. Of
eighteen years or nineteen is the bridegroom; the golden down is still
upon his lip; his kisses are not rough.

The key to understanding these verses lies in the fact that though the
poem and the tableau celebrate the 'marriage' of Aphrodite and Adonis,
the young god will 'die' on the following day; this section of the poem
thus mixes the hymeneal and the funereal in a novel way which starts
from the familiar epitaphic topoi of 'death before / instead of marriage'
and 'death as a marriage with Hades', *topoi* which exploit the similarities
between marriage and funerary ritual and which occur (unsurprisingly)
in Bion's extant *Lament for Adonis* (vv. 87ff.), but moves beyond those
topoi.[70] The hinge of the strategy is the double sense of κλίνα (v. 127) as
both 'wedding-couch' and 'funeral bier' (cf. LSJ s.v. I 2). Eighteen or
nineteen is just the age when young men die as soldiers, and this age
indeed figures in both real and literary epitaphs for young men;[71]
moreover, the peculiar pathos of death before the first beard is grown
is certainly attested as a conventional epitaphic motif by later sources,[72]
and it is not unreasonable to see that resonance here. In a way
appropriate to the whole meaning of the cult, the 'sex rôles' are reversed,
for the bridegroom is here younger than the bride and it is he, not she,
who is to die a pathetically early death; the epithet 'rosy-armed' (v.
128) is normally applied to women and so both points this reversal
and is appropriate to the female perspective of the singer and the
women admiring this essentially female festival. The Adonis cult gives
the fullest expression to the similarity and (bitter) difference between
sexual longing (πόθος) and the regret and longing which attends
death; Aphrodite is part lover, part mother mourning the death of her
young son, and the tableau representing them suggests both illicit
lovemaking ('incest') and the grandiose style of Ptolemaic funerals.
The poet has caught this strangeness with a powerful fusion of the
language of weddings and funerals, which transcends the apparent
division of the poem into hymeneal (vv. 100–31) and funereal (vv.

---

[69] I print Rossbach's emendation, though without any great confidence. Both text and
interpretation in this area of the poem are problematic.

[70] For these *topoi* in general cf. Lattimore 1962.192–4, and cf. above p. 15 on Erinna's *Distaff*.

[71] Cf. *CEG* 2.709, 739; *Anth. Pal.* 7.466 (= Leonidas LXXI G–P), 468 (= Meleager CXXV G–P).

[72] Cf. Lattimore 1962.197–8.

132–42) sections; the farewell kisses of the dirge (Bion, *Lament* 11–14, 45–50) are also the first kisses of the wedding night.

All discussion of the context of this song must begin with the close and complex association between Arsinoe II and Aphrodite.[73] In staging an Adonis festival 'Arsinoé se posait en Aphrodite et préparait son apothéose', claimed Gustave Glotz,[74] and provided that we remember (as Glotz had a tendency to forget) that we are dealing with a Theocritean poem and not a documentary acount of a 'historical' festival, I see no reason to disagree.[75] The opening invocation to a specifically Cyprian Aphrodite evokes, as has long been noted, Ptolemaic influence on the island (cf. *Id.* 17.36), and the standard dating of the Idyll to the late 270s[76] adds resonance to the encomiastic citation of Miletos and Samos (v. 126), both of which were then in the Ptolemaic orbit. There is in this poem no getting away from the ruling house. The links between Aphrodite and this house are first explicit in vv. 106–8:

Κύπρι Διώναια, τὺ μὲν ἀθανάταν ἀπὸ θνατᾶς,
ἀνθρώπων ὡς μῦθος, ἐποίησας Βερενίκαν,
ἀμβροσίαν ἐς στῆθος ἀποστάξασα γυναικός·

Lady of Cyprus, Dione's child, you, as is the report of men, did change Berenice from mortal to immortal, dropping ambrosia into her woman's breast.

I have pointed elsewhere[77] to the different levels of interpretation exposed by the phrase 'as men say'; whereas Gow and Dover look only to the fact that such phrases do not necessarily cast doubt on an assertion or may indeed strengthen one, another reading may see teasing play with the apotheosis of the Queen Mother in a tone which can readily be matched in other court poems of Theocritus. The style of the verses, with the almost jingle-effect of ἀθανάταν ἀπὸ θνατᾶς and the mannered, quasi-chiastic interplay of mortal and immortal in ἀνθρώπων ὡς μῦθος, ἐποίησας Βερενίκαν, | ἀμβροσίαν ἐς στῆθος

---

[73] There is a large bibliography: for some guidance (particularly on the Greek material) cf. F. Griffiths 1979 and 1981; Fraser 1972.I 229–46; S. B. Pomeroy, *Women in Hellenistic Egypt* (New York 1984) 30–8; Gutzwiller 1992.365–7.   [74] *REG* 33 (1920) 173.

[75] That Theocritus' poem is a literary reflection of a real, 'historical' event (for which there is no other firm evidence) is the standard critical position, cf., e.g., Weber 1993.170–1. The matter is, of course, not unimportant, but must also not be allowed to inhibit critical discussion. For the important socio-political rôle of public festivals in the early Hellenistic kingships cf. F. Dunand, 'Fête et propagande à Alexandrie sous les Lagides' in *La Fête, pratique et discours* (Centre de recherches d' histoire ancienne 42, Paris 1981) 13–40.

[76] Cf. Gow II 265.   [77] Cf. Hunter 1993.157.

ἀποστάξασα <u>γυναικός</u>, reinforces the reality of both readings. The possibility for such a 'double reading' is perhaps a marker of one kind of distinction between an Alexandrian poem and the archaic and classical literature to which Gow and Dover appeal. We find a similar 'qualification' towards the end of the song when the singer turns to the peculiar felicity of Adonis:

> ἕρπεις, ὦ φίλ' Ἄδωνι, καὶ ἐνθάδε κῆς Ἀχέροντα
> ἡμιθέων, ὡς φαντί, μονώτατος.   (Vv. 136–7)

You, dear Adonis, alone of demigods, as men say, visit both earth and Acheron.

Many of the same nuances which surrounded the previous use are also visible here: 'as men say' is at one level encomiastic, at another perhaps curiously incongruous at this moment of high praise. The 'myth' of the royal house is linked to that of Aphrodite and Adonis – Arsinoe, as the person staging the festival and thus responsible for Adonis' annual reappearance, is indeed cast in the rôle of Aphrodite – but both are subject to this pattern of different readings. Nor should this surprise us, for both cultic myth and royal apotheosis are areas where symbols and forms of language convey different things to different people and 'truth' consists in social function. Both the Adonis-myth and the apotheosis of Berenice are ideas to be exploited in various ways; both do depend crucially on 'what men say' for their significance. The trick of style which links these two ideas, therefore, points to a real affinity between them. Nevertheless, at another level, it may be here that any search for 'parody' should be directed. As Boukaios' song of praise 'failed' because it revealed the stratagems of praise, so it may be thought that the Adonis-song 'gives the game away' by revealing the possibility that the myth of Adonis' return is not literally true. Such complex tonal effects resist any simplified appeal to the taste or prejudices of any group of readers.

The verses describing Aphrodite's deification of Berenice (vv. 106–8 cited above) have a number of close analogues which the commentators cite, but Thetis' action to preserve Patroclus' body is particularly suggestive:[78]

> Πατρόκλωι δ' αὖτ' ἀμβροσίην καὶ νέκταρ ἐρυθρὸν
> στάξε κατὰ ῥινῶν, ἵνα οἱ χρὼς ἔμπεδος εἴη.
>   (*Iliad* 19.38–9)

[78] Cf. F. Griffiths 1979.122.

Through Patroclus' nostrils she dripped ambrosia and red nectar to preserve his flesh.

So too Hector's body is preserved by Aphrodite (*Iliad* 23.184–90) so that it avoids corruption:

> τὸν δ' αὖτε προσέειπε διάκτορος Ἀργειφόντης·
> "ὦ γέρον, οὔ πω τόν γε κύνες φάγον οὐδ' οἰωνοί,
> ἀλλ' ἔτι κεῖνος κεῖται Ἀχιλλῆος παρὰ νηὶ
> αὔτως ἐν κλισίηισι· δυωδεκάτη δέ οἱ ἠὼς
> κειμένωι, οὐδέ τί οἱ χρὼς σήπεται, οὐδέ μιν εὐλαί
> ἔσθουσ', αἵ ῥά τε φῶτας ἀρηιφάτους κατέδουσιν.
> ἦ μέν μιν περὶ σῆμα ἑοῦ ἑτάροιο φίλοιο
> ἕλκει ἀκηδέστως, ἠὼς ὅτε δῖα φανήηι,
> οὐδέ μιν αἰσχύνει· θηοῖό κεν αὐτὸς ἐπελθὼν
> οἷον ἐερσήεις κεῖται, περὶ δ' αἷμα νένιπται,
> οὐδέ ποθι μιαρός· σὺν δ' ἕλκεα πάντα μέμυκεν,
> ὅσσ' ἐτύπη· πολέες γὰρ ἐν αὐτῶι χαλκὸν ἔλασσαν.
> ὥς τοι κήδονται μάκαρες θεοὶ υἷος ἑῆος
> καὶ νέκυός περ ἐόντος, ἐπεί σφι φίλος περὶ κῆρι."
>
> (*Iliad* 24.410–23)

Then Hermes the guide, the slayer of Argos, answered him: 'Old man, he is not eaten yet by dogs or birds, but he still lies there in Achilleus' hut beside his ship, just as he fell. This is the twelfth day he has lain there, but his flesh is not decaying, nor the worms eating him, which feed on the bodies of men killed in war. Yes, Achilleus does drag him ruthlessly around the tomb of his dear companion every day, at the showing of holy dawn, but he cannot disfigure him. If you went there you could see for yourself how he lies there fresh as dew, and all the blood is washed from him, and there is no stain on him. All the wounds have closed where he was struck – there were many who drove their bronze into him. Such is the care the blessed gods have for your son, even for his dead body, as he is very dear to their hearts.' (Trans. Martin Hammond)

Despite Achilles' maltreatment, Hector lies in Hecuba's palace ἐρσήεις καὶ πρόσφατος, 'pristine and fresh, like one slain by the gentle darts of Apollo of the silver bow' (*Il.* 24.755–6). In his note on 23.184–91 Richardson observes that those verses and the parallel passages 'have been taken as evidence for Greek knowledge of the practice of embalming'. Be that as it may, Theocritus' evocation of Thetis' preservation of the body of Patroclus suggests to me that v. 108, 'dropping ambrosia into her woman's breast', does indeed have a reference in the world of Ptolemaic funerary practice. Perhaps it merely gratifies Alexandrian Greeks with their own familiarity with Egyptian mummification, brilliantly finding Homeric precedent for this practice, but perhaps also there is more. Alexander's body must have been preserved in some way, whatever truth lies behind the extant accounts,[79] and it is hardly bold to imagine that the early Ptolemies (and their queens) followed suit. We know little of the burial arrangements of the early Ptolemies, but Fraser noted that, before Philopator built the central *Sema* of the royal house, 'it seems likely that . . . the sanctuaries of the individual deified members . . . were in close proximity to the Sema of Alexander'.[80] We must remember that it was the deification of Arsinoe herself which seems to have marked a major turning-point in the development of the royal cult, and the deification of her mother may have been an altogether less grand, 'more Greek' affair.[81] Nevertheless, we are dealing here not with the documentary history of that cult, but with poetic evocations of it. Such an evocation of funerary practice would be, of course, encomiastic of Arsinoe as well as of her mother, as the current queen is credited with this arrangement and thus fulfils at the 'real' level the function of Thetis and Aphrodite in Homer and of Aphrodite at the most straightforward level of Theocritus' poem. Here too light is shed upon the description of Berenice made 'immortal from mortal' (v. 106), for such an endless continuation of how the 'dead' looked when 'alive' is precisely the point of mummification (cf. Diod. Sic. 1.91.7).

Here too, however, Theocritus forges links between Adonis and the royal house. Patroclus and Hector are the most obvious examples of what Jean-Pierre Vernant has termed the 'beautiful death' of the warrior, that death in battle which guarantees perpetual youth and beauty.[82] In the case of the slain warrior 'all is beautiful' (πάντα καλά, *Iliad* 22.73); he lies, an object of wonder and desire in death as he was in life (cf. *Iliad* 24.410–23, Tyrtaeus fr. 10.21–30 West). Adonis 'the beautiful', who is always both bridegroom and lost lover, is not a martial hero, indeed in some ways is the very antithesis of such a hero, for whom hunting and warfare are two sides of the same coin;[83]

---

[79] Cf. esp. Quintus Curtius 10.10.9–13; Strabo 17.1.8. We may compare the story of Agesilaos taken back to Sparta preserved in wax 'because there was no honey' (Plut. *Ages.* 40.3, cf. P. Cartledge, *Agesilaos and the Crisis of Sparta* (London 1987) 334). [80] Fraser 1972.I 225.

[81] Evidence and bibliography in Weber 1993.252–4.

[82] Cf. J.-P. Vernant, *Mortals and Immortals* (Princeton 1991) 60–74, 84–91.

[83] Cf. M. Detienne, *The Gardens of Adonis* (Hassocks 1977) 66–7; F. Griffiths 1981.255 'Adonis.. .surpasses paragons of assertive masculinity like Ajax and Agamemnon . . . for he alone participates in the triumph of the cyclic female principle over death.' It is tempting to relate Detienne's whole construction of the 'anthropology of spices' to Egyptian practices of mummification in which the body was filled with spices; I have resisted the temptation.

nevertheless in death he lies, like Hector and Patroclus – and in another way like Berenice – in perpetual youth, his beauty, like theirs, preserved for ever by divine grace. Like Hector and Patroclus also, Adonis' death brings particular grief to those who loved him. Hector indeed is the subject of the most famous scene of organised female lamentation in Greek literature (*Il.* 24.719–76), and thus a comparison with Adonis is not created *ex nihilo*. It may even be that the description of Hector as Ἑκάβας ὁ γεραίτατος εἴκατι παίδων, 'the eldest of Hecuba's twenty sons' (v. 139), is a specifically Hellenistic variation of Hecuba's address to Hector in her lamentation as ἐμῶι θυμῶι πάντων πολὺ φίλτατε παίδων, 'by far the dearest of all my sons in my heart' (*Il.* 24.748).[84] As for Patroclus, in this very same lamentation Hecuba notes that, despite his efforts, Achilles was unable to raise Patroclus from the dead, and Patroclus' ghost appears to plead for burial in a famous scene of *Iliad* 23.[85]

The catalogue of demigods[86] has attracted critical censure principally because the heroes listed do not really fall into a category of ἡμίθεοι, 'half-gods', comparable to Adonis.[87] We can, of course, never expect strict comparability when the great figures of the past are evoked in poetry as *exempla*, but the apparent difficulty here is that, whereas consolation usually works by invoking greater figures who have suffered equally or more (Achilles citing Niobe, for example), here it may be thought that Adonis' status is already qualitatively different from (and higher than) the other figures listed. The more usual procedure may be well illustrated from a very interesting epitaph in choliambics

---

[84] Homer's Priam explicitly says that he had 19 sons 'from one womb', i.e. by Hecuba, but the Theocritean scholiast cites Simonides for the number 20 (*PMG* 559); for discussion and catalogues of known names cf. van der Kolf, *RE* 22.1844–7; Roscher s.v. Priamos 2937–40; Richardson on *Il.* 24.495–7. I suspect that 20 arose by a (? humorous) interpretation of the Homeric verses in which Hector is counted separately from 'the 19'; thus τῶν πολλῶν is taken on this view not as 'correct[ing] the emotional exaggeration of 494' (Macleod) but as meaning 'these many'. Leaf *ad loc.* indeed seems to exclude Hector from the grand total of 50. If we do have an allusion to a scholarly dispute, then this would be another reason to be cautious about dismissing the Adonis-song as mediocre hackwork. I record as a curiosity Legrand's suggestion (Legrand 1898.95 n. 1) that 20 has replaced the Homeric 19 for metrical reasons.

[85] Gow notes the possible influence of the ghost scene, but not of *Iliad* 24.

[86] It may be thought somewhat surprising that, as far as I know, deletion of vv. 136–42 has never been proposed, for v. 143 would follow perfectly well after v. 135.

[87] After death Adonis is a 'demi-god' in one sense, but as applied to the figures of the catalogue this term must principally denote 'heroes', 'figures of the heroic age', a usage perhaps deriving from Hes. *WD* 160. Dover refers to 13.69, although the Argonauts as a group *were* notoriously 'sons of gods'. Cf. further Hunter 1993.103, 127–8. The discussion of the catalogue in W. Atallah, *Adonis dans la littérature et l'art grecs* (Paris 1966) 130–2 is too general to be helpful.

(Bernand 71) for a young man, probably from Alexandria, and to be
dated to the late Hellenistic or early imperial period.[88] In the first,
unfortunately broken, section the young man is praised as 'alone among
men (cf. 15.137) . . . he surpassed in virtue all those of his age . . . a
child who seemed an old man in his wisdom'. In the better preserved
section of the poem his mother is told to stop grieving for the most
familiar of reasons:

> οὐδεὶς γὰρ ἐξήλυξε τὸν μίτον Μοιρῶν,
> οὐ θνητός, οὐκ ἀθάνατος, οὐδ' ὁ δεσμώτης,
> οὐδ' αὖ τύραννος βασιλικὴν λαχὼν τιμήν
> θεσμοὺς ἀτρέπτους διαφυγεῖν ποτ' ὠιήθη·
> Φαέθοντα Τιτὰν οὐκ ἔκλαυσ', ὅτ' ἐκ δίφρων
> ἀπ' οὐρανοῦ κατέπεσεν εἰς πέδον γαίης;
> Ἑρμῆς δ' ὁ Μαίας οὐκ ἔκλαυσ' ἐὸν παῖδα
> Μυρτίλον ἀπὸ δίφρων κύμασιν φορούμενον;[89]
> οὐδ' αὖ Θέτις τὸν στεναρὸν ἔστενεν παῖδα,
> ὅτ' ἐκ βελέμνων θνῆσκε τῶν Ἀπόλλωνος;
> ὁ δ' αὖ βροτῶν τε καὶ θεῶν πάντων ἄναξ[90]
> Σαρπηδόν' οὐκ ἔκλαυσεν, οὐκ ἐκώκυσεν;
> οὐδ' αὖ Μακηδὼν ὁ βασιλεὺς Ἀλέξανδρος,
> ὃν τίκτεν Ἄμμων θέμενος εἰς ὄφιν μορφήν;

No one escapes the thread of the Moirai, no mortal, no immortal, not
the prisoner,[91] not even the tyrant with his kingly power has ever
thought to flee from the laws which cannot be changed. Did not Ti-
tan weep for Phaethon, when he fell out of the chariot from heaven
to earth? Did not Hermes, the son of Maia, weep for his son Myrtilos
carried away by the waves out of his chariot? Did not Thetis grieve
for her mighty son, when he was killed by the arrows of Apollo? Did
not the lord of all men and gods weep for Sarpedon, did he not lament? Did not the Macedonian, King Alexander, the son of Ammon
who took the form of a snake to beget him?

---

[88] For the text cf. also J. Rusten, I. C. Cunningham, and A. D. Knox, *Theophrastus, Characters; Herodas, Mimes; Cercidas and the Choliambic Poets* (Cambridge, Mass. 1993) 494–7. Bernand gives a full bibliography, together with many parallels from other epigrams; I will not repeat that material here. It would obviously be nice to believe that the young man died at the age of eighteen (cf. Theocritus' Adonis), but the interpretation of ΔΕΧΟΚΤΟ on the stone in line 6 is disputed, cf. Bernand pp. 287, 289.

[89] I do not think that the sense of this line implies corruption despite the 'faulty' metre, for which cf. πάντων ἄναξ three lines below and perhaps ἀνήρ at the end of v. 3 (although ἀνήρ might there have been intended); I am inclined to attribute the trimeters to the poet.

[90] Cf. previous note.

[91] The sense 'gaoler' (cf. Kassel–Austin on Cratinus fr. 201) is not, I think, an impossible alternative. An anonymous referee, however, draws attention to a very similar collocation at Arrian, *Anab.* 3.22.5.

Adonis has, however, escaped death, at least partially; although it is not strictly true that his regular alternation between earth and the Underworld is a unique privilege,[92] the hymn suggests that even 'dying' for part of the year redounds to Adonis' glory. Theocritus' mythological catalogue turns the rhetoric of the epitaph on its head, while evoking its simple, repetitive style. It measures Adonis' glory against the heroes of epic and tragedy: not just Hector and Patroclus from Homer, but ἔπαθ' (v. 138) hints at representations of Agamemnon's fate on the tragic stage, where *pathos* was critical, and βαρυμάνιος is clearly chosen to point to the circumstances of Ajax's suicide, most famous in antiquity from Sophocles' tragedy. Notable by his absence is the greatest hero of them all, Achilles, whose consolations to Priam in *Iliad* 24 hover over the epitaph quoted above, in which he himself becomes a consolatory example. The presence of his son, Neoptolemos/Pyrrhos,[93] however, is presumably dictated by more than the desire for alliteration with Patroclus. His beauty is praised to his father in the *Odyssey* (*Od.* 11.522), and after his death he became the object of cult at Delphi;[94] there are, therefore, points of contact with Adonis. By escaping safe from the war (v. 140) Neoptolemos did not enjoy 'the beautiful death' to which Adonis has laid claim. For a Greek the *Iliad* is the obvious text from which consolatory exempla may be chosen, as in the epitaph quoted above, but in the context of Idyll 15 as a whole, we can hardly fail to read this list in metaliterary terms also.

A poem that began as a reworking of Sophron has opened out to embrace the whole of human history ('the Lapiths and the Deucalions of an earlier age'), just as the epitaph ranges from the pre-Olympian legend of Phaethon to Alexander. As the court of Philadelphus and Arsinoe is the *telos* to which Greek history has been moving, as Adonis surpasses the heroes of the past, so Theocritean mime lays claim to unexpected literary grandeur. Not for long, though; and not perhaps with complete seriousness. When Gorgo and Praxinoa have had their glimpse of another world, of a different kind of *mimesis*, they withdraw back to their own realm to wait for another year. Mime, after all, can

---

[92] Cf. Gow on v. 137.

[93] The name Pyrrhos is first attested for the *Cypria* (fr. 16 Davies). We are perhaps to be conscious of the etymology of this name, 'ruddy', just as is the colour (πυρρά) of the down around Adonis' lips (v. 130). It is, moreover, at least a strange coincidence that Deucalion's wife was called Πύρρα.

[94] One source indeed, Pausanias 1.4.4, reports that cult honours were first paid to him after he brought assistance against the Gaulish invasion in 278; it may, therefore, be that there is an element of topicality in the reference to him in Theocritus 15.

never replace the centre, whether that be literary (Homer) or political (the Ptolemaic palace); mime must always live at the edge, on the margins (cf. vv. 7–8), because it needs the centre in order to define its own place.

CHAPTER 5

Idyll 18 and the lyric past

In the introductory chapter we considered how social changes not only led to changes in the nature of literary production, but must also have impressed upon learned poets, particularly those in touch with the scholarly activity of cataloguing and classifying poetry,[1] how much of the literary heritage had been lost. This sense of loss must have been particularly sharp in the case of lyric, especially choral,[2] poetry, for here it was not merely the social occasion which belonged to a past world, but the music and dancing were largely lost also. Although choirs still performed all over the Greek world, Alexandrian poets no longer wrote for them; they wrote poems to be recited and subsequently read.[3] Their 'choral' poetry was now largely in hexameters or elegiac couplets. Everywhere one looked, the evidence that new choral lyric poetry, composed by major poets, was a thing of the past (and had been really since the end of the fifth century) was unmistakable. The diminution in the rôle of the chorus in Attic drama, a diminution manifested in the use in tragedy of ἐμβόλιμα, i.e. odes which could be reused from one tragedy to another, both reflected and drew particular attention to the change. When texts not only of Menander but also of Euripides were marked simply with ΧΟΡΟΥ and the words of the choral performances were not preserved with the rest of the text,[4] the gulf between the present and the past

---

[1] We have no evidence for scholarly activity on the part of Theocritus (cf. above p. 14), but he was associated with the Ptolemaic court where such activity flourished, and that seems to me sufficient.

[2] It seems clear that – whatever the actual archaic position – Hellenistic scholarship made no firm distinction between choral and monodic poetry (cf., e.g., Pfeiffer 1968.283; M. Davies, 'Monody, choral lyric, and the tyranny of the hand-book', *CQ* 38 (1988) 52–64), as it was 'function' which mattered most in poetic classification. I shall, however, be considering various passages which suggest that *poets* at least were interested in the different possibilities of performance mode.

[3] Cf. above p. 4. For Corinna cf. below p. 149.

[4] For discussion and bibliography cf. E. Pöhlmann, 'Der Überlieferungswert der χοροῦ-Vermerke in Papyri und Handschriften', *WJA* 3 (1977) 69–81; Hunter 1979.

must have seemed particularly wide to those with a sense for literary history.

This gulf was merely accentuated by the frequency with which the texts of early poetry refer to the musical circumstances of performance. Thus, for example, Alcman's famous *partheneion* (with which we shall be presently concerned) is intensely 'self-reflexive' in the choir's concern with itself and its leaders, its ornaments, and the conditions of its performance, and Pindar too is full of allusions to the music and dancing which accompanied the words.[5] Moreover, it was not merely lyric texts which must have seemed to evoke a lost world; archaic and classical art was everywhere full of representations of music and dance, and we perhaps pay too little attention to how painted and sculptural representations of the past may have shaped literary ones. Epic poetry too gave a privileged place to choral performances – the dancing and the wedding-procession on Achilles' shield,[6] the Delian festival of the *Hymn to Apollo*, the dances of the Muses which open Hesiod's *Theogony*. So it is that in Hellenistic poetry a reference to dance, particularly the performance of female choirs,[7] may act as a marker of the archaic, even though the contemporary world was also filled with traditional choral singing and dancing. In Idyll 18, for example, the 'interlacing feet' (if περιπλέκτοις is the correct reading in v. 8) of the maidens evoke such things as the 'flashing feet' (μαρμαρυγάς . . . ποδῶν) of the Phaeacians at which Odysseus marvelled (*Od.* 8.265). The mixture of dancing and harmonious singing in the Idyll points to a prior world known only from its poetry, of which texts at least had survived, and art. Moreover, the frequent appearance in Hellenistic (and Roman) poetry of myths in which young girls are carried off from such choirs confirms this resonance.[8] These are (often explicitly) foundation stories from an immemorial time and are only to be grasped in poetry and song; that gods themselves (particularly Muses and nymphs) engage in these performances merely reinforces the 'otherness' and 'pastness' of such stories.

---

[5] For a recent evaluation cf. W. Mullen, *Choreia: Pindar and Dance* (Princeton 1982). The recent controversy over the mode of Pindaric performance (choral or monodic?) does not really affect the issue here, as we are concerned with Hellenistic perceptions.

[6] Theocr. 18.8 ὑπὸ δ' ἴαχε δῶμ' ὑμεναίωι possibly echoes *Il.* 18.493 πολὺς δ' ὑμέναιος ὀρώρει.

[7] For these choirs cf. Calame 1977. For a recent survey of the whole field cf. S. H. Lonsdale, *Dance and Ritual Play in Greek Religion* (Baltimore/London 1993).

[8] Such stories do, of course, also figure prominently in archaic and classical poetry and prose; this does not, however, detract from their particular significance for the later period.

THE LYRIC PAST AND THE *ARGONAUTICA*

One text which is centrally concerned with such representations of the past is the *Argonautica* of Apollonius, an epic which depicts on a broad canvas the foundations and early history of Greek culture. Apollonius tells a quest myth of self-definition in which the finest of the 'Panhellenes' recover a talisman wrongly held by barbarians; this traditional tale is accompanied by an all-embracing aetiology of Greek customs and cult. Such customs and cult are, of course, conceived as belonging to a world even before Homer had defined its contours. Among the Argonauts is Orpheus, by tradition the first singer, and his performances may act as validating models for subsequent history; so also the dances and hymns of the Argonauts as they travel around the world carry the same aetiological potential as their other actions. A survey of some relevant pasages will, I hope, provide a suitable background for the related exercise in cultural archaeology which Theocritus undertakes in Idyll 18.

(a) At 1.536ff. Apollonius describes the Argonauts rowing away from Iolkos:

οἱ δ᾽, ὥς τ᾽ ἠίθεοι Φοίβωι χορὸν ἢ ἐνὶ Πυθοῖ
ἤ που ἐν Ὀρτυγίηι ἢ ἐφ᾽ ὕδασιν Ἰσμηνοῖο
στησάμενοι, φόρμιγγος ὑπαὶ περὶ βωμὸν ὁμαρτῆι
ἐμμελέως κραιπνοῖσι πέδον ῥήσσωσι πόδεσσιν·
ὣς οἱ ὑπ᾽ Ὀρφῆος κιθάρηι πέπληγον ἐρετμοῖς
πόντου λάβρον ὕδωρ, ἐπὶ δὲ ῥόθια κλύζοντο.

(1.536–41)

Like young men who set up the dance in Phoibos' honour at Pytho or perhaps Ortygia or by the waters of the Ismenos, and to the music of the lyre beat the ground around the altar with the rhythmic tap of their swift feet, just so did the oars slap the rough water of the sea to the sound of Orpheus' kithara.

The choral performances to which this rowing from the distant heroic age is compared might belong as easily to Apollonius' own day as to a romantically imagined past, but the poeticising place names, the archaic Apolline *phorminx*,[9] echoes of Homer (*Il.* 18.567–72, the

---

[9] Although high poetry, particularly epic, tends to use the Homeric word φόρμιγξ for stringed instruments of more than one kind, we should not miss the archaising flavour of this Apolline and Orphic instrument, which had long since ceased to have any but antiquarian interest, cf. Maas–Snyder 1989.1–30, West 1992.50–3. At 24.110 Heracles is taught on the 'boxwood *phorminx*' by 'Eumolpus, son of Philammon' whose name clearly evokes the very distant past; I suspect, but cannot prove, that 'boxwood' there points to a simple, unelaborated, 'old-fashioned'

vineyard scene) and perhaps also a Callimachean aetiology (*h.* 3.240–5, ancient Ephesian dances for Artemis)[10] all reinforce the sense of remote 'otherness' which these dances evoke.

(b) This same passage from Callimachus' *Hymn to Artemis* may also have contributed to the description of the armed dance performed by the Argonauts on Mt Dindymon:

> ἄμυδις δὲ νέοι Ὀρφῆος ἀνωγῆι
> σκαίροντες βηταρμὸν ἐνόπλιον εἱλίσσοντο
> καὶ σάκεα ξιφέεσσιν ἐπέκτυπον, ὡς κεν ἰωὴ
> δύσφημος πλάζοιτο δι᾿ ἠέρος ἣν ἔτι λαοὶ
> κηδείηι βασιλῆος ἀνέστενον. ἔνθεν ἐσαιεὶ
> ῥόμβωι καὶ τυπάνωι Ῥείην Φρύγες ἱλάσκονται.
>
> (1.1134–9)

Taking their cue from Orpheus, all the young heroes leapt and danced an armed dance and beat their swords on their shields so that the ill-omened sound of the continuing lamentation of the people for their king should be lost in the air. For this reason the Phrygians still worship Rheia with tambourines and drums.

This explicitly aetiological performance is preceded by the dedication of a very ancient wooden cult-image (1.1117–22), a sacrifice performed with garlands of oak-leaves (a detail not just aetiological, but also 'primitive'), and also by the report of a hymn which the Argonauts sang to the Great Mother (1.1125–31). The whole scene therefore evokes the deepest recesses of the past, here captured by the word βηταρμός, which is found nowhere else, but is obviously formed from the Homeric βητάρμων, a word used for the Phaeacian dancers of the *Odyssey*.[11] Thus a by-form of an ancient *glossa* is used to describe an ancient practice.

(c) After Polydeuces' victory over Amycus the Argonauts celebrate with song, again wearing the garlands of nature:

> ξανθὰ δ᾿ ἐρεψάμενοι δάφνηι καθύπερθε μέτωπα
> ἀγχιάλωι †τῆι καὶ τῆι περὶ† πρυμνήσι᾿ ἀνῆπτο,
> Ὀρφείηι φόρμιγγι συνοίμιον ὕμνον ἄειδον

---

instrument. πύξινος occurs only once in Homer, at *Il.* 24.269 in the same *sedes* of a yoke (ζυγόν); it is curious that *Il.* 24.268 κὰδ δ᾿ ἀπὸ πασσαλόφι ζυγὸν ἥιρεον ἡμιόνειον is very like a repeated Odyssean verse about a *phorminx* (*Od.* 8.67, 105). A ζυγόν was, of course, also part of a *phorminx*.

10 Not discussed by E. Eichgrün, *Kallimachos und Apollonios Rhodios* (diss. Berlin 1961). E. Livrea, *Helikon* 8 (1968) 447, takes *Inc. Lesb.* 16 Voigt as the model, but the occurrence of ἐμμελέως in both passages does not establish the case.

11 *Od.* 8.250, 383; cf. *LfgrE* s.v., Chantraine, *DE* s.v.

ἐμμελέως· περὶ δέ σφιν ἰαίνετο νήνεμος ἀκτὴ
μελπομένοις· κλεῖον δὲ Θεραπναῖον Διὸς υἷα.

(2.159–63)

On the shore the boat was tied to a laurel-tree; they plucked its leaves to crown their fair brows, and in harmony sang a hymn to the accompaniment of Orpheus' lyre. All around in the windless air the coast rejoiced in their song. It was the Therapnaian son of Zeus whom they celebrated.

Fränkel[12] made the attractive suggestion that this ὕμνος to Polydeuces[13] was to be seen as the origin of the epinician ode; whether this is correct or not, a hymn in unison to the accompaniment of Orpheus' lyre is plainly intended to evoke the world of archaic performance.[14]

(d) A different kind of performance is evoked at 2.701–13 after the appearance of Apollo at Thynias:

ἀμφὶ δὲ δαιομένοις εὐρὺν χορὸν ἐστήσαντο,
καλὸν Ἰηπαιῆον' Ἰηπαιηόνα Φοῖβον
μελπόμενοι. σὺν δέ σφιν ἐὺς πάις Οἰάγροιο
Βιστονίηι φόρμιγγι λιγείης ἦρχεν ἀοιδῆς·
ὥς ποτε πετραίηι ὑπὸ δειράδι Παρνησοῖο
Δελφύνην τόξοισι πελώριον ἐξενάριξε,
κοῦρος ἐὼν ἔτι γυμνός, ἔτι πλοκάμοισι γεγηθώς –
ἱλήκοις· αἰεί τοι, ἄναξ, ἄτμητοι ἔθειραι,
αἰὲν ἀδήλητοι· τὼς γὰρ θέμις· οἰόθι δ' αὐτὴ
Λητὼ Κοιογένεια φίλαις ἐνὶ χερσὶν ἀφάσσει –
πολλὰ δὲ Κωρύκιαι νύμφαι Πλειστοῖο θύγατρες
θαρσύνεσκον ἔπεσσιν, ἰὴ ἴε κεκληγυῖαι,
ἔνθεν δὴ τόδε καλὸν ἐφύμνιον ἔπλετο Φοίβωι.

(2.701–13)

As the meat burned, they arrayed a broad dance in celebration of the brilliant Phoibos, the *Hiepaiion Hiepaiion*. With them the noble son of Oiagros sang a clear song to the accompaniment of his Bistonian lyre. He sang how once at the foot of the rocky ridge of Parnassos the god killed the monstrous Delphyne with his bow, when a young boy still in his nakedness, still rejoicing in long curls – be gracious, please! Eternally, lord, your hair is uncut, eternally it remains unravaged. So does holy law proclaim, for only Leto herself, daughter of Koios, may hold it in her dear hands – and the Korykian nymphs, daughters of Pleistos, urged him on, shouting '*Hie, hie*'; this is the source of Phoibos' lovely title.

---

[12] Fränkel 1968. 164.

[13] Some critics follow the scholiast in taking 'the Therapnaian son of Zeus' to be Apollo, but cf. Vian, *Notes complémentaires ad loc.*

[14] συνοίμιος occurs only here; is it intended to have a quasi-technical flavour?

What is apparently envisaged here is that the crew dance and sing the refrain of the paean, the *hie hie Paiion*, while Orpheus sings the aetiological foundation narrative of the killing of the Delphic serpent.[15] The scene as a whole has clear links to the foundation narrative of the Delphic shrine in the *Homeric Hymn to (Pythian) Apollo*. In the archaic hymn, Apollo commands his future priests to build an altar on the beach and then to follow him up to the shrine:

αὐτὰρ ἐπεὶ πόσιος καὶ ἐδητύος ἐξ ἔρον ἔντο,
βάν ρ᾽ ἴμεν· ἦρχε δ᾽ ἄρα σφιν ἄναξ Διὸς υἱὸς Ἀπόλλων,
φόρμιγγ᾽ ἐν χείρεσσιν ἔχων ἐρατὸν κιθαρίζων,
καλὰ καὶ ὕψι βιβάς· οἱ δὲ ῥήσσοντες ἕποντο
Κρῆτες πρὸς Πυθὼ καὶ ἰηπαιήον᾽ ἄειδον,
οἷοί τε Κρητῶν παιήονες οἷσί τε Μοῦσα
ἐν στήθεσσιν ἔθηκε θεὰ μελίγηρυν ἀοιδήν.

(*h. Apollo* 513–19)

When they had set aside their desire for drink and food, they went off; Lord Apollo, the son of Zeus, led them, holding his lyre (*phorminx*) in his hands and playing a lovely tune as he pranced graceful and high. The Cretans followed to Pytho, dancing and singing the *Ie Paiion*, as do Cretan paean-singers and those into whose hearts the Muse has placed sweet-voiced song.

Here Apollo does not merely lead the procession, he also leads the song in his own honour; Apollonius offers a modern rewriting of this scene, and one in which the ancient 'otherness' of the performance competes with the modern sophistication of the elaborate interplay of voices.[16] Such interplay is to some extent compensation for what has been lost. If we can no longer hear the choirs and see their dances, we can at least hear the poet perform in a way we cannot hear Homer; the interlacing of poetic voices has taken the place of the harmonious singing and 'interlacing feet' of archaic choirs.

  (e) Outside the cave on Drepane in which Jason and Medea consummate their marriage, the Argonauts, again crowned with foliage and again to the accompaniment of Orpheus' lyre, sing an epithalamian (4.1155–60).[17] On the following day, the people of the countryside come to observe the celebration:

---

[15] Contrast the much briefer narrative of paean singing at *Il.* 1.472–4.

[16] Cf. Hunter 1986; 1993.150–1.

[17] The song, as in Theocritus 18, is called *hymenaios*, although originally that was the song accompanying the bride on her journey to her new home; even in the classical period, however, the distinction is not always preserved, cf. R. Muth, '"Hymenaios" und "Epithalamion"' *WS* 67 (1954) 5–45; Contiades-Tsitsoni 1990.29–31.

θάμβευν δ' εἰσορόωσαι ἀριπρεπέων ἡρώων
εἴδεα καὶ μορφάς, ἐν δέ σφισιν Οἰάγροιο
υἱὸν ὑπαὶ φόρμιγγος ἐυκρέκτου καὶ ἀοιδῆς
ταρφέα σιγαλόεντι πέδον κρούοντα πεδίλωι.   1195
νύμφαι δ' ἄμμιγα πᾶσαι, ὅτε μνήσαιντο γάμοιο,
ἱμερόενθ' ὑμέναιον ἀνήπυον· ἄλλοτε δ' αὖτε
οἰόθεν οἶαι ἄειδον ἑλισσόμεναι περὶ κύκλον,
Ἥρη, σεῖο ἕκητι· σὺ γὰρ καὶ ἐπὶ φρεσὶ θῆκας
Ἀρήτηι πυκινὸν φάσθαι ἔπος Ἀλκινόοιο.   1200

(4.1192–1200)

1196 μνήσαιτο Brunck

They were struck with wonder at the sight of the handsome form of
the glorious heroes, and among them the son of Oiagros who beat the
ground in rapid time with his glittering sandal to the tuneful sound
of his lyre and his song. Whenever the Argonauts sang of marriage,
all the nymphs blended their voices with them in the lovely wedding-
hymn. At other times the nymphs sang and danced by themselves in
a circle, in your honour, Hera; for it was you who put into Arete's
mind the idea of revealing Alkinoos' careful decision.

Two different kinds of performance seem to be described here. In one,
the nymphs sing the marriage refrain Ὑμὴν ὦ Ὑμέναιε at the
appropriate moments of the Argonauts' song, i.e. there are male and
female choirs with the male taking the major part;[18] in the other the
nymphs themselves sing and dance in honour of Hera, the most
important of the deities who presided over marriages. There is,
however, much to be said in favour of Brunck's μνήσαιτο in 1196 (i.e.
'whenever Orpheus sang of marriage');[19] with this textual change,
Apollonius would then be describing a virtuoso kitharodic performance
by Orpheus as solo singer and instrumentalist, with a female choir
merely joining in for the refrain.

(f) A closely related kind of performance is the description of how
Orpheus saved the crew (except for Boutes) from the peril of the Sirens:

ἀπηλεγέως δ' ἄρα καὶ τοῖς
ἴεσαν ἐκ στομάτων ὄπα λείριον· οἱ δ' ἀπὸ νηὸς

[18] For male and female *choroi* together cf., e.g., Hes. *Aspis* 278–85, Call. *h.* 4.304–6, Catullus 62.
West 1992.40 notes that there is no evidence for men and women singing in unison until late
sources; Apollonius' text may, however, envisage the possibility.
[19] This is particularly the case if we do not adopt Fränkel's transposition of 1182–1200 after
1169, a transposition which puts both song descriptions together as occurring during the
wedding-night. Livrea seeks to meet Fränkel's point by reference to the *diegertika* sung on the
morning after the wedding (cf. below p. 160 n. 83), but some doubts remain. Without the
transposition, the plural verb with the Argonauts as subject is a very harsh change.

ἤδη πείσματ᾽ ἔμελλον ἐπ᾽ ἠιόνεσσι βαλέσθαι,
εἰ μὴ ἄρ᾽ Οἰάγροιο πάις Θρηίκιος Ὀρφεύς,
Βιστονίην ἐνὶ χερσὶν ἑαῖς φόρμιγγα τανύσσας,
κραιπνὸν ἐυτροχάλοιο μέλος κανάχησεν ἀοιδῆς,
ὄφρ᾽ ἄμυδις κλονέοντος ἐπιβρομέωνται ἀκουαὶ
κρεγμῶι· παρθενίην δ᾽ ἐνοπὴν ἐβιήσατο φόρμιγξ.
νῆα δ᾽ ὁμοῦ Ζέφυρός τε καὶ ἠχῆεν φέρε κῦμα
πρυμνόθεν ὀρνύμενον· ταὶ δ᾽ ἄκριτον ἵεσαν αὐδήν.

(4.902–11)

For the Argonauts too the Sirens opened their mouths in pure liquid
song as soon as they saw them. The men made ready to throw the
ship's cables to the shore, and would have done so, had not Thracian
Orpheus, the son of Oiagros, taken up his Bistonian lyre in his hands
and played a fast rendition of a quick-rolling tune, so that its re-
sounding echo would beat in their ears, thus blurring and confound-
ing the other song. The lyre overpowered the virgin voices, and the
ship was carried forward by the combined efforts of the Zephyr and
the lapping waves which came from astern; the Sirens' song became
quite unclear.

Despite ἀοιδῆς in 907, it seems that Orpheus' performance here is
solely instrumental (cf. 909); μέλος (907) will therefore mean 'tune' or
'melody' rather than 'song'.[20] The rolling rhythm (ἐυτροχάλοιο)[21] is
manifested in the pure dactyls of 907–8 which are brought to an
abrupt halt by κρεγμῶι at the head of 909, announcing the victory of
the lyre over the Sirens' voices. Formally, there is a competition
between Orpheus and the Siren 'choir', but the scene is conceived
rather as one in which the instrumental music drowns out the choir's
words and makes them ἄκριτον (911).[22] Such a scenario is very
familiar from the history of Greek music. It was a common
(conservative) complaint against 'the new music' which first came to
prominence in the late fifth century – a music characterised by
instrumental virtuosity and a kind of vocal coloratura – that not only
did it break down traditional rhythmical and harmonic distinctions,
but it also pushed the actual words into a very secondary position; the
breaking of the link between rhythmical and linguistic structures

---

[20] Cf. 1.578; H. Färber, *Die Lyrik in der Kunsttheorie der Antike* (Munich 1936) 15–16; Livrea *ad loc.*; H. Koller, '*Melos*', *Glotta* 43 (1965) 24–38.
[21] The metaphor may be related to 'the chariot of song'. T. B. L. Webster, *Hellenistic Poetry and Art* (London 1964) 75–6 attractively suggested an allusion to the τροχός of wax in the Homeric Siren episode (*Od.* 12.173).
[22] For other aspects of this scene cf. Goldhill 1991.298–300.

allowed 'instrumentalists' to go their own way.[23] Plato, a stern critic of such developments, highlights 'speed' as one of the features of this new type of playing:

Nor would the Muses ever combine in a single piece the cries of beasts and men, the clash of instruments, and noises of all kinds, by way of representing a single object; whereas human poets, by their senselessness in mixing such things and jumbling them up together, would furnish a theme for laughter to all the men who, in Orpheus' phrase, 'have attained the full flower of joyousness'. For they behold all these things jumbled together, and how, also, the poets rudely sunder rhythm and gesture from tune, putting tuneless words into metre, or leaving tune and rhythm without words, and using the bare sound of harp or flute, wherein it is almost impossible to understand what is intended by this wordless rhythm and harmony, or what noteworthy original it represents. Such methods, as one ought to realise, are clownish in the extreme in so far as they exhibit an excessive craving for speed, mechanical accuracy, and the imitation of animals' sounds, and consequently employ the *aulos* and the *kithara* without the accompaniment of dance and song; for the use of either of these instruments by itself is the mark of the tasteless trickster. (*Laws* 2 669d–e, trans. R. G. Bury, adapted)[24]

Of such purely instrumental performances we can, of course, recover almost nothing, but references to, and fragments of, closely related kitharodic 'turns' are not uncommon. The conclusion of Timotheus' *Persians*, our most complete text from such a performance, celebrates the poet's innovations:

> πρῶτος ποικιλόμουσος 'Ορ-
> φεὺς χέλυν ἐτέκνωσεν
> υἱὸς Καλλιόπας ∪ –
> – × Πιερίαθεν·
> Τέρπανδρος δ' ἐπὶ τῶι δέκα
> ζεῦξε μοῦσαν ἐν ὠιδαῖ
> Λέσβος δ' Αἰολία νιν 'Αν-
> τίσσαι γείνατο κλεινόν·
> νῦν δὲ Τιμόθεος μέτροις
> ῥυθμοῖς τ' ἐνδεκακρουμάτοις
> κίθαριν ἐξανατέλλει,
> θησαυρὸν πολύυμνον οἴ-
> ξας Μουσᾶν θαλαμευτόν·
>
> (*PMG* 791. 221–33)

[23] For brief accounts cf. Gentili in Gentili–Pretagostini 1988.9–10; West 1992. 356–72.
[24] Cf. also *Laws* 7 812d–e.

First did Orpheus, son of Kalliope, a cunning artificer of music,[25] give birth to the tortoise-shell on Pieria. After him, Terpander yoked the Muse to ten songs;[26] Aeolian Lesbos gave birth to him, a source of fame for Antissa. But now, Timotheus causes *kitharis* to rise again in metres and in eleven-stringed rhythms; he has opened the Muses' secret treasure-house of songs.

By describing Orpheus as ποικιλόμουσος, 'cunning artificer of music', Timotheus claims the authorising founder of *kithara* music for his own musical project; it is not age which matters (cf. vv. 213–15), but the spirit of adventure. In a famous fragment of the comic poet Pherecrates, Music herself complains of the outrages done to her by 'the new musicians', and she describes those outrages in terms of sexual violence. The passage need not be cited in full, as a few verses will give the flavour:

ἐμοὶ γὰρ ἦρξε τῶν κακῶν Μελανιππίδης,
ἐν τοῖσι πρῶτος ὃς λαβὼν ἀνῆκέ με
χαλαρωτέραν τ' ἐποίησε χορδαῖς δώδεκα.

κακά μοι παρέσχεν οὗτος, ἅπαντας οὓς λέγω
παρελήλυθεν, ἄγων ἐκτραπέλους μυρμηκιάς.
κἂν ἐντύχηι πού μοι βαδιζούσηι μόνηι,
ἀπέδυσε κἀνέλυσε χορδαῖς δώδεκα.
            (Pherecrates fr. 155.3–5, 22–5 K–A)

Melanippides started my troubles. He was the first of them: he grabbed me and pulled me down, and loosened me up with his twelve strings. . . . The things [Timotheus] did to me were worse than all the others put together, with those perverted ant-crawlings he went in for. And when he found me out for a walk by myself, he stripped me and undid me with his twelve strings. (Trans. A. Barker, adapted)

Apollonius seems to evoke similar sexual images in the punning language of v. 909, παρθενίην δ' ἐνοπὴν ἐβιήσατο φόρμιγξ, 'the lyre overpowered the virgin voices'. Thus, paradoxically, Orpheus is here portrayed as a modern virtuoso[27] whose playing deafens the audience and drowns out the choir; archaic harmonies are replaced by agonistic disharmony. In turning Orpheus into a master of 'modern

---

[25] This is my inadequate attempt to convey Timotheus' adjective which combines suggestions of Orpheus' skill with his performance of 'ever-changing' tunes (like Timotheus himself).

[26] The meaning is disputed, cf. A. Barker, *Greek Musical Writings I: The Musician and his Art* (Cambridge 1984) 96.

[27] For a similar picture of Simonides in Theocritus 16 cf. above pp. 101–2.

music' Apollonius' brilliant conceit mingles the mythical past with 'the modern age' in a way typical of the whole epic.

The *Argonautica* thus offers a whole array of images of archaic song and dance, and those images are powerful constituents of Apollonius' total evocation of a distant, heroic world; they share too, however, in that mixing of temporal frames which was central to Apollonius' epic project. In Idyll 18, Theocritus too depicts the choral music of the past to evoke the world of heroic story.

A SONG FOR SPARTA

Idyll 18 reconstructs an epithalamian sung by a choir of twelve Spartan girls outside the wedding-chamber of Helen and Menelaos. A notice in Philodemus (*De musica* 68.37–41 Kemke) suggests that new epithalamia were no longer being written in the first century, and whatever this actually means – weddings, of course, continued to be central sites for song, although prose was increasingly the principal mode of encomium –[28] it is likely that already in Theocritus' day the form, as well as the setting, of Idyll 18 was recognisably archaic. We have already observed that the great age of lyric poetry barely survived the fifth century.[29] Isolated exceptions are, of course, always to be expected: the choral lyrics of the Boeotian poetess Corinna (*PMG* 654–89) may date from the third century BC rather than from the age of Pindar, but this will not significantly alter the general picture.

Like Idyll 12, Idyll 18 includes the aetiology of a rite, though unusually the participants are made conscious of the fact that they are beginning a tradition.[30] A brief narrative introduction sets the scene in a far distant past (ποκα v. 1), like the *Herakliskos* (Idyll 24), and that past world is marked by the evocation of elaborate singing and dancing (vv. 7–8). ἄρα, 'then', in v. 1 has caused considerable academic head-scratching,[31] but it seems best explained, like the similar case at 22.27,[32] as marking the poet's control over his narrative – he has chosen where in the fabric of myth to begin his

---

[28] For some of the ramifications of this change cf. Rossi 1971.78–80.   [29] Cf. above p. 3.

[30] Vv. 43, 45 πρᾶται . . . πρᾶται; cf. further below p. 161. For Idyll 12 cf. below pp. 190–1.

[31] Cf. e.g. Kaibel 1892.259; Wilamowitz 1906.141; Merkelbach 1957.20–1; Dover *ad loc.*

[32] At 22.27 ἄρα does not 'mark the narrative which follows as depending on the decision to celebrate Polydeuces first' (Gow), but rather marks the fact that the narrative does not 'begin at the beginning' (unlike the *Argonautica* to which the verse may in fact allude). Cf. below on the probable reference in 18.1 to the *Helen* of Stesichorus.

song.[33] It is tempting to go further by connecting this particle with the report in the scholia that some things (τινα) in Idyll 18 have been taken over from the *Helen* of Stesichorus of Himera, one of the great figures of archaic lyric poetry (first half of the sixth century). Two narratives in late sources may give us some information about this poem.[34] A Homeric scholiast informs us that Stesichorus (*PMGF* 190) told how Tyndareos extracted from Helen's suitors an oath that the unlucky ones would come to the aid of the successful suitor if the latter was wronged after the marriage; Paris then abducted Helen and the Trojan expedition was launched in accordance with the oath. Secondly, Pausanias ascribes to Stesichorus (*PMGF* 191) the story that Iphigeneia was really the child of Helen and Theseus, conceived when Theseus abducted Helen before her marriage to Menelaos, a relationship from which Helen was rescued by the Dioscuri, who brought her back to Sparta. Although neither of these stories is stated explicitly to be derived from the *Helen*, such a speculation seems hardly bold, and these narratives may be used to confirm what we would in any case have assumed on the basis of the Stesichorean texts we possess, namely that the *Helen* was an expansive narrative from which Theocritus has selected a small, though perhaps central, incident, namely the marriage of Helen and Menelaos. Recently published papyri of Stesichorus have confirmed the monumental nature of his narrative poems, which were 'in effect lyric epics',[35] probably performed solo, like the hexameter epics of the rhapsodes; his *Oresteia* was in at least two books, and the *Geryoneis* ran to over 1,300 verses.[36] The only certain fragment of any note to have survived[37] from the *Helen* (*PMGF* 187) confirms that the wedding of Helen and Menelaos was indeed described in that poem; the metre is dactylic, and so Theocritus' hexameters are themselves metrically

---

[33] H. White, *QUCC* 32 (1979) 108, explains (without reference to earlier discussions) that the particle 'implies the existence of "antefatti" which the poet deliberately omits to narrate'. This is clearly true, though it does not go far enough. My approach is basically that outlined by Effe 1978.74 n. 58.

[34] I omit from consideration here the difficult problems of Stesichorus' 'palinodes' and the possibility that other known fragments of this poet are to be assigned to the *Helen*.

[35] M. L. West, *Greek Lyric Poetry* (Oxford 1993) xvi. For a recent assessment cf. G. Arrighetti, 'Stesicoro e il suo pubblico', *MD* 32 (1994) 9–30.

[36] Cf. the stichometric mark at s27 Davies; the poem from which the famous 'Lille Stesichorus' on the Theban myth survives (*PMGF* 222(b), cf. below p. 155) ran probably well beyond the 300 verses guaranteed by a stichometric mark.

[37] M. L. West, *ZPE* 4 (1969) 148, tentatively suggested that 'Ibycus s166 Davies' came from Stesichorus' *Helen*; even if this is not correct, that broken fragment can offer us another glimpse of the 'lyric Sparta' which Theocritus has sought to re-create in Idyll 18.

'analogous' to the archaic model. If indeed Theocritus wants us to think of Stesichorus' *Helen*[38] and the narratives quoted above do refer to that poem, then μναστεύσας (v. 6) and the reference to the other suitors (v. 17) give us some indication of what parts of Stesichorus' poem have 'preceded' and been omitted by Theocritus. To what extent these narratives also support an 'ironic' reading of Idyll 18 will be considered presently.

However great the extent of the debt to Stesichorus, it is obvious that Theocritus has also used both the motifs of popular wedding-songs and other literary evocations of those motifs in archaic lyric.[39] The opening structure of narrative followed by hymeneal song has been seen to have a close analogue in the opening of a poem of Bacchylides on the wedding of Idas and Marpessa:

Σπάρται ποτ' ἐν ε[
ξανθαὶ Λακεδα[ιμονι . . .
τοιόνδε μέλος κ[. . .
ὅτ' ἄγετο καλλιπά[ραιον
κόραν θρασυκάρ[διος Ἴδας
Μάρπησσαν . . .
(Bacchylides 20. 1–6 Sn.–M)

Once in . . . Sparta blonde [maidens] sang the following song, when bold Idas married lovely Marpessa . . .

Even if this poem was not a direct model for Theocritus, it serves as a useful reminder that the form, as well as the substance, of Idyll 18 is essentially a re-creation.[40] Beyond this fragment, two obvious debts stand out. One is to Sappho, the poet *par excellence* of erotic poetry in general and epithalamia in particular;[41] Sappho's wedding-songs almost certainly included dactylic hexameters (cf. frr. 105–6 Voigt), and her fragments provide many parallels for the encomiastic motifs

---

[38] I can hardly fail to mention the possibility that χορὸν ἐστάσαντο in v. 3 alludes to the archaic poet; for the etymology of his name cf. *Suda* σ 1095.

[39] Contiades-Tsitsoni 1990.128–9 quotes a modern Greek 'Wecklied' which throws amusing light on vv. 9–11 of Theocritus' poem: 'Do you hear, do you hear, Mr Bridegroom, what your mother tells you? Don't eat too much, don't drink too much, or else you will go to bed and fall asleep.'

[40] This is important as the structure of 'narrative + song' is often considered a particularly Theocritean form; cf. R. Pretagostini, 'La struttura compositiva dei carmi teocritei', *QUCC* 34 (1980) 57–74.

[41] Cf., e.g., Contiades-Tsitsoni 1990.68–109. For possible borrowings from Sappho in Idyll 18 add to the standard commentaries Kaibel 1892, Merkelbach 1957, and J. Mesk, 'Sappho und Theokrit in der ersten Rede des Himerios', *WS* 44 (1924/5) 160–70. For Theocritus and Lesbian poetry in general cf. below pp. 171–86.

of Idyll 18. In fr. 44 Voigt we have the remains of a relatively extensive narrative, in a stichic length with clear affinities to the dactylic hexameter, of the arrival of Hector and Andromache in Troy for their wedding; choirs of *parthenoi* are, of course, part of the festivity (vv. 25–6). Sappho's importance for the writing of literary wedding-songs is seen perhaps most clearly later in Catullus 61 and 62.[42] The other crucial archaic model is Alcman (late seventh / early sixth century), the great lyric poet of archaic Sparta and a figure of the greatest interest for subsequent centuries. Similarities between the presentation of Helen in Idyll 18 and that of the chorus-leader Hagesichora in Alcman's 'Louvre Partheneion' (*PMGF* 1) have long been noted,[43] and some scholars have indeed wished to identify Hagesichora or the 'dawn goddess' Ἀῶτις, to whom Alcman's poem appears to be addressed, with Helen in her manifestation as a Spartan goddess (cf. Theocr. 18.26–8).[44] Certainly the 'Louvre Partheneion' offers a striking analogy to many of the images from Idyll 18:

> ἐγὼν δ' ἀείδω
> Ἀγιδῶς τὸ φῶς· ὁρῶ
> F' ὥτ' ἄλιον, ὅνπερ ἄμιν
> Ἀγιδὼ μαρτύρεται
> φαίνην· ἐμὲ δ' οὔτ' ἐπαινῆν
> οὔτε μωμήσθαι νιν ἀ κλεννὰ χοραγὸς
> οὐδ' ἀμῶς ἐῆι· δοκεῖ γὰρ ἦμεν αὔτα
> ἐκπρεπὴς τὼς ὥπερ αἴτις
> ἐν βοτοῖς στάσειεν ἵππον
> παγὸν ἀεθλοφόρον καναχάποδα
> τῶν ὑποπετριδίων ὀνείρων·
>
> ἦ οὐχ ὁρῆις; ὁ μὲν κέλης
> Ἐνετικός· ἀ δὲ χαίτα
> τᾶς ἐμᾶς ἀνεψιᾶς
> Ἀγησιχόρας ἐπανθεῖ
> χρυσὸς ὡς ἀκήρατος·
> τό τ' ἀργύριον πρόσωπον,
> διαφάδαν τί τοι λέγω;
>
> (*PMGF* 1.39–56)

I sing the radiance of Agido: I see her shining like the sun which Agido summons to witness us. But the glorious leader of the chorus

[42] Cf. P. Fedeli, *Catullus' Carmen 61* (Amsterdam 1983).

[43] Cf., e.g., Crusius, *RE* 1.1569; Maas, *RE* 9. 132; A. Griffiths 1972; Calame 1977. 1 91–2, 333–41, II 123–6; G. Nagy, *Pindar's Homer. The Lyric Possession of an Epic Past* (Baltimore/London 1990) 345–6.

[44] So Calame loc. cit., following a tentative speculation of C. M. Bowra, *Greek Lyric Poetry* 2nd ed. (Oxford 1961) 54–5.

prevents me from praising or blaming her, for she herself stands out as clearly as if you set a horse among flocks, a great, prize-winning steed with thunder in its hooves, one of the horses that appear in dreams under rocks. Do you not see? The horse is Venetic: the hair of my cousin Hagesichora blooms bright like pure gold, and her silvered face . . . Why should I say it explicitly?

This poem was probably the first in the Alexandrian edition of Alcman and thus not only particularly well-known, but also 'marked' in a special, programmatic way; that Theocritus was thinking specifically of this poem of Alcman is not improbable, though not to be assumed on present evidence. Alcman was known in the third century as a composer of wedding-songs[45] and was clearly a poet of considerable interest to the Alexandrians;[46] works entitled *On Alcman* were written by Sosibios of Sparta (*FGrHist* 595 F6) and by Philochorus (*FGrHist* 328 T1), both probably older contemporaries of Theocritus, and possibly also at the same period by the Peripatetic scholar Chamaileon of Heraclea Pontica (cf. frr. 24–5 Wehrli).[47] It is noteworthy that when, at the end of the *Lysistrata*, Aristophanes wished to evoke the world of Spartan celebration, he did so with 'para-Alcmanic' verse presenting Helen as ἁγνὰ χοραγὸς εὐπρεπής, 'holy and beautiful chorus-leader' (v. 1315).[48] Already in classical and later antiquity, then, female choruses and songs composed for them by Alcman were considered to be particularly characteristic of archaic Sparta. As with Sappho, some of Alcman's verse appears to have been stichic, including stichic dactylic hexameters (cf. *PMGF* 26),[49] and so Theocritus' 'sung' hexameters again provide an appropriate form of mimetic analogy.

Alcman has a further importance for Idyll 18, and this concerns the language of the poem. Idyll 18 is normally classed with the 'pure Doric' poems of Theocritus on the basis of very few certain Homerisms[50] and some striking dialect features such as the genitive τεοῦς in v.41.[51]

---

[45] Leonidas, *Anth. Pal.* 7.19.1 (= *HE* 2321); for a survey of possible signs of these poems among the fragments cf. Contiades-Tsitsoni 1990.46–63.

[46] Cf., e.g., Alexander Aetolus, *Anth. Pal.* 7.709 (= 1 G–P = 9 Powell).

[47] Chamaileon also wrote 'On Stesichorus' (frr. 28–9 Wehrli).

[48] See esp. Wilamowitz 1900.88–92, and Henderson's notes *ad loc.*

[49] For the evidence cf. Haslam on *POxy.* 3209.

[50] Cf. Di Benedetto 1956.54; for the general issues involved cf. above pp. 28–45.

[51] This form also occurs at 11.25 in the mouth of the Sicilian Cyclops, and is otherwise quoted from Sophron and Corinna; cf. the related τεῦς, which occurs in Epicharmus, Corinna, and Theocritus (Gow on 2.126). In 18.41 the strong dialect form may give an affective emotional tone as the choir promise Helen that they will long for her in her absence 'as milk-fed lambs long for the teat of their mother ewe'.

The poem's concern with dialect is made explicit in v. 48.[52] There are, however, no real signs in the transmission of Idyll 18 of traditional 'Attic' ways of representing diagnostic features of Laconian Doric such as σ for θ.[53] Our earliest witnesses to the text, *POxy*. 3550 and 3552 of the second century AD, offer a familiar mixture of different Doric forms, e.g. both -οισα and -ουσα participles in the same text.[54] Nevertheless, if the language of Idyll 18 looks very like the language of the 'bucolic' poems, there is no need to assume that the intended effect is the same, and analogical *mimesis* of the language of Alcman seems in this case a hypothesis worth pursuing.

Modern debate about the language of Alcman has concerned the extent to which it is a basically Doric *Kunstsprache* of a kind familiar for other early lyric poets, i.e. one showing strong influence from both the aeolic and the epic traditions; the argument has largely concerned the degree to which Alcman's language was faithful to the Laconian vernacular. The matter cannot be considered in any detail here;[55] we would give much to be sure of the linguistic form of the text of Alcman available to Theocritus, although the first-century AD text of the 'Louvre Partheneion' probably brings us in fact quite close to the Alexandrian edition of the poet. What does seem crucial is that the grammatical tradition constantly cites Alcman as a 'Doric' poet, sometimes as *the* Doric poet;[56] though he is also, of course, adduced as an example of Laconian, it is the Dorism of his poems which dominates the learned tradition. If it is safe to assume that the seeds of this tradition were already sown in the third century, then an obvious reason for the language of Idyll 18 appears. The anonymous passer-by of vv. 47–8 will read Δωριστί, 'in Dorian', not 'in Laconian', or even 'in the language of Amyklai' (12.13), because it is the Dorian heritage and a Dorian tradition that the poem celebrates.[57] It is perhaps worth adding that Praxinoa, one of the Syracusan housewives of Idyll 15, also seems to assert that the Peloponnese is the

---

[52] Cf. further below.

[53] In v. 33 *POxy*. 3552 (2nd cent. AD) offers δαιδαλιω for δαιδαλέωι, but editors prefer to see here a phonological error rather than a genuine Dorism, or even Laconism, cf. Molinos Tejada 1990.96.

[54] Both papyri do, however, offer the form Ἑλάνα rather than Ἑλένα in the Theocritean text (although inconsistently so)_: Ελένα is otherwise the universal form in Laconian inscriptions and texts. For discussion cf. Gallavotti 1984.9–10; Molinos Tejada 1990.111–13.

[55] For the arguments cf. D. L. Page, *Alcman, The Partheneion* (Oxford 1951) 102–63; Risch 1954; Nöthiger 1971.126–8; A. C. Cassio, 'Alcmane, il dialetto di Cirene e la filologia alessandrina', *RFIC* 121 (1993) 24–36. For a recent comparison of Alcman and Theocritus cf. Abbenes 1995.

[56] Cf. Risch 1954.26–8; Cassio 1993.   [57] Cf. below p. 166.

home of 'true Doric' (15.90–3),[58] and so the symbolic power of the figure of Alcman is not to be too narrowly confined to the provincially Laconian. The language of Idyll 18, therefore, is not intended to reproduce as a historical exercise 'the language of Alcman', but rather to offer a poetic language which, while having much in common with the language of Alcman, functions as mimetically analogous to the archaic poet.

After language, form. Archaic lyric poetry is either monostrophic, i.e. composed in metrically identical single stanzas, or triadic, i.e. composed in repeated units of strophe–antistrophe–epode; antiquity ascribed the 'invention' of triadic composition to Stesichorus, and stanzas and triads are, as I have noted, already marked on the 'Lille Stesichorus' of the later third century. Whether or not Alcman's 'Louvre Partheneion' is triadic has been debated,[59] but it is certainly composed in responding 14-line stanzas, and whatever the colometry (or lack of it) might have been in texts of the early and middle third century, there seems no good reason to doubt that Theocritus and his contemporaries broadly understood the stanzaic nature of early lyric.[60] Attempts, however, to divide Theocritus' poems into stanzas as part of his imitation of the lyric manner have a notoriously unhappy history, particularly in the nineteenth century.[61] No advance has been made since the powerful discussion of Wilamowitz,[62] who dismissed earlier attempts to find a strophic pattern in Idyll 18 as 'vollkommene Begriffsverwirrung'. As others had before him, he accepted that vv. 26–37 were formed from four groups of three verses and that vv. 43–8 consisted of three distichs; like the distichs of the songs in Idyll 10 and the distichs and triplets of Idyll 3, these small units were designed 'to recall the musical effect of song', but the overall structure of what was essentially *epos* had nothing to do with (big or small) stanzas. Nevertheless, there are signs which might at least encourage us to look again. The interest of Hellenistic poets in stanzaic and quasi-stanzaic effects is clear not merely from Theocritus'

---

[58] Cf. Arena 1956.9.

[59] On the structure of this poem cf. most recently V. Hinz, *ZPE* 99 (1993) 15–16.

[60] This is denied by Bohnenkamp 1972.118, but cf. below p. 174. I would not, of course, wish to deny that there may be important differences between poetry composed free from the influence of Alexandrian scholarship on early lyric and poetry which reflects that interest.

[61] Helpful bibliography at Gow II 16 n. 2. To cite but one example for Idyll 18: Ahrens divided the wedding-song into 'stanzas' of 7 verses (9–15), 3 (16–18), 7 (19–25), 6 (26–31), 6 (32–7), 6 (38–42, with a lacuna of two half-verses), 6 (43–8), 5 (49–53), 5 (54–8). A more recent division into 'verse paragraphs' at Cairns 1979.203, and cf. also Sanchez-Wildberger 1955.38.

[62] Wilamowitz 1906.137–51; cf. also Legrand 1898.386–95.

use of the refrain in Idylls 1 and 2, but also from Callimachus' hymns. The *Hymn to Apollo* begins with three verse paragraphs or stanzas of eight verses (1–8, 9–16, 17–24) and one of seven (25–31) before the 'hymn proper'; that poem concludes with two paragraphs of eight verses (97–104, 105–12) and the farewell to the god (v. 113).[63] The *Hymn to Demeter* is similarly divisible into 23 + 92 (= 23 × 4) + 23.[64] In the light of this, I offer a tentative suggestion about Idyll 18.

As transmitted,[65] the wedding-song of Idyll 18 is fifty verses long (vv. 9–58), and major punctuation easily allows a division into five verse paragraphs each of ten verses (9–18, 19–28, 29–38, 39–48, 49–58). Of these paragraphs vv. 39–48 deal with the rite to be inaugurated on the following morning, and vv. 49–58 are the *envoi* framed by χαίροις . . . χαρείης. Vv. 9–18 are addressed to Menelaos and concern his good fortune; vv. 19–28 are concerned with praise of Helen, moving, by way of v. 21, from address to Menelaos to the chorus' own concerns, and are framed by the patterning of Ζανός τοι θυγάτηρ . . . Ἑλένα; vv. 29–38 are again praise of Helen. That such a pattern is deliberate seems more than likely. The fact that there is no major sense-break after vv. 18 and 28 and that the break after v. 38 separates a μέν from a δέ are not strong arguments against the proposed arrangement; these phenomena can, for example, easily be paralleled from the various ways in which Alcman relates sense to stanzaic structure. A more potent objection might perhaps be developed on the basis of the undeniable patterning of vv. 26–37 and 43–8 into small 'song-like' units, of the kind discussed by Wilamowitz and others; it might be thought that these groupings are incompatible with larger ten-verse units. I see, however, no reason why these two structurings cannot co-exist. Within archaic lyric itself, of course, there are many 'groupings' which cut across strophic divisions, although their formal marking may not be as strong as, say, the very mannered parallelisms of 18.43–4 and 18.45–6. This doubleness of structure in Idyll 18 is in fact a marked product of a culture which has, to an important extent, lost touch with the musical and rhythmical aspects of the archaic performance evoked by the poem; this 'over-determined' formal structure is indeed another kind of compensation for that loss, somewhat analogous to the interplay of voices in Orpheus' hymn to Apollo in *Argonautica* 2 (above p. 144). It is also, of course, a phenomenon of a culture in which writing and reading played a central rôle which they

[63] Cf. Wilamowitz 1924.ɪɪ 82–3; Cairns 1979.123–4.　　[64] Cf. Hopkinson's edition p. 11.
[65] On the difficulties of vv. 21–5 cf. below pp. 159–60.

did not have in the archaic 'model period'. These overlaid structures are the formal counterparts of what at a textual level is the mingling of (primarily) Stesichorus, Alcman, and Sappho into a reconstructive blend. Idyll 18 is thus a composite text, both allusively and structurally.

With the hindsight of literary history, we can also see that Idyll 18 is 'generically composite': by its conclusion the *hymenaios* has taken on many of the features of the hymn. These two encomiastic 'genres' were of course always closely related, and late lexical sources offer ὕμνος as one of the etymologies of ὑμέναιος, defining the latter as a species of the former;[66] whether or not this etymology was current in the third century, the two words are juxtaposed sufficiently often to cause us to suspect that some affinity between them was felt.[67] The importance of hymnic form in Idyll 18 is clear in the prominence of Helen over her husband, a prominence which completely destroys any balance between the pair.[68] This prominence is the result of the Spartan setting and Spartan concerns of the poem – particularly the reworking of Alcman's maiden-songs – and it is to these concerns which I now turn.

Antiquarian interest in traditional Spartan culture was matched, at least for a while, by a political interest when, in the early 260s, Philadelphus supported Athens and Sparta in the so-called Chremonidean War against Macedonia.[69] The Sparta which Theocritus depicts, however, is a mythical place caught for ever in a golden age of ritual evoked by familiar landmarks; Idyll 18, like the closely related Spartan passage of Callimachus' *Hymn to Athena* (vv. 21–32),[70] may be thought of as a kind of cultural rescue-archaeology which depends upon a vision of Sparta derived from books rather than from personal observation. Our scattered sources, most notably Pausanias, do allow us to sense something of what was in those books, but much must inevitably remain speculative.

---

[66] Cf. *Etym. Mag.* 776.42–3 Gaisford, Eustathius on *Il.* 18.493; the other standard etymologies are from ὁμοῦ ναίειν or ὁμονοεῖν (cf. Theocr. 18.51–2), or make a link with the female ὑμήν.

[67] Cf. Soph. *Ant.* 813–16; Eur. *IT* 367; Leonidas loc. cit. (n. 45 above).

[68] Contrast, e.g., Men. Rhet. III 403.26–30 Spengel (p. 142 R–W), where the emendation suggested by Russell and Wilson finds strong support in Theocr. 18.32–7.

[69] Antiquarian interest: e.g., E. Rawson, *The Spartan Tradition in European Thought* (Oxford 1969) 81–93, though Rawson is strangely silent about poetry. Chremonidean War: e.g., H. Hauben 'Arsinoé II et la politique extérieure de l' Égypte' in *Egypt and the Hellenistic World* (Studia Hellenistica 27, Louvain 1983) 99–127; P. Cartledge in P. Cartledge and A. Spawforth, *Hellenistic and Roman Sparta. A Tale of Two Cities* (London/New York 1989) 35–7; F. Walbank in *CAH* 2nd ed., VII.1, pp. 236–40; C. Habicht, *Athen in hellenistischer Zeit* (Munich 1994) 144.

[70] For the links between these poems cf., e.g., F. Griffiths 1979.89; Bulloch on Call. *h.* 5.23–8.

Helen and Menelaos were honoured with cult both at Sparta and at the village of Therapne near Sparta;[71] at Sparta, Helen's shrine was near 'the tomb of Alcman' and next to a shrine of Heracles said to have been established after he killed the sons of Hippokoön, which is the subject of the myth of the 'Louvre Partheneion' (Pausanias 3.15.2–3). Also near the 'tomb of Alcman' was an area called 'Platanistas' ('The Plane Trees') where ephebic contests were held (Paus. 3.14.8), and modern scholars are surely correct to link this place with the plane-tree cult of Helen which is described in Idyll 18. The Spartan Δρόμος, 'Racetrack' (18.39), which plays such a central rôle in the choir's life and the rite which they found, was next to the site of 'Menelaos' house' (Paus. 3.14.6), outside which, we may assume, the epithalamian of Idyll 18 is imagined to be sung; nearby also was a shrine to Helen's brothers, the Dioscuri, and the Graces. The geography of Idyll 18 is therefore the sacred geography of old Sparta.

The choir itself consists of twelve girls, 'the leading ones of the city', who will not merely found a cult in Helen's honour but also, we may reasonably suppose, be the first 'priestesses' of that cult.[72] We should perhaps be reminded of the Διονυσιάδες, a band of young Spartan women who offered sacrifice together with the Λευκιππίδες, the priestesses of Hilaira and Phoibe, who were called πῶλοι, 'foals', and who are associated by Pausanias with a running contest.[73] The Leukippides themselves are constantly associated with Helen in references to Spartan cult (cf. Ar. *Lys.* 1307–15, Eur. *Hel.* 1465–7), and Theocritus may well be alluding to a known (or believed) association of young Spartan women. More broadly, it is important that Sparta appears to have had a rich, priestly caste which reserved important priesthoods to itself;[74] the 'leading women of the city' (v. 4), who pray for the passage of wealth ἐξ εὐπατριδᾶν εἰς εὐπατρίδας may well belong to this priestly aristocracy. There is certainly abundant evidence from the archaic and classical periods for a wealthy Spartan aristocracy;[75] ancient sources

---

[71] Texts collected by S. Wide, *Lakonische Kulte* (Leipzig 1893) 340–6; add H. W. Catling and H. Cavanagh, 'Two inscribed bronzes from the Menelaion, Sparta', *Kadmos* 15 (1976) 145–57. For further discussion and bibliography cf. Gow on vv. 43–8 and I. Malkin, *Myth and Territory in the Spartan Mediterranean* (Cambridge 1994) 47–8.

[72] Cf. further below pp. 160–1.

[73] Paus. 3.13.7, Hesychius δ 1888; the Dionysiades were connected with Idyll 18 by Wide op. cit. (n. 71) 344 n. 4. Cf. in general Calame 1977.1 323–41.

[74] Cf. Spawforth in Cartledge–Spawforth (above n. 69) 164, though the evidence for the Hellenistic period is not as strong as one would wish.

[75] Evidence collected by G. E. M. de Ste Croix, *The Origins of the Peloponnesian War* (London 1972) 137–8; P. A. Rahe, *Historia* 29 (1980) 386.

in fact comment upon the value placed upon wealth in Sparta (cf. Pl. R. 8 548a–b, Arist. Pol. 2 1269b23–4). Thus the prayer to Zeus for 'unceasing prosperity' (v. 52) and the comparison of Helen to a Thessalian horse (v. 30) are not just topoi of epithalamia and of Spartan partheneia (cf. Alcman fr. 1.45–51, Ar. Lys. 1302–21), but are part of the evocation of archaic 'eupatrid' Spartan life; horse-breeding indeed 'occupied a special place in Lakonian life'.[76]

More difficult problems, however, confront us in vv. 22–5:

ἀμὲς γὰρ πᾶσαι συνομάλικες, αἷς δρόμος ωὑτός
χρισαμέναις ἀνδριστὶ παρ' Εὐρώταο λοετροῖς,
τετράκις ἑξήκοντα κόραι, θῆλυς νεολαία,
τᾶν οὐδ' ἅτις ἄμωμος ἐπεί χ' Ἑλέναι παρισωθῆι.

> For we, the full company of her coevals, together anoint ourselves in manly fashion by the bathing places in Eurotas and run there together, a girlish band of four times sixty maids, of whom, when matched with Helen, not one is faultless. (Trans. Gow, adapted)

The difficulties which this apparently verbless sentence[77] has caused are adequately indicated by Dover's note on v. 22: 'not only does the sentence change direction, but when it does so the first person with which it began is forgotten and the demonstrative . . . is used with reference only to the appositional phrases'. Unless we postulate textual loss (? after v. 23) – a hypothesis with obvious consequences for the stanzaic arrangement I have proposed – the most natural paraphrase of these verses would seem to be, '[Helen has no peer . . .], for we who are assembled here are all the συνομάλικες, 240 maidens who exercise together, none of whom is faultless when compared to Helen.' 'The number 240 remains mysterious' as Gow observes, although it must be clear that somehow 'the 12 "leading" girls . . . speak on behalf of the entire age-group which they represent' (Dover).[78] The most likely solution seems to be that of Kuiper, who suggested that Theocritus here reflects an antiquarian tradition about archaic Sparta;[79] 'four times sixty' suggests an arrangement somewhat parallel to the βούαι or ἀγέλαι, 'herds', into which Spartan

---

[76] P. Cartledge, Sparta and Lakonia (London 1979) 174, cf. de Ste Croix loc. cit. (n. 75, with pp. 354–5).

[77] POxy. 3552 (cf. Gow I 257) reads ε]ιμες at the head of v. 22, but this looks like an attempt to 'normalise' the construction.

[78] H. White, QUCC 32 (1979) 111–13, suggested (on the basis of Call. h. 5.23–8) taking the number 240 not with κόραι but with δρόμος, so that there are only ever 12 girls; to my mind, syntax and word-order make this very improbable.

[79] 'De Theocriti carmine xviii' Mnem. 49 (1921) 223–42, at pp. 231–5.

boys were said to be ordered.[80] Beyond this guess we can hardly go, though there may be something more to be said about συνομάλικες. Parallels from other wedding-songs and references to them suggest that the primary sense should be 'Helen's coevals', such as would be expected to perform the epithalamian,[81] and, at one level, this must be the meaning. συνομάλικες may, however, also evoke the ὁμοῖοι, the Spartan ruling class, and a term which cuts across strict age-grading. This is not to say that συνομάλικες was actually a Spartan term, but rather that it forms part of the poet's historicising reconstruction. When the choir sing that any child of Helen's will be great 'if she bears a child like (ὁμοῖον) its mother' (v. 21), this not only varies pointedly the usual felicity of children who resemble their father, but also clearly alludes to the Spartan governing class: any son of Helen is bound to be one of the *homoioi*. On this interpretation Theocritus may mean to suggest that συνομάλικες, 'the coevals', were all the daughters of the Spartan aristocracy.

As for the cult of Helen itself, Martin West[82] has revived and extended a reconstruction and interpretation which starts from various indications that Helen was originally a goddess of the Sun and of fertility; her abduction, like that of Persephone, marked the onset of winter. West interpreted the rite of Idyll 18 as a spring festival[83] comparable to 'May Day' in England and similar celebrations in northern Europe which mark the coming of summer; he noted that such festivals often involve the decoration or honouring of trees and similar objects (cf. the maypole). If this hypothesis is correct – and in view of the rest of the poem it is reasonable to assume that this rite does actually have an analogue in the assumed customs of traditional Sparta – then it will reinforce the other indications in the poem that the season is late spring: the *huakinthos* in the choir's hair, and their image of themselves as suckling lambs (vv. 41–2), an image

[80] For the evidence cf. K. M. T. Chrimes, *Ancient Sparta* (Manchester 1949) 84–136. Pindar fr. 112 Sn–M describes a choir as Λάκαινα μὲν παρθένων ἀγέλα, and this will evoke peculiarly Spartan institutions.

[81] Cf. Pindar, *Pyth.* 3.17–18, Catullus 62.32 (*aequales*). It is relevant that at *Iliad* 3.175 Helen claims to miss her ὁμηλικίη ἐρατεινή.

[82] *Immortal Helen* (Inaugural Lecture, London 1975). For further speculations cf. O. Skutsch, 'Helen, her name and nature', *JHS* 107 (1987) 188–93.

[83] The scholiast takes ἦρι in v. 39 as 'in springtime' rather than 'in the morning', and this has been defended by H. White, *QUCC* 32 (1979) 113–16. White saw in this interpretation a way of avoiding the apparent difficulty that the choir seems to give itself two tasks in the morning (cf. v. 56); the reference to spring in v. 27 could, I think, be used to argue both for and against a setting of the poem in that season. Elsewhere in Theocritus ἦρι occurs only at 24.93 in the sense 'in the morning', and a striking parallel at 15.132–5 argues for that sense here.

both appropriate to Helen as a nurturing goddess and one suggesting that soon she will no longer be playing with her friends because she will have her own children to care for. It is tempting to go further and speculate that the rite which the choir founds is one which henceforth will be observed by *all* Spartan brides who, before their weddings, will pay honour to Helen as both 'original bride' and (for this reason) the protecting deity of young women and granter of fertility.[84] If so, then part of the point of the image of vv. 41–2 will be that Helen's marriage reminds the choir of their own impending rite of transition and their rapidly passing girlhood; the lambs are not merely hungry, they are separated from their mother because they are growing up.[85]

Some of the features of the Sparta of Idyll 18, such as the 'female athletics' of vv. 22–3, are familiar from our main 'Lycurgan' texts, Xenophon's *Constitution of the Spartans* and Plutarch's *Life of Lycurgus*, but more evoke the world of beauty and culture which we can glimpse in the fragments of Alcman. The toughness of 'Lycurgan' Sparta is, to an important extent, an Athenian creation, for Sparta was one of the 'other' cultures whose image was an important site for Athenian self-definition. One of Theocritus' strategies for evoking the Spartan past is a creative tension between 'Lycurgan' and 'anti-Lycurgan' images of the city; we cannot be sure what texts about Sparta Theocritus and his audience knew, and hence what images of archaic Sparta were common currency, but some inferences seem hardly bold. Thus, for example, the belief that Lycurgus made private wealth a useless commodity (Plut. *Lyc.* 10) is obviously at variance with the closing prayer and with the whole ethos of the poem. So too, the apparent belief that Spartan women left weaving to the slaves (Pl. *Laws* 7 806a, Xen. *Lac.* 1.3–4) points clearly to the 'pre-Lycurgan' world evoked by Theocritus (cf. vv. 32–4). Plutarch's account of 'Lycurgan marriage' could hardly be more different than that imagined for Helen and Menelaos:

For their marriages the women were carried off by force, not when they were small and unfit for wedlock, but when they were in full bloom and wholly ripe. After the woman was thus carried off, the lady called the *num-*

---

[84] Cf. Merkelbach 1957.21. Of particular interest is the story (Hdt. 6.61) of how devotion to Therapnean Helen changed the looks of an ugly girl who eventually married the Spartan king.

[85] The idea of Helen's 'nourishing' presence may bring to mind the image in Sappho fr. 96 Voigt of the beloved girl compared to the moon which brings out the dew which causes flowers to bloom.

pheutria took her in charge, cut her hair off close to the head, put a man's cloak and sandals on her, and laid her down on a pallet, on the floor, alone, in the dark. Then the bridegroom, not impotent from too much drinking, but quite sober, having eaten as usual at the public mess (*phiditia*), slips stealthily into the room, unties the bride's girdle, and carries her over to the bed. After spending a short time with her, he goes away in an orderly fashion to his usual quarters to sleep with the other young men. And he continues to do this . . . visiting his bride by stealth . . . not for a short time only, but long enough so that some Spartans have become fathers before they have seen their wives in daylight. This practice not only taught restraint and moderation, but united husbands and wives when their bodies were full of creative energy and their affections new and fresh, not when they were sated and dulled by constant intercourse; there was always left behind in their hearts some residual spark of mutual longing and delight. (Plut. *Lyc.* 15.3–5, trans. Perrin, adapted)

This passage might also lend colour to the choir's teasing suggestion that Menelaos had had too much to drink before going to bed with Helen;[86] Xenophon too (*Lac.* 5.4–7) notes that the *sussitia* system put a rein on excessive drinking. Whereas the 'Lycurgan' husband spends only a brief part of his wedding-night with his bride, Menelaos and Helen will clearly be inseparable all night long. The prayer that the happy couple be granted εὐτεκνία (v. 51) draws colour from one of the most striking features of the Lycurgan system, the eugenic regulations which aimed at promoting healthy and strong children.[87] Here again a standard *topos* of the epithalamian is given a particular Spartan slant. The same may be true of the prayer for mutual φιλότης and πόθος (vv. 54–5). Both Xenophon (*Lac.* 1.5) and Plutarch (*Lyc.* 15.5, quoted above) note how Lycurgan restrictions upon marital intercourse increased a couple's desire with consequent eugenic effects. By itself Theocritus' εὐτεκνία could denote 'the blessing of a child/children' or 'healthy/strong children' or 'many children', a range of meanings which is activated by the prayer to Leto whose children, Apollo and Artemis, were notoriously few in number but all-powerful in effect, as Niobe found to her cost (*Il.* 24.603–17). Classical Sparta offered public encouragement to the production of multiple children in order to increase the population,[88] and though the children of Menelaos and Helen were not for the most part destined to become major

---

[86] Cf. also n. 39 above.

[87] Cf. Xen. *Lac.* 1.4–8. V. 21, ἢ μέγα κά τι τέκοιτ', εἰ ματέρι τίκτοι ὁμοῖον, is curiously paralleled by Xen. *Lac.* 1.3, where the hope is for women μεγαλεῖον . . . τι γεννῆσαι.

[88] Cf. Arist. *Pol.* 2 1270b1–5; P. Cartledge, *CQ* 31 (1981) 95–6; id., *Agesilaos and the Crisis of Sparta* (London 1987) 168–9.

figures of Greek mythology, we may well see another 'Spartan' feature here.[89]

If there is a 'Spartan' reading of Idyll 18, there may well also be a Ptolemaic one. Helen, especially the chaste Helen of Stesichorus and Euripides, was closely associated with Egypt and was the object of cult there.[90] She and her brothers, the Dioscuri, have an important place in Alexandrian poetry, and not only do Helen and Aphrodite–Arsinoe share similar powers and inhabit similar spheres,[91] but there are also clear indications that the women of the royal house, Helen, and Aphrodite together formed a composite model of ideal motherhood and womanhood (cf. esp. 15.110–11).[92] Kuiper[93] suggested long ago that the idealising picture of the mutual affection of Helen and Menelaos in Idyll 18 may be intended to point to the ideal couple of Philadelphus and Arsinoe, and Griffiths has elaborated upon this suggestion in an important discussion.[94] Griffiths noted that there are close links between many of the themes in Idyll 18 and those of Idyll 17, the encomium for Philadelphus; in one sense, of course, this is hardly surprising as encomiastic *topoi* are, as it were, epithalamic *topoi* which have been fulfilled – in the encomium children *are* like their parents, rulers *are* rich and happy, and so on. Nevertheless, the persistent recurrence of certain themes is indeed noteworthy. The stress on the lineage of the Ptolemaic house (17.13ff.) perhaps finds an echo in the repeated εὐπατρίδαι of 18.53; Ptolemy's mother, Berenice, is, like Helen, very closely associated with Aphrodite (17.34–52), and Ptolemy's parents are the very model of the mutual affection for which the Spartan choir prays (cf. 17.38–40). Many possible links must remain purely speculative, because the generality of the *topoi* involved permits a purely generic explanation. Thus, for example, the association of Zeus with great wealth which we find in both poems

---

[89] Homer explicitly says that Hermione was Helen's only child (*Od.* 4.12–14), but Hesiod (fr. 175 M–W), Sophocles (*El.* 539), and the Theocritean scholiast know others of whom we know little except for their names.

[90] Cf. Visser 1938.19–20; Gow II 348. Plutarch (*Hdt.* 12) asserts that Helen and Menelaos still receive 'many honours among the Egyptians', but this may be a tendentious memory of the Alexandrian cult.

[91] Cf. G. Basta Donzelli, 'Arsinoe simile ad Elena (Theocritus Id. 15, 110)', *Hermes* 112 (1984) 306–16.   [92] On these verses cf. above pp. 131–2.   [93] Art. cit. (n. 79) 226–7.

[94] F. Griffiths 1979.86–91; cf. also Gutzwiller 1992.367. C. Vatin, *Recherches sur le mariage et la condition de la femme mariée à l'époque hellénistique* (Paris 1970) 78–81, sought to reconstruct Ptolemaic court marriage ceremonial on the basis of the marriage of Jason and Medea in *Arg.* 4, Catullus 64, and a fragmentary epithalamian for Arsinoe (*SH* 961); curiously he has nothing to say about Idyll 18. One verse survives of a Callimachean treatment of Arsinoe's wedding (fr. 392, where see Pfeiffer's notes).

(17.75, 18.52) was naturally traditional, particularly in hymnic contexts.[95]

Outside Sparta, Helen's reputation was not always that of the faithful and loving wife, and we have seen that in Stesichorus Helen had already had a child by Theseus when she marries Menelaos; if we remember this, then some of the choir's praise of Menelaos' singular felicity will seem to carry a distinctly ironic charge. It is therefore hardly surprising that an 'ironic' reading of the poem as a whole has found critical favour. The clearest exposition of this reading is that of Effe,[96] part of whose account may simply be quoted:

> ... the observation that Menelaos had shut his bride in (5f.) makes the reader think with a smirk that he ought to have done that later also ... When the text says that the bride will belong to Menelaos forever (14f.), then the reader knows better ... It is not chance that the words with which Helen is praised as unique among Achaean women echo the corresponding praise of Penelope in the *Odyssey* (21.107) ... the author's irony cannot be missed. Ambivalent also is the conventional praise of the bride's beauty (22ff.), given that this caused so much suffering. ... The choir's prayer to Aphrodite to grant the young couple mutual love is not only ironised by the reader's knowledge of the future, but particularly ... because it was Aphrodite who promised Helen to Paris in return for his support in the goddesses' beauty contest. The final verse, Ὑμὴν ὦ Ὑμέναιε, γάμωι ἐπὶ τῶιδε χαρείης, once again makes clear the dissonance between wish and reality.

This case can be strengthened in various ways, and not merely by reference to the version of the story of Helen used by Stesichorus. The children of Helen and Menelaos were destined to remain mere mythological cyphers, except for Hermione, whose story, as Attic tragedy knew it, was an unhappy mixture of polyandry and attempted murder.[97] Helen's subsequent 'elopement' with Paris – itself clearly in origin an aetiology for Spartan marriage by ἁρπαγή – is perhaps foreshadowed by v. 37, 'Helen on whose eyes are all desires', and Helen herself would seem to be a paradigmatic problem for a Lycurgan Sparta which claimed to know no adultery because wives were freely shared in the interests of producing the best children (Plut. *Lyc.* 15.9–10).

A variant of the 'ironic reading' has been proposed by Jacob

---

[95] Cf., however, Call. *h.* 1. 91–6 where the Ptolemaic context is undeniable.

[96] Effe 1978.74–6 (my translation).

[97] Cf. Eur. *Andr.*; Sophocles, *Hermione* (evidence in *TrGF* 4.192–3).

Stern,[98] who sees the poem as epitomising 'the ambiguities in Helen's character'. The two halves of the poem which suggest a mortal and then a divine Helen, a beautiful woman who can be compared to a slender tree but then in fact a tree-goddess, point also to alternative futures for her: the desperate unhappiness with Paris *and* the immortality of Spartan legend. We might almost say that, in evoking both of these Helens, the poem reconstructs both Stesichorus' *Helen* and the infamous 'palinode'. The attraction of such a reading is that, whereas a straightforwardly 'Spartan' or 'Ptolemaic' reading places a seemingly intolerable burden of control upon the text, forcing readers to exercise their minds in a selective way hard to credit even for rhetorically oriented ancient readers, a *simple* 'ironic' reading – which should not be dismissed just because it so obviously suits modern sensibility – ignores many of the contrary indications of the text. The irony created by Idyll 18 is related to the familiar technique of writing the 'before' of a famous 'after': the song of the young and lovesick Cyclops, whose words are to turn out to be truer than he knows, is perhaps the most famous Theocritean example.[99] That poem exploits our knowledge – derived from epic and drama – of what came later, but it does not (unless our ignorance of Philoxenus causes us to go badly wrong)[100] reveal the unbridgeable gap between the Theocritean text and the legendary performance which it seeks to re-create. Here lies an important difference between Idyll 11 and Idyll 18. A wedding-song or cult performance is tied to the shared communal beliefs and values of the society in which it is performed. The marriage of Helen and Menelaos as an imitable model of marital perfection, even of only hoped-for perfection, is fine within a historical community which had shaped their image in this way. Outside that society, however, or re-created as an exercise in historical imagination, the picture becomes blurred and subject to interference from the audience's knowledge of other models and other systems. Theocritus could not re-create, even had he wanted to, an exact model of the songs of archaic Greece, not principally because of the loss of music or metre, but because the audience had gained in knowledge, and a different audience necessarily meant a very different song.

---

[98] 'Theocritus' *Epithalamium for Helen*', *RBPh* 56 (1978) 29–37.

[99] On this technique in general see A. Barchiesi, 'Future reflexive: two modes of allusion and Ovid's *Heroides*', *HSCP* 95 (1993) 333–65.   [100] Cf. above p. 6.

In choosing Helen as one of the figures of legend with whom to associate the ruling house, the Ptolemies asked their Greek subjects to practise a process of selective memory, of constant choice between alternatives. This dynamic political process is closely analogous to the very process of reading and interpretation, which also involves continual choice as to what is or is not relevant, and hence also a continual ignoring of 'meaning' which would cause interference or disturbance. Idyll 18 not only dramatises this process by taking as its subject perhaps the most famously 'difficult' marriage in Greek legend, but it also challenges us to read, like the anonymous passer-by, 'in Dorian fashion', i.e. to set aside stories of Helen's wantonness and celebrate the glorious goddess. As the choir looks to the future, they are given a kind of second sight in which Δωριστί acknowledges that there will be 'another' Helen, far less worthy of reverence. Not, of course, that Theocritus imagines that we will forget this other Helen; the obvious ironies of the poem keep her insistently before us.[101]

I referred earlier to Idyll 18 as a form of cultural rescue-archaeology, but it will now be clear that this poem itself is a kind of 'site' where excavation may hope to lay bare the different strata which have gone into its composition. Unlike an archaeological site, however, there is no virtue and indeed no point in seeking to keep the strata distinct. Through this poem the past has dripped and trickled until the whole text is saturated, and it is no longer possible to allot particular elements to particular chronologies. It will not be hard to think of other examples of this phenomenon from the high poetry of the third century.

---

[101] The text of 18.48 has been much debated, but the details do not, I hope, affect the interpretation offered here. If ἀνανέμειν, 'read', is indeed (or was believed to be) principally Doric (cf. Gow *ad loc.*), then this reinforces, rather than explains, Δωριστί.

CHAPTER 6

For the love of boys: Idylls 12, 29, and 30

THE PAEDERASTIC PAST

Nowhere perhaps is Theocritus more obviously the conscious heir to a rich poetic tradition than in the paederastic poetry of Idylls 7, 12, 13, 29, and 30.[1] In order to appreciate the place of these poems in the Theocritean corpus, it will be necessary to consider briefly the changing context of paederastic verse. As far at least as archaic erotic poetry is concerned, it is often difficult, and may be misguided, to seek to distinguish homoerotic poems on grounds of form, genre, occasion, or motif from poems of heterosexual desire. Apart from the elegiac verses of, probably, very varying date and provenance which are gathered in what is now called 'Theognis, Book 2', the amount of extant paederastic verse from the archaic and classical periods is actually quite small.[2] From the middle of the sixth century survive a few relevant fragments of Ibycus (*PMG* 288)[3] and Anacreon (*PMG* 346, 357, 359, 360),[4] and from the previous generation a couple of isolated paederastic couplets are ascribed to Solon (frr. 23 and 25 West).[5] Early fifth-century poetry of this kind is best illustrated for us by several passages of Pindar,[6] and the recently recovered elegiacs of Simonides.[7] Theocritus' debt to these archaic traditions will be the central concern of this chapter; nevertheless, it is not merely the poetic tradition that we must consider with regard to these poems of Theocritus.

---

[1] For the authenticity of Idyll 30 cf. below pp. 172, 175.   [2] Cf. Dover 1978.195–6.
[3] Note also *PMG* 282.40–8 (the beauty of Troilus as a model for Polycrates?), 289 (the rape of Ganymede), and *SLG* 227 which may be paederastic.
[4] Note also *PMG* 378. For the later biographical tradition of Anacreon as a lover of boys cf. Rosenmeyer 1992.17–18.   [5] Cf. E. Bethe, *RhM* 62 (1907) 441.
[6] Cf. below pp. 183–4. There is a full treatment of the paederastic theme of Olympian 1 in E. Krummen, *Pyrsos Hymnon. Festliche Gegenwart und mythisch-rituelle Tradition als Voraussetzung einer Pindarinterpretation* (Berlin/New York 1990) 184–204.   [7] Cf. above p. 26.

The classical period saw the production of a considerable body of philosophical and quasi-philosophical prose writing on the subject of *eros*. This work is best represented for us by the *Lysis*, *Symposium*, and *Phaedrus* of Plato, the *Symposium* of Xenophon, and the 'erotic discourse' preserved under the name of Demosthenes.[8] Although we should be wary of being misled by the chance survival of a group of texts with similar concerns, the fact that these works tend to privilege paederastic desire over heterosexual desire[9] and are, broadly speaking, associated with education and the cultivation of the high ideals of traditional *arete*, may well have meant that the cultural resonance of this type of *eros* and the poetry celebrating it were more strongly marked as 'different' in the following Hellenistic period than in the archaic and classical periods. In the Hellenistic period, paederasty remained a focus for philosophic moralising, as it offered new contexts in which to rework Plato's stern contrasts between the 'true *eros*', which leads towards educational and philosophic progress, and the base pursuit of bodily pleasure.[10] Even in the earlier periods, of course, the relevant texts emanate from élite circles and are associated with social institutions of a narrow focus, such as the aristocratic symposium or the athletic games, and therefore the difference between periods is not to be exaggerated. Nevertheless, there seem to be grounds for wondering whether paederastic subject-matter *might* carry with it a strong sense of the past, which could be activated when a poet so wished; we shall see that Theocritus exploited this sense of the past to the full.

An obvious place to look both for this sense of the past and for the possible influence of 'philosophical' writing about *eros* is the narrative of Heracles' loss of Hylas in Idyll 13:

> ἀλλὰ καὶ Ἀμφιτρύωνος ὁ χαλκεοκάρδιος υἱός,
> ὃς τὸν λῖν ὑπέμεινε τὸν ἄγριον, ἤρατο παιδός,
> τοῦ χαρίεντος Ὕλα, τοῦ τὰν πλοκαμῖδα φορεῦντος,
> καί νιν πάντ' ἐδίδασκε, πατὴρ ὡσεὶ φίλον υἱόν,
> ὅσσα μαθὼν ἀγαθὸς καὶ ἀοίδιμος αὐτὸς ἔγεντο·
> χωρὶς δ' οὐδέποκ' ἦς, οὔτ' εἰ μέσον ἆμαρ ὄροιτο,
> οὔθ' ὁπόχ' ἁ λεύκιππος ἀνατρέχοι ἐς Διὸς Ἀώς,
> οὔθ' ὁπόκ' ὀρτάλιχοι μινυροὶ ποτὶ κοῖτον ὁρῷεν,

---

[8] On such works cf. F. Lasserre, "Ἐρωτικοὶ λόγοι' *MH* 1 (1944) 169–78; Hunter 1983a.132; S. Goldhill, *Foucault's Virginity* (Cambridge 1995).

[9] Antisthenes, however, is credited with a περὶ παιδοποιίας ἢ περὶ γάμου ἐρωτικός ('On the production of children, or on marriage; an essay on *eros*'), and Theophrastus wrote at least two *erotika* (frr. 557–68 Fortenbaugh) from which anecdotes covering the full range of human and animal love are cited.

[10] There is much valuable information in the commentaries of Livrea and Lomiento on Cercidas fr. 6. For that fragment's reference to '*pothos* which is equal' cf. below pp. 180–1.

σεισαμένας πτερὰ ματρὸς ἐπ' αἰθαλόεντι πετεύρωι,
ὡς αὐτῶι κατὰ θυμὸν ὁ παῖς πεπονᾱμένος εἴη,
†αὐτῶι δ' εὖ ἕλκων† ἐς ἀλαθινὸν ἄνδρ' ἀποβαίη.

(13.5–15)

The bronze-hearted son of Amphitryon – he who withstood the savage lion – he too loved a boy, charming Hylas with his tresses still unshorn. And as a father teaches his beloved son, so did Heracles teach Hylas everything which he himself had learned and thus had become noble (*agathos*) and renowned in song (*aoidimos*). He never parted from him, neither at noon's onset, nor when dawn with her white steeds sped upward to the halls of Zeus, nor when the chickens looked twittering to their roosting-place as on the smoke-stained perch their mother shook her wings – so that the boy might be fashioned to his mind and . . . come to the true measure of a man.[11]

Here Heracles' aim is said to be the instruction and moral improvement of Hylas, just as in the normative model of 'good paederasty' put by Plato into the mouth of Pausanias (*Symp.* 184c5) the *eromenos* should become 'better either with respect to wisdom or to some other part of *arete*'. This tradition is exploited for humorous purposes in Idyll 5 when the 'obscene' banter of two rustics echoes the 'high' language of *charis*:

ΚΟ. ἀλλ' οὔτι σπεύδω· μέγα δ' ἄχθομαι εἰ τύ με τολμῇις
ὄμμασι τοῖς ὀρθοῖσι ποτιβλέπεν, ὅν ποκ' ἐόντα
παῖδ' ἔτ' ἐγὼν ἐδίδασκον. ἴδ' ἁ χάρις ἐς τί ποχ' ἕρπει·
θρέψαι καὶ λυκιδεῖς, θρέψαι κύνας, ὥς τυ φάγωντι.
ΛΑ. καὶ πόκ' ἐγὼν παρὰ τεῦς τι μαθὼν καλὸν ἢ καὶ ἀκούσας
μέμναμ', ὦ φθονερὸν τὺ καὶ ἀπρεπὲς ἀνδρίον αὔτως;
ΚΟ. ἀνίκ' ἐπύγιζόν τυ, τὺ δ' ἄλγεες· αἱ δὲ χίμαιραι
αἵδε κατεβληχῶντο, καὶ ὁ τράγος αὐτὰς ἐτρύπη.

(5.35–42)

comatas I'm in no hurry; but I am very upset that you should have the audacity to look me in the face – I was your teacher when you were still a boy. That's gratitude (*charis*) for you! Bring up puppies, nay wolf-cubs, to devour you.

lakon When can I remember learning or hearing anything good (*kalon*) from you, spiteful brute that you are!

comatas When I buggered you – that produced some pain! The she-goats bleated in mockery, and the he-goat mounted them.

In this passage, the bucolic context allows the poet to place the language of 'noble paederasty' under the most severe examination; we shall see that in Idylls 12, 29, and 30 also Theocritus probes the

[11] The text at the beginning of v. 15 is very uncertain.

ever-present possibility of opening a gap between the traditional language and ideals of paederasty and the reality of sexual desire. In Idyll 13, however, the point lies in the fact that Heracles was not just Hylas' *erastes*, but was in fact his surrogate father (v. 8) as he himself had killed Hylas' real father – a fact which Theocritus chooses to omit. It is therefore unsurprising that older critics saw in Heracles' paedagogical motives an example of the 'displaced fathering' of 'Dorian' paederasty, in which the older man trained the younger in both military and civic virtue.[12] There is, however, an obvious analogy, which *erastai* can exploit for their advantage,[13] between the paternal relationship and the 'classical' mode of paederasty, and so it is hardly necessary to invoke 'Dorian' traditions here. Besides, whatever historical developments lie behind 'Dorian paederasty', Idyll 13 is more likely to yield to literary explanations. More recent criticism has therefore stressed the humour and irony with which Theocritus treats the passion of the 'bronze-hearted son of Amphitryon'.[14] This is clearly an important aspect of the poem – particularly as Heracles is somehow to be analogous to the poet himself and to Nicias, the addressee – but we must be wary of leaping from the fact that the figure of Heracles is certainly ironised and that the story of Hylas is in part a story of transition from the rôle of *eromenos* to that of the male partner in heterosexual relations[15] to the notion that paederastic desire itself is, at least in literature, somehow 'out of date'. It could indeed carry with it the sense of the past to which I have referred, but the paederastic verses of the *Greek Anthology* (to say nothing of the later Greek novels) would seem to suggest that, at least as far as literature is concerned, this was not an inevitable resonance.[16] Not only do the motifs of heterosexual and paederastic epigrams

---

[12] Cf. Wilamowitz 1906.175. The issues raised by the notion of 'Dorian paederasty' are well beyond the scope of this book: for some guidance cf. Dover 1978 and 1988; P. Cartledge, 'The politics of Spartan pederasty' *PCPS* 26 (1981) 17–36; H. Patzer, *Die griechische Knabenliebe* (Wiesbaden 1982).

[13] Thus the advice of Theognis 1049–54, 'as a father to his son', is very likely from an *erastes* to his *eromenos*. Those verses are not in fact unlike 29.10–24 in tone and import.

[14] Cf. e.g. D. J. Mastronarde, 'Theocritus' Idyll 13: love and the hero', *TAPA* 99 (1968) 273–90; Gutzwiller 1981.19–29; ead. 1991.107; Goldhill 1991.248–9.

[15] For discussion and bibliography cf. Hunter 1993.38–41.

[16] The implications of Phanocles fr. 1 Powell are unclear in this regard. The case of Callimachus would, as always, require special treatment; for some extraordinary speculations about him cf. Fraser 1972.1 790–2. Cairns 1979.22 believes that the topic had become 'bourgeois' in the Hellenistic period. For 'casual' references to paederasty in Theocritus cf. 2.44, 150 (where the use of ἀνήρ for the expected παῖς deserves more attention than it has received), [8.47], and Epigram 3.

overlap extensively, but the earliest anthologists, such as Meleager, made no obvious distinction between these categories, mixing up epigrams of both kinds in books of *erotika*.[17] Nevertheless, it is to this period that we owe the first important poetic reflections of the theme of 'homo- vs. heterosexual love',[18] a theme which partly constructs the opposition between Lycidas and Simichidas in Idyll 7, and the fact that the three poems to be considered in this chapter rewrite archaic poetry in an overt manner which is distinguishable in important ways from the exploitation of prior texts in the rest of the corpus does suggest that Theocritus at least used an 'archaic' potential latent in the paederastic subject-matter. Hellenistic poetry is indeed 'studiously bisexual',[19] but it was no less alert to the available nuances of sexual behaviour than to any other cultural field. Idyll 23, a poem of probably late date (? first century BC) and uncertain authorship, tells how a statue of Eros took revenge on an *eromenos* whose disdain caused the suicide of an *erastes*; here too we may perhaps be dealing with a story set in an uncertain past with the paradigmatic force of an aetiology.

To move from these literary considerations to conclusions about social change is, of course, extremely difficult. The 'archaism' of these poems cannot be considered in isolation from the gradually increasing freedom with which literature explored heterosexual, particularly female, desire;[20] this freedom may have offered poets the possibility, rather than the necessity, of associating paederasty with 'the archaic' and heterosexual desire with 'the new', almost regardless of the social facts lying behind such a construction. Already in Aristophanes' *Clouds* (late fifth century), the paederastic interests of 'the Old Education' are given remarkable prominence, even though his 'modern' opponent casually juxtaposes 'boys' and 'women' as two of life's pleasures (v. 1073).[21]

IDYLLS 29 AND 30

The later biographical tradition had no doubt that Alcaeus of Lesbos (late seventh / early sixth century) had written paederastic verse. Horace's picture of him,

---

[17] Cf. A. Cameron, *The Greek Anthology from Meleager to Planudes* (Oxford 1993) 24–8.
[18] Cf. Asclepiades, *Anth. Pal.* 12.17 (= xxxvII G–P).   [19] A. Henrichs, *ZPE* 39 (1980) 22.
[20] Cf. Hunter 1993.46–7.
[21] Cf. Dover's edition pp. lxiv–vi. 'The New Education' illustrates 'the constraints of nature' from heterosexual adultery because his concern is with the ability to defend oneself in court (vv. 1075–82); nevertheless, the difference between the two opponents cannot be overlooked.

Liberum et Musas Veneremque et illi
semper haerentem puerum canebat
et Lycum nigris oculis nigroque
    crine decorum   (*Carm.* 1.32.9–12)

is amply confirmed by other sources.[22] Unfortunately, no single verse
from among the tattered scraps of his poetry which have reached us
can be securely identified as paederastic; even the Alcaic quotation
with which Idyll 29 begins, οἶνος, ὦ φίλε παῖ . . . καὶ ἀλάθεα (fr. 366
Voigt), lacks all context, however tempting it might be to assume that
the poem from which it was taken was paederastic. To refuse to
believe that antiquity did in fact know such verses might seem
excessively sceptical, and the circumstantial case does not depend
upon Idylls 29 and 30 alone.[23] Nevertheless, this is an area where
untested assumptions may be particularly dangerous.

    As far as textual transmission allows us to judge in such matters,[24]
Idylls 29 and 30 are written in an Aeolic dialect, although with an
important element of non-Aeolic poetic forms, and in stichic verse
units which we know to have been used by Sappho and Alcaeus. Idyll
29 is composed in the so-called 'Sapphic fourteen-syllable'
$(\times \times - \cup\cup - \cup\cup - \cup\cup - \cup \times)$ in which the whole of the second
book of the Alexandrian edition of Sappho[25] was composed; fragments
of Alcaeus in this metre also survive.[26] Idyll 30, like Idyll 28, is
composed in what is now usually designated the 'greater asclepiad'
$(\times \times - \cup\cup - - \cup\cup - - \cup\cup - \cup \times)$;[27] in this metre was composed
the third Alexandrian book of Sappho, and there are again
corresponding fragments of Alcaeus.[28] The related shorter verse in
which a glyconic is 'extended' by only one choriamb

---

[22] Cf. Page 1955.294–5, Nisbet and Hubbard on v. 11. Of particular importance for Theocritus
may have been the monograph *On Alcaeus* by Dicaearchus (frr. 94–9 Wehrli).

[23] It has been attractively suggested (e.g. Krevans 1983.214) that the paederastic song of
Lycidas in Idyll 7, with its repeated reference to Mytilene, points directly to Lesbian
love-lyric; this may well be true, but the new Simonides at least complicates the picture (cf.
above p. 26), and Sappho is as likely a point of reference as Alcaeus. F. Griffiths 1981.249–50
considers Idylls 29 and 30 to be 'ambitious adaptations of Sappho – as paederastic poems'. In
principle this is a nice idea, but the links with Alcaeus and Asclepiades look too strong.

[24] For the problem in general cf. above pp. 35–6.

[25] This edition was largely the work of Aristophanes of Byzantium and thus later than
Theocritus, cf. Pfeiffer 1968.205; S. Nicosia, *Tradizione testuale diretta e indiretta dei poeti di Lesbo*
(Rome 1976) 29–32.

[26] Sappho: Hephaestion 23.15 Consbruch; Alcaeus: frr. 141, 365, and (probably) 38 Voigt.

[27] Idyll 30 allows a pyrrhic ($\cup\cup$) base, whereas 28 (like, apparently, Alcaeus) does not.
Whether or not this should be added to the cumulative case against authenticity may be debated.

[28] Cf. Alcaeus frr. 50, 340–8 Voigt.

(x x — ∪∪ — — ∪∪ — ∪ x) was called the 'asclepiad' by ancient metricians; those who explain the name do so from the fact that it was used by Asclepiades,[29] although it is usually exemplified from Alcaeus.[30] The ancient names for the verse of Idylls 28 and 30 were the 'Sapphic sixteen-syllable' or the *choriambicum asclepiadeum*. Unless the model verse cited by a late metrician (*SH* 215) really is by Asclepiades, nothing in lyric by that poet survives;[31] nevertheless, it is not unlikely that this is purely a matter of chance,[32] and Gow and Page rightly note that 'a good many of [Asclepiades'] epigrams might, so far as theme and sentiment go, have been handled in lyrics like those of Theocritus'.[33] It is also relevant that a propemptic fragment of Callimachus in Doric dialect and 'greater asclepiads' survives:

ἀ ναῦς ἀ τὸ μόνον φέγγος ἐμὶν τὸ γλυκὺ τᾶς ζόας
ἅρπαξας, ποτί τε Ζανὸς ἱκνεῦμαι λιμενοσκόπῳ
(fr. 400 = *HE* 1343–4)[34]

O ship, which has snatched away the sole sweet light of my life, by Zeus who watches over harbours I beg you . . .

In the light of Callimachus' other erotic verse, it seems very probable that this propempticon was paederastic (cf. Lycidas' song in Idyll 7), as is an epigram of Meleager (*Anth. Pal.* 12.52 = LXXXI G–P) which seems indebted to it. There is then a serious, though circumstantial, case for believing that Asclepiades wrote paederastic verse in the Lesbian manner, presumably in imitation of Alcaeus.[35] Asclepiades certainly echoes Alcaeus in *Anth. Pal.* 12.50 (= XVI G–P) (unhappy love, although the gender of the beloved is not specified), and the opening of *Anth. Pal.* 12.135 (= XVIII G–P), οἶνος ἔρωτος ἔλεγχος, 'wine finds out love', may, like the opening of Idyll 29, be intended as a quotation of οἶνος . . . καὶ ἀλάθεα. Thus Idylls 29 and 30 may be not merely re-creations of Alcaeus' verse, but also imitations of earlier such re-creations. At any rate Theocritus seems to acknowledge

---

[29] Cf. (implicitly) Trichas *apud* Hephaestion 390.2 Consbruch (= *SH* 215); Atil. Fort., *Gramm. Lat.* VI 283.7, 295.19–20.

[30] Cf. Hephaestion 33.6 Consbruch; Trichas loc. cit. On the naming of stichic units cf. above pp. 4–5.

[31] *Anth. Pal.* 13.23 (= Epigram XXXIII G–P) is an epodic mixture of iambic lengths.

[32] For lyric in Hellenistic literary poetry cf. West 1982.149; Fantuzzi 1993a. 64–5; Parsons 1992.14–16; above p. 4.   [33] *HE* II 115.

[34] μόνον, ζόας, Ζανὸς Bentley: μον, ζωᾶς, Ζηνὸς Pal.

[35] Of Asclepiades' surviving poetry, *Anth. Pal.* 12.17 and 12.36 (= XXXVII and XLVI G–P) are paederastic, but of doubtful authenticity, and the priamel of *Anth. Pal.* 5.169 (= I G–P) could as well be homo- as heterosexual.

Asclepiades as an older model poet in the programmatic seventh Idyll (vv. 39–40). If it is correct that these poems have both an archaic and a post-classical model, then it will emerge that such a layered textuality would be completely in keeping with the central strategy of the poems themselves.

Comparison with Idyll 28 unfortunately makes the situation more, rather than less, uncertain. Idyll 28 is an address to a distaff which the poet is to present to the wife of his friend Nicias on a visit to Miletos. Hopkinson well characterises it as 'an exotic production . . . in Aeolic metre by a Dorian for an Ionian destination'.[36] What is important here is that, despite its dialectal and metrical form, virtually all the parallel material that may be adduced for this poem comes from Hellenistic epigram.[37] When every allowance for the state of our knowledge of archaic poetry has been made, it appears most probable that whereas the form of the poem is, broadly speaking, archaic, its subject-matter is post-classical. That this is also true for Idylls 29 and 30 is not to be assumed, but can hardly be ruled out.

The form of these poems is only 'broadly speaking' archaic because both the grammatical tradition[38] and the papyri (which all date from the Christian era)[39] suggest a division of the stichic poems of Sappho and Alcaeus into distichs. Sense-breaks do not, however, necessarily correspond with any division into distichs or quatrains, any more than there is a necessary sense break at the end of a stanza in the stanzaic poems. Lobel[40] saw it as significant that both 29 and 30 have a verse total divisible by four, because 'there is strong reason to believe that the *four-lined* stanza was a fundamental element in Alcaeus' method of composition'; here again, however, the possibility that we are dealing with chance must always be borne in mind.[41] However that may be, it is clear that in Idyll 29 four initial couplets are followed by a powerfully rhetorical monostich:[42]

πῶς ταῦτ' ἄρμενα, τὸν φιλέοντ' ὀνίαις δίδων;

How is this fair, to cause pain to the one who loves you?

[36] Hopkinson 1988.172.
[37] Cf. Cairns 1976. Cairns speculates about 'archaic models' (pp. 301–2) but his own helpful collection of evidence seems to tell a clear story.
[38] Hephaestion (cf. Sappho, Test. 228 Voigt) notes that Sappho composed 'greater asclepiads' in distichs.
[39] Cf., e.g., Alcaeus 38 and 50 Voigt; there is a full discussion in Bohnenkamp 1972.103–21.
[40] ΣΑΠΦΟΥΣ ΜΕΛΗ (Oxford 1925) xvi.   [41] Cf. Bohnenkamp 1972.115–16.
[42] So rightly Wilamowitz 1906.138. I cannot, however, follow his division of the rest of the poem.

This is then followed by a further three couplets (vv. 10–15), and then a triplet (vv. 16–18); textual problems cloud what follows, but vv. 21–4 look like a quatrain (or two couplets), and vv. 25–30 hang together in both sense (a version of the 'gather ye rosebuds' *topos*) and syntax as a single unit. The poem closes with a further set of five couplets (vv. 31–40). It seems clear, then, that this poem does seek to evoke the small verse-groupings of Lesbian lyric, with which Theocritus would of course have been familiar, whether or not the texts which he used were marked into such groupings;[43] the evocation is, however, only partial and is not allowed to dictate the structure of the whole. As so often in the Theocritean corpus, *mimesis* is something quite other than a striving for 'accurate reproduction'. As for Idyll 30, an initial quatrain is followed by three couplets and then a monostichic introduction to the lover's address to his *thumos* (v. 11). The speech itself consists of three couplets followed by a six-verse section (vv. 18–23) where further sub-division would be pointless, and it is followed by a monostichic conclusion (v. 24) and then the speech of the *thumos* which also defies sub-division. Here the case is less clear than with Idyll 29, and the chance that the observable structuring is accidental correspondingly greater. This may add something to the case for at least caution in the matter of this poem's authenticity.

Idyll 29 begins with a 'motto' from Alcaeus (fr. 366 Voigt), which is also one of the most trite pieces of Greek sympotic wisdom. The triteness characterises the speaker unflatteringly, but the Alcaic motto also compels us to read the poem against our knowledge of archaic paederastic verse and presents us with a speaker who self-consciously sets himself within the archaic ethos. It will emerge that this is not the only occasion when the principal character of Theocritus' paederastic verse seeks to legitimate his passion by adopting the authenticating voice of archaic verse. As I have already noted, we cannot tell just how much Alcaeus there actually is in this poem. The plea for openness and faithful dedication could easily have appeared in the Lesbian poet (cf., e.g., Theognis 87–90), but much else seems to derive from a later period. Denys Page's warning that 'we must certainly not *assume* [my italics] that the Aeolic love-poems

---

[43] Cf. Wilamowitz loc. cit., R. Stark, *Maia* 15 (1963) 380–1. The assertion of West, 1982.149, '[Hellenistic poets] were not in general concerned to write pseudo-song, either strophic or astrophic, but rather to widen the repertory of stichic and distichic metres available for literary purposes', requires modification, at least in the case of Theocritus. Cf. further above pp. 155–7 on Idyll 18.

of Theocritus are faithful to their models either in matter or in spirit'[44] is surely justified. It seems *a priori* likely that Theocritus, like Horace after him,[45] exploited the difference in period and social setting between his own time and that of his model for particular poetic effects. Without more knowledge of the archaic model, we will only ever be able to speculate about the nature of those effects, but some headway may be possible.

The monologue of Idyll 29 seems to be set at a symposium, which is already well advanced (μεθύοντας, v. 2). This is the setting which we may suppose both for Alcaeus and for most Theognidean paederastic verse.[46] In the course of the speech, however, the importance of the setting seems to fade somewhat, but may be refocused at the end as the lover threatens revenge if his pleas fall on deaf ears:

τότα δ' οὐδὲ κάλεντος ἐπ' αὐλείαις θύραις
προμόλοιμί κε, παυσάμενος χαλέπω πόθω.
(Vv. 39–40)

then, having ceased from the desire which is hard to bear, I would not come to the house-door, not even if you should call me.

'Then' apparently refers to the time when the boy has grown up and lost his youthful charms (vv. 25–30), for it is hard to believe that even this speaker would threaten the boy with 'if you don't do as I urge, I will give up wanting you' – a threat which the boy might well wish carried out. The scholiast takes the doors in these verses to be those of the boy's house, so that the lover imagines a time when the young man – now no longer so sought after – actively invites his *erastes* to call; καλεῖν, 'call', 'invite', is almost a technical term in this sense in erotic relations of all kinds.[47] The specificity of αὐλείαις ('outside-door') and the compound προμόλοιμι ('come out'), however, suggest rather that the door in question belongs to the speaker's house (so Gow etc.), so that the lover threatens not even to answer a visit from his former

---

[44] Page 1955.295.

[45] The treatment of the Alcaic motto of *Carm.* 1.37 (*nunc est bibendum*) by E. Fraenkel, *Horace* (Oxford 1957) 159 leaves something to be desired. As we have only two verses of Alcaeus' poem, the assertion that 'after the first clause . . . there is in the ode no further reminiscence of Alcaeus' may seem incautious; who is to say that, for example, the abuse of vv. 10–12 did not have some parallel in Alcaeus?

[46] Particularly close to Idyll 29 is Theognis 1299–1304; cf. also 1305–10, 1327–34. For the sympotic context of the Alcaic motto of 29.1 cf. W. Rösler, 'Wine and truth in the Greek *symposion*' in O. Murray and M. Tecuşan (eds.), *In Vino Veritas* (London 1995) 106–12.

[47] Cf. 2.101, 116, 3.7; Asclepiades, *Anth. Pal.* 5.134 (= XIII G–P); Ter. *Eun.* 46–9 etc.

eromenos. Such a threat marks the speaker's delusion, for the circumstances of such a visit are hard to imagine. What is envisaged is a fate something like that which Horace foresees for Lydia, whose charms are now fading:

in uicem moechos anus arrogantis
flebis in solo leuis angiportu
Thracio bacchante magis sub inter-
        lunia uento

            (*Carm.* 1.25.9–12)

In your turn, old and worthless, you will weep at the disdain of the young men, as the Thracian wind riots around the deserted alley on moonless nights.

Like Lydia, the Theocritean *eromenos* will in the future have to solicit 'custom', although the Greek poem lacks the savage visualisation of the Horatian ode. In their introduction to Horace's poem, Nisbet and Hubbard note that it 'has affinities with the . . . *paraclausithyron* . . . [which] sometimes contains . . . predictions that the beauty of the lady will fade, and prayers that she will then suffer in turn'.[48] By foreshadowing a time when the young man will himself be *exclusus*, the poet refocuses the scene so that we may, if we wish, imagine *the speaker* to be currently in this position. This is not to say that the poem is a version of the *paraclausithuron*, like, say, the song of the goatherd in Idyll 3; rather, the poet evokes different situations from the repertory of erotic poetry with a fluidity which is to become more familiar in the longer poems of the Roman elegists.[49]

The *erastes* of Idyll 29 appeals to his 'dear boy' through a set of values which are very familiar in the Theognidean corpus: the need for openness, for true and lasting *philia*, and the importance of good public reputation (vv. 21–2). He claims to speak with the wisdom of age (vv. 10–11), and out of concern for the young man. I have already noted how the opening 'motto' shows us that he sees his love in historical perspective. The same could be said for his wish that he and the *pais* should become Ἀχιλλέιοι φίλοι, that is inseparable friends like Achilles and Patroclus, whose friendship, at least as it was

[48] Cf. also Cairns 1972.85–9.
[49] Cf., e.g., D. Kennedy, *The Arts of Love* (Cambridge 1993) 18–21 on Tibullus 1.2. Asclepiades seems to have been an important figure in the development of the Hellenistic *paraclausithuron* (cf., e.g., S. Tarán, *The Art of Variation in the Hellenistic Epigram* (Leiden 1979) 52–114; Krevans 1983.216–17), and this too may be added to the case for this poet's importance in the traditions of Idyll 29.

conceived in the classical period,[50] grew out of an *erastes–eromenos* relationship.[51] Such a wish may seem at least ironised by the vividness with which the speaker has already described the young man's promiscuity – in vv. 14–18 he is a bird who hops from one branch[52] to another – and this sense of irony is certainly strengthened by the speaker's vision of himself as a Heracles:

νῦν μὲν κἀπὶ τὰ χρύσια μᾶλ' ἕνεκεν σέθεν
βαίην καὶ φύλακον νεκύων πεδὰ Κέρβερον
(vv. 37–8)

though now for you I would go to fetch the golden apples or Cerberus, the guard of the dead . . .

The golden apples of the Hesperides and the trip to the Underworld were traditionally Heracles' greatest tasks, the ones which in differing traditions represented the final steps towards immortality.[53] Heracles was a notorious *erastes* of both women and boys,[54] and an epic poet called Diotimos, who may well have written before Theocritus, wrote a poem in which Eurystheus was the hero's *paidika* and the labours were presumably represented as acts of devotion of the kind imagined by the speaker of Idyll 29.[55] The humorous self-aggrandisement of this projection into the mythic sphere has a close analogue in Idyll 12.[56] We may well wonder whether this speaker was ever 'made of iron' (29.24).[57]

Not only is the speaker's delusion revealed by the terms in which he images the relationship, but the true nature of his desires seeps out

[50] The 'classic' treatment seems to have been Aeschylus' *Myrmidons*, cf. Dover 1978.197–8. An interest in the relations of Achilles and Patroclus 'before' the *Iliad* would be typical of Hellenistic poetry, cf. above p. 165.

[51] F. Cairns, *Hermes* 105 (1977) 131–2, concludes from this poem that the theme of lifelong *philia* arising from an erotic relationship was found in early Greek lyric. The conclusion may be correct, but the argument is a very dangerous one; cf. above p. 176.

[52] The temptation to see a *double entendre* in κλάδος should probably not be resisted, cf. perhaps *Anacreontea* 18.13 West, Lat. *ramus* (discussed by J. N. Adams, *The Latin Sexual Vocabulary* (London 1982) 28); the *double entendre* is helped by the phallic ὅρπετον in v. 13 (cf. Ar. *Eccl.* 909 (with Ussher's note); Adams op. cit. 30–1), which rewrites Sappho fr. 130 Voigt in a quite new mode. The idea of the beloved as a little bird may develop from the comparison of Erotes to birds, cf. 15.120–2; Bion fr. 13; Longus, *D&C* 2.7.1; Hunter 1983a.132–3.

[53] Cf. Bond on Eur. *HF* 394–9.

[54] For the latter cf. Idyll 13; Antisthenes frr. 24–5 Caizzi; Xen. *Mem.* 2.1.24; *POxy.* 3723 (discussed by P. J. Parsons, 'Eine neugefundene griechische Liebeselegie', *MH* 45 (1988) 65–74); Plut. *Amat.* 17.761d–e etc.

[55] Cf. Ath. 13 603d = *SH* 393; for the dating cf. U. von Wilamowitz, *Euripides Herakles* (Berlin 1889) I 310 n. 78; *HE* II 106.   [56] Cf. below pp. 190–4.

[57] μόλθακον (v. 24) is lightly ironic in view of this word's associations with the 'softness' of pretty boys, cf. 7.105, Dover 1978.79; the point is made by ἀπάλω in the following verse.

from the coded language of *eros* in which they are couched. The boy's beauty (vv. 16, 25 'by your soft mouth') may cause us to suspect that the speaker's desire for constant and unique access to the young man's body is at least as great as any concern for his reputation, education, and *philia*. The chance for a poet to exploit these two ways of seeing paederastic *eros* arose not merely from the 'euphemistic' language of *charis* which marked the literary expression of such relationships, but also from the philosophical tradition which sought to distinguish a 'good' *eros*, which aimed at *arete* and in which the physical gratification of the *erastes* was not the principal focus, from a 'bad' *eros* in which the older man's lust for such gratification was the main motive.[58] Any relationship could, broadly speaking, exemplify either kind of *eros*, depending on the circumstances and motive of the representation; what the *erastes* may see (or claim to see) as a concern for *arete* and *kleos*, others (including the *eromenos*) may see as sexual pestering (ἐνοχλεῖν, v. 36). The importance of generic factors is made clear by a fragment of the Middle Comedy poet Amphis:

> τί φήις; σὺ ταυτὶ προσδοκαῖς πείσειν ἐμέ,
> ὡς ἔστ' ἐραστὴς ὅστις ὡραῖον φιλῶν
> τρόπων ἐραστής ἐστι, τὴν ὄψιν παρεὶς
> σώφρων τ' ἀληθῶς; οὔτε τοῦτο πείθομαι
> οὔθ' ὡς πένης ἄνθρωπος ἐνοχλῶν πολλάκις
> τοῖς εὐποροῦσιν οὐ λαβεῖν τι βούλεται
>
> (Fr. 15 K–A)

What do you say? Do you expect me to believe that there is a lover who fancies a pretty boy, but loves only his character, while ignoring his looks and being really chaste? I believe this no more than I believe that a poor man who constantly pesters the rich doesn't want something

In this fragment we can see the early stages of the tradition which culminates in the familiar figure of the lecherous moralist (Eumolpus in Petronius' *Satyrica*, for example). The 'two voices' of Idyll 29 are a different exploitation of the possibilities for deconstruction offered by the classical literary representation of 'noble' paederasty. Here again we may suspect that this kind of irony was not one which Theocritus found in his archaic models.

The lover's happiness is totally at the mercy of the beloved's whim:

---

[58] Cf. above p. 168.

κὦταν μὲν σὺ θέλῃς, μακάρεσσιν ἴσαν ἄγω
ἀμέραν· ὅτα δ' οὐκ ἐθέλῃς σύ, μάλ' ἐν σκότωι.

(Vv. 7–8)

When you are willing, my day is equal to that of the blessed gods;
but when you are unwilling, I am plunged in darkness.

This happiness, however, is constituted by the young man's physical
compliance; 'be willing' means 'be willing <to allow me sexual
access>'.[59] So too, the hyperbole of vv. 7–8 finds its closest parallels
in triumphant effusions of sexual conquest. Thus Dioscorides rejoices
that he 'became immortal' through a particularly enjoyable sexual
act with Doris (*Anth. Pal.* 5.55 = v G–P),[60] and Propertius more than
once hopes for 'immortality' of a similar kind.[61] Thus it is the tension
between, on the one hand, the physicality of the lover's desire and, on
the other, the archaic ethos to which he claims to aspire and the
archaic form in which that desire is expressed which lies at the heart of
the poem's power.

One further aspect of this tension deserves notice here. The lover
warns the boy that he should return his love, μοι τὦραμένωι συνέραν
ἀδόλως σέθεν, 'return my love which is without guile' (v. 32). συνερᾶν,
'to join in *eros*', is a very unusual verb in such a context.[62] In the
'classical' paederasty described by Pausanias in Plato's *Symposium* the
emotion which the *erastes* seeks in the *eromenos* is *philia*.[63] ἀντερᾶν, 'to
love in return', is found in a heterosexual context in Xenophon (*Symp.*
8.3),[64] and after Theocritus the verb is used by Bion in a relevant context:

> ὄλβιοι οἱ φιλέοντες ἐπὴν ἴσον ἀντεράωνται.
> ὄλβιος ἦν Θησεὺς τῶ Πειριθόω παρεόντος,
> εἰ καὶ ἀμειλίκτοιο κατήλυθεν εἰς Ἀΐδαο·
> ὄλβιος ἦν χαλεποῖσιν ἐν Ἀξείνοισιν Ὀρέστας
> ὤνεκά οἱ ξυνὰς Πυλάδας ἄιρητο κελεύθως·
> ἦν μάκαρ Αἰακίδας ἑτάρω ζώοντος Ἀχιλλεύς·
> ὄλβιος ἦν θνάισκων ὅ οἱ οὐ μόρον αἰνὸν ἄμυνεν.

(Fr. 12 Gow)

---

[59] For this use of the simple verb cf. *Anth. Pal.* 12.29.1 (= *HE* 42), and perhaps Catullus 8.7
    (where notice the imagery of the following verse, *fulsere uere candidi tibi soles*).
[60] Cf. Straton, *Anth. Pal.* 12.177.6 ἀποθειωθείς.
[61] 2.14.10, 2.15.37–40. Note that this latter passage also uses the motif of the beloved's
    'willingness', *mihi si secum talis concedere noctes | illa uelit*. Rothstein *ad loc.* cites Plaut. *Curc.* 167
    sum deus, but there the point is somewhat different.
[62] At Eur. *Andr.* 223, *PMG* 902.1, and Plut. *Ages.* 20 the sense is different. The meaning of the
    Menandrean title ἡ Συνερῶσα is unclear.
[63] Cf. Dover 1978.52–3; the joke at Xen. *Hiero* 11.11 is an important witness (if correctly
    understood).   [64] Cf. ἀντιφιλεῖν in *CEG* 2.530 (fourth century).

Happy are lovers whose love finds equal return. Happy was Theseus when Peirithous was there, even if he had to descend to fierce Hades. Happy in the terrible Pontus was Orestes, because Pylades undertook the voyage with him. Blessed was Achilles, descendant of Aiakos, while his companion was alive; happily he would have died because he did not protect him from grim fate.

The equal partnership which Bion illustrates from the realm of myth is precisely the kind of relationship summoned up by the archaising fantasy of the speaker of Idyll 29. Our classical sources do, of course, hold out the hope for such lifelong relationships,[65] but it is really only in the vision of the *Phaedrus* that the *eromenos* himself feels *eros*, which he himself calls *philia* (255c–e), and the lovers lead a life 'of blessedness and harmony' (μακάριος καὶ ὁμονοητικὸς βίος, 256b1). Here again, then, it seems likely that we can trace a particularly Hellenistic element in the ideas of Idyll 29. In marking the poem's distance from its archaic models, it also marks the unreality of the speaker's wishes. The appeal to the brevity of youthful beauty and to the inevitable onrush of time (vv. 25–30) are ironically pathetic in a poem that evokes a *kleos* which lives for ever. Historical process makes short work of the fragility of the individual. The attempt to re-create the past, whether in form or ethos, can never be more than a partial and distorting *mimesis*.

In turning to Idyll 30, it is necessary to note that, but for a few scraps on the Antinoopolis papyrus, this lacunose and corrupt text is preserved in only one manuscript, which was not published until 1866. In a number of places there is real doubt not just about the text but also about the general sense of what the poet intended. There is a broad tendency in Theocritean scholarship to regard extensive corruption as a marker of spurious authenticity, and we have already noted metrical and structural features which, though of little weight by themselves, might lend force to a cumulative case against this poem. Nevertheless, the case against Theocritean authorship is very far from proved, and the poem clearly belongs with the other texts considered in this chapter.

Idyll 30 begins with a lament by a miserable and ageing lover who is suffering with passion for a boy. A recent sight of the boy has caused new pain, and he narrates how he came home and reproved his *thumos*

---

[65] Cf., e.g., Pl. *Symp.* 183e5–6 (Pausanias); Xen. *Symp.* 8.18–19 (where there is the revealing phrase ἐρῶντες τῆς φιλίας).

for its wantonness;[66] the *thumos* replies that it is powerless to do anything against Eros, who conquers even Zeus and Aphrodite. As in Idyll 29, we suspect that the lover is suffering from delusion as well as passion. In vv. 7–8 he describes his recent encounter with the young man:

> ἔχθες γὰρ παρίων ἔδρακε λέπτ᾽ ἄμμε δι᾽ ὀφρύων,
> αἰδέσθεις προσίδην ἄντιος, ἠρεύθετο δὲ χρόα·

> For yesterday as he passed by he gave me a quick glance from be-
> tween his lids; he was too shy to look me in the face and he blushed;

The coy glance and the blush may indeed be a sign of proper *aidos*, but the boy may also be flirting to torment his lover (cf. Ar. *Clouds* 980). Such self-delusion sits well with a strategy of blaming the *thumos* for behaviour inappropriate to the age of the speaker; like the morally weak (ἀκρατής) man of the philosophic tradition, the speaker is unable to resist the call of desire: his *thumos* is stronger than his reason. The irony of the poem lies in the fact that it is the speech of the *thumos* which is then characterised by an appeal to reason, whereas the lover hectors his *thumos* like a comic father lecturing his wayward son.[67] This separation of the *thumos* from the self may go back to such things as the conversations of the Homeric hero with his *thumos*, and it is perhaps best known from Medea's famous monologue in Euripides' tragedy where, however, the basic sense of *thumos* seems to be 'anger' (*Med.* 1056–80); together with the separation of the self from the *psuche*, it seems, however, to have become something of a *topos* of Hellenistic love epigram.[68] Thus 'Plato' too blames his *thumos* for stupid behaviour (though of a rather different kind):

> νῦν, ὅτε μηδὲν Ἄλεξις ὅσον μόνον εἶφ᾽ ὅτι καλός,
>   ὦπται, καὶ πάντηι πᾶς τις ἐπιστρέφεται.
> θυμέ, τί μηνύεις κυσὶν ὀστέον, εἶτ᾽ ἀνιήσηι
>   ὕστερον; οὐχ οὕτω Φαῖδρον ἀπωλέσαμεν;
>   (Epigram VI Page)

---

[66] I follow Hutchinson 1988.167 n. 40 in rejecting Gow's doubts that this is indeed the scenario envisaged; the parallel poem in Meleager (cf. below) is strong support for this view. Hutchinson is also correct that εἰσκαλεῖν is not the expected verb in this context; he tentatively suggests δὴ καλέσαις and I have toyed with ἐγκαλέσαις.

[67] Cf. perhaps Ter. *Ad.* 685–95.

[68] Cf. Meleager, *Anth. Pal.* 12.132a, 5.24 (= XXI, XLI G–P), Philodemus, *Anth. Pal.* 5.131 (= XI G–P) etc. Walsh 1990 has much of interest on this subject, although the focus of his discussion is rather different.

Now, when I had merely said that Alexis was pretty, everyone is on fire and everyone turns to him. My soul (*thumos*), why do you show a bone to dogs, only to suffer afterwards? Is not this how we lost Phaidros?[69]

and Meleager conducts a conversation with his *thumos* along very similar lines to that of Idyll 30:

βεβλήσθω κύβος· ἅπτε· πορεύσομαι. – ἠνίδε τόλμαν·
οἰνοβαρές, τίν' ἔχεις φροντίδα; – κωμάσομαι,
κωμάσομαι. – ποῖ, θυμέ, τρέπηι; – τί δ' Ἔρωτι λογισμός;
ἅπτε τάχος. – ποῦ δ' ἡ πρόσθε λόγων μελέτη;
– ἐρρίφθω σοφίας ὁ πολὺς πόνος· ἓν μόνον οἶδα
τοῦθ', ὅτι καὶ Ζηνὸς λῆμα καθεῖλεν Ἔρως.

(*Anth. Pal.* 5.131 = xix G–P)

Cast the die! Light the torches! I shall be on my way.' 'Look at this recklessness. What do you have in mind, drunken sot?' 'I shall go on a *komos*, on a *komos*.' 'Where, my soul (*thumos*), are you off to?' 'What has Love to do with reason (*logismos*)? Quickly light the torches!' 'Where is all your training in argument?' 'The long labours of education can be damned. All I know is that Eros also brought low the high mind of Zeus.'

Already in Homer[70] the *thumos* urges action ('but if your great *thumos* urges you on . . .') and may be the seat of erotic desire (*Od.* 18.212). In what survives of archaic lyric it, more often than the *psuche*, is the seat of desire.[71] The address to the *thumos* or the *psuche* becomes familiar in all literary genres;[72] the earliest surviving example in an erotic context may be in Simonides (fr. eleg. 21 West), but of particular interest is a famous fragment of Pindar:

χρῆν μὲν κατὰ καιρὸν ἐρώ-
    των δρέπεσθαι, θυμέ, σὺν ἁλικίαι·
τὰς δὲ Θεοξένου ἀκτῖνας πρὸς ὄσσων
μαρμαρυζοίσας δρακείς
ὃς μὴ πόθωι κυμαίνεται, ἐξ ἀδάμαντος
ἢ σιδάρου κεχάλκευται μέλαιναν καρδίαν κτλ.

(Fr. 123 Sn–M)

---

[69] ἀπωλέσαμεν should, I think, be regarded as a true plural, 'you and I lost'.

[70] On the *thumos* in archaic poetry cf., e.g., J. Bremmer, *The Early Greek Concept of the Soul* (Princeton 1983), esp. 54–6; Onians 1951.44–50; C. P. Caswell, *A Study of Thumos in Early Greek Epic* (Leiden 1990); S. D. Sullivan, 'Person and θυμός in the poetry of Hesiod', *Emerita* 61 (1993) 15–40; id., 'The relationship of person and θυμός in the Greek lyric poets (Part One)' *SIFC* 87 (1994) 12–37.

[71] Cf. Anacreon, *PMG* 375; Sappho fr. 1.4, 18, 27 Voigt; Alcaeus fr. 283.4 Voigt. For the *psuche* cf. Anacreon, *PMG* 360.4 and perhaps Sappho fr. 62.8 Voigt.

[72] Cf. F. Leo, *Der Monolog im Drama* (Abh. Göttingen 10.5, Berlin 1908) 94–113.

> My soul, you must pluck the flowers of love at the right time, when
> in your prime; but the man who can behold the sparkle in the flash-
> ing eyes of Theoxenos and not be carried away on a wave of desire,
> indeed his black heart is forged of adamant or iron . . .

Here, as in Idyll 30, the speaker seeks to reason with his *thumos*,
apparently on the grounds of his age, but concludes by acknowledging
the irresistible attractions of Theoxenos. Vv. 2ff., 'but the man who
can behold . . .', are unlikely to be the answer of the *thumos*,[73] but this
passage does use the 'voice of reason' and the 'voice of desire' in a way
which clearly foreshadows Idyll 30 and which may shed some light on
the nature of Theocritus' poetic reconstruction.

The speech of the Theocritean *thumos*, like that of Aphrodite
(another externalised 'inner voice'?) in Sappho fr. 1, is 'pronouncedly
urbane'[74] and wittily persuasive in the constructed opposition between
its own feebleness and lightness and the 'great mind of Zeus and of the
Cyprian-born herself' which is no match for Eros; the latter are
'brought low' whereas the former is 'lifted up and swiftly carried away':

ταῦτα γάρ, ὤγαθε,
βόλλεται θέος ὃς καὶ Δίος ἔσφαλε μέγαν νόον
καὔτας Κυπρογενήας· ἔμε μάν, φύλλον ἐπάμερον
σμίκρας δεύμενον αὔρας, ὀνέλων ὦκα φόρει <πνόαι>.

(30.29–32)

> For this, my friend, is the will of that god who brought low the great
> mind of Zeus and of the Cyprian-born herself. Me with a breath he
> lifts and swiftly bears away, like a leaf that lives but for a day and is
> the sport of lightest airs.

The comparison of the *thumos* to a leaf draws upon Glaukos' famous
comparison of the generations of men to the generations of leaves
(*Iliad* 6.145–9); this comparison is the opening of Glaukos' reply to
Diomedes' expression of unwillingness to fight with him if Glaukos is
a god, because fighting with gods has disastrous consequences. The
Homeric context thus reinforces the point of the Theocritean verses.
φύλλον ἐπάμερον, 'a leaf that lives but for a day', looks to the Iliadic
passage to suggest the insignificance of the single individual, the
single ἐφήμερος, and thus suggests how trivial a task it is for Eros to
carry off such a thing. From the archaic period on, however, we find
the *thumos* itself (like the *psuche*) conceived as a kind of breath or

---

[73] If they were, μέν would have to be 'emphatic' and δέ would mark the adversative opening of a
riposte (cf. Denniston 1954.166–7, 361).   [74] Hutchinson 1988.169.

breeze;[75] this conception here becomes one in which the 'breath' which sports with the *thumos* is *Eros*, himself as proverbially fickle as the breezes. As beauty may be described in terms appropriate to a 'breeze' or emanation from the beloved,[76] the 'breeze' of v. 32 resonates both inside and outside the comparison: the smallest 'whiff' of a desirable boy is sufficient to undo all the good intentions of the lover.

There is one further detail of the poem which may help us to gauge its distance from any archaic models. In v.2 the lover describes his passion as a recurrent fever:

τετόρταιος ἔχει παῖδος ἔρος μῆνά με δεύτερον

a quartan passion for a boy has held me for two months now

Gow rightly notes that the 'resemblance between his love and the fever resides in its intermittency, not in the length of the intervals between the attacks'. Such an epigrammatic conceit follows easily after νοσήματος, but it is at least curious that the same notion recurs in Callimachus' famous description of the illnesses which prevent Cydippe's father from marrying her off:

δειελινὴν τὴν δ' εἷλε κακὸς χλόος, ἦλθε δὲ νοῦσος,
    αἶγας ἐς ἀγριάδας τὴν ἀποπεμπόμεθα,
ψευδόμενοι δ' ἱερὴν φημίζομεν· ἣ τότ' ἀνιγρή
    τὴν κούρην Ἀίδεω μέχρις ἔτηξε δόμων.
δεύτερον ἐστόρνυτο τὰ κλισμία, δεύτερον ἡ παῖς
    ἑπτὰ τεταρταίωι μῆνας ἔκαμνε πυρί.
τὸ τρίτον ἐμνήσατο γάμου κάτα, τὸ τρίτον αὖτις
    Κυδίππην ὀλοὸς κρυμὸς ἐσωικίσατο.
                                         (Call. fr. 75.12–19)

In the afternoon an evil pallor came upon her; the disease seized her, which we banish on the wild goats and which we falsely call the holy disease. That grievous sickness then wasted the girl even to the halls of Hades. A second time the couches were spread; a second time the maiden was sick for seven months with a quartan fever. A third time they thought of marriage; a third time again a deadly chill settled on Cydippe.

[75] Cf. *Il.* 21. 386 δίχα δέ σφιν ἐνὶ φρεσὶ θυμὸς ἄητο ('in two ways did the *thumos* in their chests blow like the wind'); Onians 1951.44–50; and Caswell op. cit. (n. 71); for the *psuche* in this context cf. also E. Vermeule, *Aspects of Death in Early Greek Art and Poetry* (Berkeley 1979) 7–11 (with nn. on pp. 212–13).   [76] Cf. Onians 1951.73–4; Richardson on *h. Dem.* 276.

With Callimachus' poem – in which, it is worth noting, the poet also separates himself from his *thumos* in order to reprove its behaviour (vv. 4–7) – Idyll 30 shares not merely the quartan fever but also δεύτερον, though used in different senses. In Callimachus τεταρταίωι, 'quartan', is to be given its full medical flavour, as it follows the (ironically misleading) medical sophistication of vv. 12–14 and comes as part of a detailed 'case history' in which the numeration of months is important. 'Healing' finally comes through an intervention of Apollo, though Apollo the prophet rather than Apollo the doctor. In Idyll 30, however, there is no such complex nest of resonance, and this may strengthen the argument for Callimachean influence.[77] As with Idyll 29, therefore, this poem is constructed of textual layers from both the recent and the distant past, and these lend both historical perspective and historicising irony to the pain of unrequited passion.

IDYLL 12

Idyll 12 begins, as we have seen, with a marker of its Ionic dialect.[78] The explanation for the dialect of the poem has naturally been sought in the literary models presupposed by the poem. Wilamowitz[79] noted that it was natural to think of Anacreon, but was puzzled because the opening verses seemed to rework a surviving fragment of Sappho:

> ἦλθες, †καὶ† ἐπόησας, ἔγω δέ σ' ἐμαιόμαν
> ὂν δ' ἔψυξας ἔμαν φρένα καιομέναν πόθωι
> (Fr. 48 Voigt)

> You came . . . I desired you, and you cooled my heart which was burning with desire.

A reworking of Sappho in a quite different idiom would hardly surprise in Theocritus, but we will see that there are in fact grounds for doubting whether Sappho really is behind these verses; we may have to do with an accidental similarity. If, however, Sappho is in fact evoked here, the point will be that, whereas the Sapphic speaker is 'cooled' (i.e. sexually satisfied) by the arrival of the beloved, the

---

[77] It may be worth noting that Aristainetos' version of the story of Acontius and Cydippe gives prominence to Cydippe's *aidos* and blush (1.10.40–5 Mazal); so too the charm of Acontius' cheeks is described (1.10.8–9), and the motif of lovers stepping into his footprints (1.10.13–14) perhaps helps with the difficult vv. 3–4 of Idyll 30. There is thus some reason to suspect Callimachean influence on Idyll 30. Note that Acontius himself was the object of paederastic attention (frr. 68–9 Pfeiffer).   [78] Cf. above pp. 40–1.

[79] Wilamowitz 1906.179.

speaker of Idyll 12 merely finds greater emotional torment. As for any debt to Anacreon, it is obviously tempting to imagine that Theocritus would imitate the Ionian singer of wine and boys, who was also to be included in the Alexandrian canon of lyric poets; the hexameter form of the poem may be ascribed both to general poetic trends in the third century[80] and to the now familiar impulse towards partial rather than complete *mimesis* of archaic models. No explicit echoes of what we possess of Anacreon can be identified, but one of the poems of the so-called *Anacreontea*, a collection ranging in date from Hellenistic to Byzantine times, is at least suggestive:[81]

δότε μοι, δότ' ὦ γυναῖκες
Βρομίου πιεῖν ἀμυστί·
ἀπὸ καύματος γὰρ ἤδη
προδοθεὶς ἀναστενάζω·
δότε δ' ἀνθέων, ἑλίνου·
στεφάνους δότ' οἷς πυκάζω
τὰ μέτωπά μου, 'πικαίει.
τὸ δὲ καῦμα τῶν ἐρώτων,
κραδίη, τίνι σκεπάζω;
παρὰ τὴν σκιὴν Βαθύλλου
καθίσω· καλὸν τὸ δένδρον,
ἀπαλὰς δ' ἔσεισε χαίτας
μαλακωτάτωι κλαδίσκωι·
παρὰ δ' αὐτὸ νέρθε ῥοιζεῖ
πηγὴ ῥέουσα Πειθοῦς.
τίς ἂν οὖν ὁρῶν παρέλθοι
καταγώγιον τοιοῦτο;

> (*Anacreontea* 18 West)

Ladies, give me, give me some Bromian to gulp down, for I am already betrayed by the heat and am groaning. Give me flowers and vine leaves; give me garlands to wreathe my brow, for I am on fire. With what, my heart, shall I ward off the fierce heat of the Loves? I shall sit in the shade of Bathyllos: it is a fine tree, and soft is the hair it waves on the tenderest of branches; nearby whispers a flowing spring of Persuasion. Who could see such a resting-place and pass it by?

Here the poet seeks shade from the heat of love in the *locus amoenus* of the beloved;[82] common to both poems (as to Sappho fr. 48) is the idea of the presence of the beloved offering cooling release from the heat of

---

[80] Cf. above p. 4.
[81] I give West's text, as the relevant issue is not affected by the textual uncertainties of the Anacreontic.   [82] Cf. Rosenmeyer 1992.199–201.

passion. Theocritean influence upon the Anacreontic cannot be ruled out, but it is hardly necessary to assume it, any more than we need suppose that the Anacreontic motif was found in Anacreon himself. Nevertheless, the shared motifs do nothing to lessen the likelihood that Anacreon is an important source for Idyll 12. It is, however, also worth noting that, unlike the Anacreontic, Idyll 12 also gestures towards the curious paradox that the presence of the beloved both cools and heats:

> τόσσον ἔμ᾽ εὔφρηνας σὺ φανείς, σκιερὴν δ᾽ ὑπὸ φηγόν
> ἠελίου φρύγοντος ὁδοιπόρος ἔδραμον ὥς τις.
>
> (Vv. 8–9)

so has your appearance gladdened me, and under the shady oak I ran as a traveller when the sun burns

By refusing explicitly to say 'I ran *to you*' and by the use of φανείς, which in context evokes the appearance of the sun, the speaker's delusion that the presence of the beloved will actually bring anything but temporary relief is brought into sharp focus; the boy's arrival may well merely stoke new fires.[83] The immediately following wish for mutual devotion, which must be predicated upon the current absence of such devotion, makes the reality of the speaker's condition clear.

Beyond Anacreon, scholars have looked for the sources of Idyll 12 in Lesbian lyric[84] or in the elegiac tradition.[85] One poet who deserves particular attention is Theognis; the inclusion of Megarian traditions in the poem (vv. 27–37) might be thought most obviously to point to that elegist. I begin by gathering some of the elements common to both Idyll 12 and the Theognidean corpus.

The opening verses of Theocritus' poem share a number of features with Theognis 1249–52:

> παῖ, σὺ μὲν αὔτως ἵππος, ἐπεὶ κριθῶν ἐκορέσθης,
>   αὖθις ἐπὶ σταθμοὺς ἤλυθες ἡμετέρους
> ἡνίοχόν τε ποθῶν ἀγαθὸν λειμῶνά τε καλὸν
>   κρήνην τε ψυχρὴν ἄλσεά τε σκιερά.

Boy, you are just like a horse: now that you are filled full of barley, you have returned to my stall, longing for a good rider and a lovely meadow, a cooling spring and shady groves.

---

83 Cf. S. T. Kelly, 'On the twelfth Idyll of Theocritus', *Helios* 7 (1979/80) 55–61, p. 59. There is an excellent appreciation of Idyll 12 in Walsh 1990.18–20, although his reading differs from mine in significant respects.   84 Cf., e.g., Giangrande 1971.

85 Cf., e.g., Legrand 1898.250; Ruijgh 1984.57 (although his specific reference to Antimachus and Philetas seems improbable).

Here the returning (αὖθις . . . ἤλυθες) *eromenos* is said by a (perhaps self-deceiving) *erastes* to desire the *locus amoenus* which the latter can offer. The harsh expression of v.1249, 'now that you are stuffed with barley', shows that the boy is returning from other *erastai*.[86] If the opening of Idyll 12 is read with this passage in mind, our natural suspicion that the boy in the Theocritean poem has been neither on a journey nor 'ein dreitägiges Schmollen'[87] but with another *erastes* is considerably strengthened. The voices of both the Theognidean verses and of Idyll 12 are self-deceiving, but whereas the archaic voice maintains the appearance of control, the Hellenistic voice openly confesses emotional dependence and lack of control. This is particularly clear in the verses which express the speaker's joy in terms of the difference between preferred and rejected specimens in the same category:

> ἤλυθες, ὦ φίλε κοῦρε· τρίτηι σὺν νυκτὶ καὶ ἠοῖ
> ἤλυθες· οἱ δὲ ποθεῦντες ἐν ἤματι γηράσκουσιν.
> ὅσσον ἔαρ χειμῶνος, ὅσον μῆλον βραβίλοιο
> ἥδιον, ὅσσον ὄις σφετέρης λασιωτέρη ἀρνός,
> ὅσσον παρθενικὴ προφέρει τριγάμοιο γυναικός,
> ὅσσον ἐλαφροτέρη μόσχου νεβρός, ὅσσον ἀηδών
> συμπάντων λιγύφωνος ἀοιδοτάτη πετεηνῶν,
> τόσσον ἔμ' εὔφρηνας σὺ φανείς . . .   (12.1–8)

You have come, dear lad; after two nights and days you have come, but those who suffer longing grow old in a day. As spring is sweeter than winter, as apple than sloe; as the ewe is deeper of fleece than her lamb; as maiden surpasses a woman three times wed; as fawn is swifter than calf; as the clear-voiced nightingale sings sweetest of all winged things – so has your appearance gladdened me . . .

The chosen images point in part to the rejuvenation of the ageing lover that brief physical satisfaction has seemed to bring: spring, a sweet apple, lambs, young girls, fawns, and calves. Such images, however, also highlight the lover's delusion when set against the knowledge that the first verse has brought us; is this young man παρθενική or τρίγαμος?[88] What kind of 'satisfaction' is he likely to offer? Moreover, the very effusion of images and measures of

---

[86] Cf. Theognis 1269; Vetta *ad loc.*; Dover 1978.58–9.

[87] Wilamowitz 1906.181. The boy has in fact only missed two full days.

[88] On these verses cf. also Cairns 1972.25. Ancient rhetoric does indeed tend to pile up such images in a way foreign to the modern manner, but generic parallels should not be taken for explanations. On the obvious parallel of A. *Ag.* 895–903 cf. the suggestive remarks of R. Seaford, *CQ* 34 (1984) 254.

difference reveals a lack of control over language which clearly reflects the speaker's emotional state.

The wish of vv. 10–21 marks the break between, on the one hand, the ecstasy of memory and the memory of ecstasy and, on the other, the nagging doubts which calmer reflection brings. The language which acknowledges the imperfect nature of the current relationship is strongly reminiscent of Theognis' famous verses (237–54) in which he promises Kyrnos immortal *kleos* through his poetry, but turns at the end to accuse the young man of deceit (*apate*). As in the wish of Idyll 12, Kyrnos will 'lie in the mouths of many' (240, cf. 12.21) and be 'a subject of song for men to come' (251–2, cf. 12.11), but it is above all Theocritus' use of the archaic ethos of *philia* which evokes Theognis and the elegiac world.[89] In Theocritus the harsh ironies of the archaic poem are replaced by a combination of wistfulness and dialectology, but the evocation of Theognis and Kyrnos as a pair whose name has in fact lived 'for ever' through reference to a poem in which the *eromenos* is explicitly accused of deceit sharpens the pathetic impossibility of the speaker's desire. Even in the glorified world of the past, it was not always easy to tell the true from the counterfeit (cf. 12.36–7). The image of the touchstone itself finds a striking parallel in Theognis (415–18 = 1164e–f):

> οὐδέν' ὁμοῖον ἐμοὶ δύναμαι διζήμενος εὑρεῖν
> πιστὸν ἑταῖρον, ὅτωι μή τις ἔνεστι δόλος·
> ἐς βάσανον δ' ἐλθὼν παρατρίβομαι ὥστε μολύβδωι
> χρυσός, ὑπερτερίης δ' ἄμμιν ἔνεστι λόγος.

> Though I search, I can find no trustworthy comrade who is like me, who does not harbour deceit. When I go to the touchstone and am rubbed like gold beside lead, the mark of excellence is upon me.

The Theognidean context of how to tell a trustworthy comrade from a deceitful one may be helpful in understanding the difficult final verses of Idyll 12:[90]

> ὄλβιος ὅστις παισὶ φιλήματα κεῖνα διαιτᾶι.
> ἦ που τὸν χαροπὸν Γανυμήδεα πόλλ' ἐπιβῶται
> Λυδίηι ἶσον ἔχειν πέτρηι στόμα, χρυσὸν ὁποίηι
> πεύθονται, μὴ φαῦλος, ἐτήτυμον ἀργυραμοιβοί.

---

[89] For *philia* in these verses of Theognis cf. Goldhill 1991.109–16.
[90] I print Gow's text, as the textual detail does not, I think, affect the point at issue.

Happy he who judges those kisses for the boys, and surely long
he prays to radiant Ganymede that his lips may be as the Lydian
touchstone whereby the moneychangers try true gold to see it be not
false.

The lucky judge in the kissing-contest awards the prize to the boy
whose kisses are sweetest (v. 32), but he *should* be able to distinguish
'real' kisses, that is those of a *pais* who is 'golden' (vv. 16, 36) and thus
emotionally committed to his *erastes*, from 'false' ones which are the
kisses of deceitful and promiscuous boys; such a distinction, for which
the judge would require a 'touchstone mouth', would make the contest
really worthy of Diokles ὁ φιλόπαις. The theme of the impossibility of
telling from a kiss what mind lies behind it – despite frequent prayers
for such a favour (v. 35) – betrays also the deluded insecurity of the
speaker of the poem. How is he to know what his young man's attitude
to him is? He too is now enjoying sweet kisses, but for how long?

There is then a strong *prima facie* case for the importance of
Theognis in the understanding of Idyll 12.[91] This importance is not
purely one of literary *mimesis*, but speaks to the central concerns of the
Theocritean poem. These concerns are the fragile relationship
between the past and the present – a concern most obvious in the
aetiology of the Megarian Diokleia – and between the present and the
future (vv. 10–23). It is perhaps unsurprising that there is no other
evidence for the Diokleia;[92] comparable perhaps is the exchanging of
oaths by Boeotian *erastai* and *eromenoi* at the tomb of Iolaos, an *eromenos*
of Heracles (Aristotle fr. 97R). The Theocritean kissing-contest
establishes for the speaker the reality of his fantasy of recovering the
past; aetiology thus (as often) forms a bridge between past and
present which explains the importance of the past. As long as the
Diokleia is celebrated the speaker may hope for similar fame, and a
similarly fulfilled relationship. Nevertheless, the very obscurity of the
rite (perhaps known only from learned compilations of 'local customs')
suggests that this Megarian festival is itself a feature of the archaic
world, here evoked as part of a wistful harking back to a 'golden' age.
This, like the poetry of Theognis and the nautical prowess of the
Megarians (v. 27), which transports us back to the period of
colonisation,[93] sets the desire of the speaker within the whole context

---

[91] Note also ὤνησας (v. 26) paralleled at Theognis 1265, and for αἰνέων (v. 23) cf. Theognis
1327 (where Dover 1978.58 retains the articulation of the transmitted text as σαίνων).

[92] For some speculations cf. B. Sergent, *Homosexuality in Greek Myth* (London 1987) 169–73.

[93] Cf. Ap. Rhod. *Arg.* 2.746–51; Call. fr. 43.51–2.

of historical process. This is not simply a matter of laughing at the pretensions of an absurd rustic,[94] but rather of measuring the specific case of one *erastes* and one *eromenos* against the whole spread of 'paederastic time'. In looking to a future fame, the speaker assimilates that fame to what is already a long distant past, recoverable only in the archaeology and dialectology of that past. It is this distortion of time frames which is signalled by the use of Theognis, just as the Alcaic motto sets the direction of Idyll 29.

In the course of this assimilation the poem covers the Greek mainland from Thessaly to the Peloponnese (vv. 13–14), touching in its course at both Megara and Attica. Amyklai and Thessaly evoke the authorising paederastic relationships of Apollo and Hyakinthos and of Achilles and Patroclus,[95] thus creating a mythical paradigm for the speaker's desire in a way which seems to foreshadow the developments of Roman elegy. The latter paradigm is perhaps reinforced by an echo in vv. 17–18 of Achilles' wish for Patroclus and himself:[96]

> αἲ γὰρ, Ζεῦ τε πάτερ καὶ Ἀθηναίη καὶ Ἄπολλον,
> μήτε τις οὖν Τρώων θάνατον φύγοι, ὅσσοι ἔασι,
> μήτε τις Ἀργείων, νῶιν δ' ἐκδῦμεν ὄλεθρον,
> ὄφρ' οἶοι Τροίης ἱερὰ κρήδεμνα λύωμεν.
>
> (*Iliad* 16.97–100)

> O father Zeus and Athene and Apollo, would that not one of the Trojans should escape death, and not one of the Argives, but we two should avoid destruction, so that alone we might untie the sacred crown of Troy.

This 'childish and impossible prayer' (as the T-scholiast calls it), which was athetised by Zenodotus and Aristarchus as a 'paederastic' interpolation,[97] helps us to see how hopeless is the position of the Theocritean speaker. Whereas the relationship of Achilles and Patroclus did become a theme of song for all future generations (v. 11), the *erastes* and *eromenos* of Idyll 12 remain for ever unnamed; the speaker's wish is as futile as that of the Homeric Achilles proved to be. It is historical process which remains, ageless like the gods (vv.

---

[94] So Giangrande 1971. Cairns 1972.26–31 offers a much better appreciation of this aspect of the poem, although his reference to Pind. *Pyth.* 10.1–2 does not seem to help with vv. 12–14.

[95] Cf. C. Gallavotti, 'Alcmane, Teocrito, e un'iscrizione laconica', *QUCC* 27 (1978) 183–94.

[96] The closest Homeric verbal echo is probably *Il.* 12.322–4 (Sarpedon to Glaukos) εἰ μὲν γάρ ... μέλλοιμεν ἀγήρω τ' ἀθανάτω τε κτλ. The Theocritean speaker really does seek to 'heroize' his passion.   [97] On these verses cf. W. M. Clarke, *Hermes* 106 (1978) 384–5; Janko *ad loc.*

17–18), but individuals grow old (v. 2) and die (v. 19). We count the days (v. 1) because it is in days that we must measure our lives. We seek to recover the past of our imagination, just as the kissing-contest seeks to re-create the 'perfect' passion of Diokles, but the past can never be recuperated, in part of course because it is indeed our own construction. When we compare our love to that of Achilles and Patroclus, it is always the difference which comes home to us; when we seek to speak with the voice of Theognis, it is our mimetic failure which is most obvious.

It is unfortunate that appreciation of this aspect of the poem is hindered by the interpretative difficulties posed by vv. 12–14, which I give here in Gow's text:

> δίω δή τινε τώδε μετὰ προτέροισι γενέσθην
> φῶθ', ὃ μὲν εἴσπνηλος, φαίη χ' Ὡμυκλαϊάζων,
> τὸν δ' ἕτερον πάλιν, ὥς κεν ὁ Θεσσαλὸς εἴποι, ἀίτην.

> Excellent were these two among former generations, the one Inspirer (*eispnelos*), as he would be called in the speech of Amyklai, the other Hearer (*aites*), as the Thessalian would say.

As, however, there is no independent evidence for the Thessalian character of ἀίτης, Wilamowitz[98] and Gallavotti eliminated this implication from the text by printing (with minor differences) v. 14 as:

> τὸν δ' ἕτερον, πάλιν ὡς καὶ ὁ Θεσσαλὸς, εἴποι ἀίτην.

> the other Hearer (*aites*), as the Thessalian also would say.

The result of this text is that both glosses are ascribed to the speaker from Amyklai, and the Thessalian merely concurs in ἀίτης. Gallavotti[99] argued that both glosses were in fact pan-Greek and were used here to evoke famous paederastic myths (cf. above), rather than to display dialectal learning. The amount of evidence which may be adduced is very slender, but despite its appearance in Callimachus fr. 68 (set on Ionian Keos), the Spartan credentials of εἴσπνηλος seem fairly well established,[100] and that area too has as good a claim as any to ἀίτης, which means 'hearer', or perhaps 'blower', 'inspirer'.[101] As Gow's text of v. 14 is essentially what is transmitted, we might be tempted to keep

---

[98] Wilamowitz 1906.180 n. 1. Wilamowitz and Latte (1968.654) guessed that Theocritus took over the glosses from the work of Philitas (cf. above p. 17).   [99] Art. cit. (n. 96 above).

[100] For discussion cf. E. Bethe, *RhM* 62 (1907) 460–74; Onians 1951.118–19; Gow *ad loc.*; Patzer (n. 12 above) 13 n. 11; Dover 1988.123–4.

[101] Cf. Onians 1951.74–5 Dover loc. cit. It might be relevant that at Xen. *Symp.* 8.30 Ganymede's name is explained from the Homeric tag γάνυται δέ τ' ἀκούων.

it and to explain that the hapless lover is as deluded about the facts of Greek dialects as he is about his chances with the young man. However that may be, it is plain that this reaching into the archaeology of the Greek language is a further attempt to associate the speaker's passion with the glorious past. To what extent the inhabitants of Amyklai had a distinctive dialect or accent we do not know, but this small village, important only for the sanctuary of Apollo and the legends associated with it, belongs to a romanticising vision of the past, which is now as remote as the glorious future into which the speaker's fantasy projects his fame.

The paederastic verses which form 'Theognis, Book 2' may well not have been gathered together separately in any third-century text of Theognis, although our earliest witnesses suggest that 'Book 1' at least was in roughly its present shape in the early Christian centuries.[102] It has been argued that the paederastic verses cannot have been associated in the earlier period with Theognis' name, because Isocrates (*To Nicocles* 43–4) cites him, along with Hesiod and Phocylides, as an exemplary moral advisor.[103] Such an argument, however, mistakes the selective categorisation which operates in any rhetoric of citation. Theognis' poetry was immortally connected with the name of his *eromenos* Kyrnos; it was always available to be recovered as an authorising model of paederastic verse. Nevertheless, attempts to trace echoes of Theognis in paederastic Hellenistic verse have often been unconvincing or inconclusive because it is usually very common ideas and motifs which are at stake.[104] The strongest case perhaps can be made for Callimachus' 'echo' epigram (xxviii Pfeiffer = ii G–P), which seems to draw upon at least two passages of Theognis, 'Book 1' (579–82, 959–62).[105] That Callimachus' poem is a

---

[102] *POxy.* 2380 (2nd or 3rd cent. AD) preserves 254–78 and *PBerol.* 21220 (2nd cent. AD) preserves 917–33, cf. R. Kotansky, *ZPE* 96 (1993) 1–5. A. Cameron, *The Greek Anthology from Meleager to Planudes* (Oxford 1993) 14, notes that the fact that Meleager did not include any 'Theognis' in his *Garland* is 'a strong argument for dating the *Sylloge* in something like its present form before Meleager'. For the general issues raised cf. M. L. West, *Studies in Greek Elegy and Iambus* (Berlin/New York 1974) 55–8; M. Vetta, *Theognis. Elegiarum Liber Secundus* (Rome 1980) xi–xxvii.

[103] So T. Hudson-Williams, *The Elegies of Theognis* (London 1910) 89–92.

[104] For examples of such arguments cf. R. Reitzenstein, *Epigramm und Skolion* (Giessen 1893) 69–70; P. Kägi, *Nachwirkungen der älteren griechischen Elegie in den Epigrammen der Anthologie* (diss. Zürich 1917); Vetta op. cit. (n. 103) xix–xxiii. Outside the confines of paederastic verse, the strongest case can be made for Ap. Rhod. *Arg.* 4.445–9 as a reworking of Theognis 1231–4, the verses which stand at the head of our 'Book 2'. For the various views which have been put cf. Fränkel 1968.494 n. 78 and Vetta op. cit. xix–xxi. It is at least attractive to imagine that στοναχαί τε πόνοι (*uel* γόοι) τε rewrites ὤλετο μὲν 'Ιλίου ἀκρόπολις.

[105] For a recent discussion cf. A. Henrichs, *HSCP* 83 (1979) 209–10.

reworking of archaic elegy, while it proclaims its disdain for 'well-worn poetry' is an irony of a typically Callimachean kind.[106] If Theognis was indeed regarded as a principal authorising model for paederastic verse, then the irony is merely heightened.

[106] The interpretation of the epigram is of course hotly disputed, cf., e.g., Hunter 1989.37; Parsons 1992.16–17; Koenen 1993.84–9.

Epilogue

There are two important senses in which the poems with which this book has been concerned are backward-looking. First, as the opening chapter sought to describe, they seem to have close links with a vibrant poetic culture which flourished in the last half of the fourth century and the early years of the third. Most of that culture is lost to us, but the Theocritean Idylls, a designation which may itself point to the extraordinary variety of poetic 'forms' on display,[1] allow us precious glimpses of what we are missing. Secondly, of course, the poems themselves dig deeply into a (real or constructed) archaic world for much of their matter and their form; just how deeply is something that the papyri are slowly teaching us to appreciate.

The simplifying eye of literary history may see a third sense. Broadly speaking, it is true that most of the traditions recuperated in these poems disappear again after Theocritus. Theocritus himself became a classic, but it was above all the bucolic Theocritus which influenced subsequent Greek and Roman poetry. We have perhaps to wait until Horace to find again anything like the active engagement with archaic traditions which we have found in these poems of Theocritus. The many voices of Theocritus ultimately became one, which in its turn was overshadowed, at least in Rome, by the power of the Callimachean idea. That literary history is the victors' story is amply confirmed by the balance of modern writing about Theocritus. The puzzling genesis and extraordinary *Nachleben* of the bucolic poems has (unsurprisingly) attracted the bulk of critical attention, and the result (more surprisingly) has often been a blander, more unitary picture of poetic activity in this period than the evidence actually warrants; 'the Roman picture', one might almost call it. The most potent weapon with which to combat simplifying generalisations has always been the discovery of new texts: let us hope for yet more help from this quarter before too long.

---

[1] Cf. Gutzwiller 1995.

196

Bibliography

Abbenes, J. G.-J. 1995. 'The Doric of Theocritus, a literary language' in Harder–Regtuit–Wakker 1995.

Arena, R. 1956. 'Studi sulla lingua di Teocrito', *Bollettino Centro di Studi Filologici e Linguistici Siciliani* 4: 5–27.

Bechtel, F. 1923. *Die griechischen Dialekte. II: Die westgriechischen Dialekte.* Berlin.

Bernsdorff, H. 1995. 'Parataktische Gleichnisse bei Theokrit' in Harder–Regtuit–Wakker 1995.

Bing, P. 1988. *The Well-Read Muse. Present and Past in Callimachus and the Hellenistic Poets.* Göttingen.

Bohnenkamp, K. E. 1972. *Die horazische Strophe. Studien zur 'Lex Meinekiana'.* Hildesheim/New York.

Bowie, E. 1985. 'Theocritus' Seventh *Idyll*, Philetas and Longus', *Classical Quarterly* 35: 67–91.

1995. 'Frame and framed in Theocritus Poems 6 and 7' in Harder–Regtuit–Wakker 1995.

Buck, C. D. 1955. *The Greek Dialects.* Chicago.

Burton, J. B. 1992. 'The function of the symposium theme in Theocritus' *Idyll* 14', *Greek, Roman and Byzantine Studies* 33: 227–45.

Cairns, F. 1972. *Generic Composition in Greek and Roman Poetry.* Edinburgh.

1976. 'The distaff of Theugenis – Theocritus *Idyll* 28', *Papers of the Liverpool Latin Seminar* 1: 293–305.

1979. *Tibullus: a Hellenistic Poet at Rome.* Cambridge.

1992. 'Theocritus, *Idyll* 26', *Proceedings of the Cambridge Philological Society* 38: 1–38.

Calame, C. 1977. *Les Chœurs de jeunes filles en Grèce archaïque.* Rome.

Cassio, A. C. 1993. 'Parlate locali, dialetti delle stirpi e fonti letterarie nei grammatici greci' in *Dialectologica Graeca* (Madrid) 73–90.

Contiades-Tsitsoni, E. 1990. *Hymenaios und Epithalamion.* Stuttgart.

Denniston, J. D. 1954. *The Greek Particles* 2nd ed. Oxford.

Di Benedetto, V. 1956. 'Omerismi e struttura metrica negli idilli dorici di Teocrito', *Annali della Scuola Normale Superiore di Pisa* 25: 48–60.

Dover, K. J. 1978. *Greek Homosexuality.* London.

1988. 'Greek homosexuality and initiation' in *The Greeks and their Legacy.*

197

Collected Papers (London) II 115–34.

Effe, B. 1978. 'Die Destruktion der Tradition: Theokrits mythologische Gedichte', *Rheinisches Museum* 121: 48–77.

Fabiano, G. 1971. 'Fluctuation in Theocritus' style', *Greek, Roman, and Byzantine Studies* 12: 517–37.

Fantuzzi, M. 1980. 'La contaminazione dei generi letterarî nella letteratura greca ellenistica: rifiuto del sistema o evoluzione di un sistema?', *Lingua e Stile* 15: 433–50.

　1988. *Ricerche su Apollonio Rodio.* Rome.

　1993a. 'Il sistema letterario della poesia alessandrina nel III sec. A. C.' in G. Cambiano, L. Canfora, D. Lanza (eds.), *Lo spazio letterario della Grecia antica* I.2 (Rome) 31–73.

　1993b. 'Teocrito e la poesia bucolica' in G. Cambiano, L. Canfora, D. Lanza (eds.), *Lo spazio letterario della Grecia antica* I.2 (Rome) 145–95.

　1995. 'Variazioni sull'esametro in Teocrito' in M. Fantuzzi and R. Pretagostini (eds.), *Struttura e storia dell'esametro greco* (Rome) 221–64.

Fränkel, H. 1968. *Noten zu den Argonautika des Apollonios.* Munich.

Fraser, P. M. 1972. *Ptolemaic Alexandria.* Oxford.

Fuhrer, T. 1992. *Die Auseinandersetzung mit den Chorlyrikern in den Epinikien des Kallimachos.* Basel/Kassel.

Gallavotti, C. 1952. *Lingua, tecnica e poesia negli Idilli di Teocrito.* Rome.

　1984. 'Nuovi papiri di Teocrito', *Bollettino dei Classici* 5: 3–42.

　1986. 'Pap. Hamb. 201 e questioni varie della tradizione teocritea', *Bollettino dei Classici* 7: 3–36.

Gentili, B. and Pretagostini, R. (eds.). 1988. *La musica in Grecia.* Rome/Bari.

Giangrande, G. 1971. 'Theocritus' twelfth and fourth Idylls: a study in Hellenistic irony', *Quaderni Urbinati di Cultura Classica* 12: 95–113 [= *Scripta Minora Alexandrina* I 87–105].

Goldhill, S. 1991. *The Poet's Voice.* Cambridge.

　1994. 'The naive and knowing eye: ecphrasis and the culture of viewing in the Hellenistic world' in S. Goldhill and R. Osborne (eds.), *Art and Text in Ancient Greek Culture* (Cambridge) 197–223.

Griffiths, A. 1972. 'Alcman's Partheneion: the morning after the night before', *Quaderni Urbinati di Cultura Classica* 14: 7–30.

　1995. 'Customising Theokritos' in Harder–Regtuit–Wakker 1995.

Griffiths, F. T. 1976. 'Theocritus' silent Dioscuri', *Greek, Roman and Byzantine Studies* 17: 353–67.

　1979. *Theocritus at Court.* Leiden.

　1981. 'Home before lunch: the emancipated woman in Theocritus' in H. P. Foley (ed.), *Reflections of Women in Antiquity* (New York) 247–73.

Gutzwiller, K. J. 1981. *Studies in the Hellenistic Epyllion.* Königstein.

　1983. 'Charites or Hiero: Theocritus' *Idyll* 16', *Rheinisches Museum* 126: 212–38.

　1991. *Theocritus' Pastoral Analogies. The Formation of a Genre.* Madison, Wisc.

1992. 'Callimachus' *Lock of Berenice*: fantasy, romance, and propaganda', *American Journal of Philology* 113: 359–85.

1995. 'The evidence for Theocritean poetry books' in Harder–Regtuit–Wakker 1995.

Halperin, D. M. 1983. *Before Pastoral: Theocritus and the Ancient Tradition of Bucolic Poetry*. New Haven and London.

Harder, M. A., Regtuit, R. F., Wakker, G. C. (eds.).1993. *Callimachus* (*Hellenistica Groningana* I). Groningen.

1995. *Theocritus* (*Hellenistica Groningana* II). Groningen.

Herington, J. 1985. *Poetry into Drama. Early Tragedy and the Greek Poetic Tradition*. Berkeley.

Hopkinson, N. 1988. *A Hellenistic Anthology*. Cambridge.

Horstmann, A. E.-A. 1976. *Ironie und Humor bei Theokrit*. Meisenheim am Glan.

Hunter, R. L. 1979. 'The comic chorus in the fourth century', *Zeitschrift für Papyrologie und Epigraphik* 36: 23–38.

1983a. *Eubulus, The Fragments*. Cambridge.

1983b. *A Study of Daphnis & Chloe*. Cambridge.

1986. 'Apollo and the Argonauts. Two notes on Ap. Rhod. 2, 669–719', *Museum Helveticum* 43: 50–60.

1989. *Apollonius of Rhodes, Argonautica Book III*. Cambridge.

1992. 'Writing the God: form and meaning in Callimachus, Hymn to Athena', *Materiali e discussioni* 29: 9–34.

1993. *The Argonautica of Apollonius. Literary Studies*. Cambridge.

1995a. 'Mime and mimesis: Theocritus, *Idyll* 15' in Harder–Regtuit–Wakker 1995.

1995b. 'Plautus and Herodas' in L. Benz (ed.), *Plautus und die Tradition des Stegreifspiels* (Tübingen) 155–69.

1995c. 'The divine and human map of the Argonautica', *Syllecta Classica*.

1995d. 'Written in the stars: poetry and philosophy in the *Phainomena* of Aratus', *Arachnion* 2 (September 1995).

Hutchinson, G. 1988. *Hellenistic Poetry*. Oxford.

Kaibel, G. 1892. 'Theokrits ΕΛΕΝΗΣ ΕΠΙΘΑΛΑΜΙΟΝ', *Hermes* 27: 249-59.

Koenen, L. 1993. 'The Ptolemaic king as a religious figure' in A. W. Bulloch et al. (eds.), *Images and Ideologies: Self-definition in the Hellenistic World* (Berkeley) 25–115.

Köhnken, A. 1965. *Apollonios Rhodios und Theokrit*. Göttingen.

Krevans, N. 1983. 'Geography and the literary tradition in Theocritus 7', *Transactions of the American Philological Association* 113: 201–20.

forthcoming [book about ancient poetry books].

Kuchenmüller, W. 1928. *Philetae Coi reliquiae*. Diss. Berlin.

Kunst, C. 1887. *De Theocriti versu heroico*. Leipzig.

Kurz. A. 1982. *Le Corpus Theocriteum et Homère. Un problème d'authenticité (Idylle 25)*. Bern and Frankfurt.

1991. 'Idylle 22 de Théocrite: quelques réflexions à propos d'une conjecture de Wilamowitz (v. 170)', *Museum Helveticum* 48: 237–47.

Latte, K. 1968. *Kleine Schriften*. Munich.

Lattimore, R. 1962. *Themes in Greek and Latin Epitaphs*. Urbana.

Laursen, S. 1992. 'Theocritus' Hymn to the Dioscuri, unity and intention', *Classica et Mediaevalia* 43: 71–95.

Legrand, P. E. 1898. *Étude sur Théocrite*. Paris.

Maas, M. and Snyder, J. M. 1989. *Stringed Instruments of Ancient Greece*. New Haven and London.

Magnien, V. 1920. 'Le syracusain littéraire et l'Idylle xv de Théocrite', *Mém. Soc. Ling.* 21: 49–85, 112–38.

Meincke, W. 1965. *Untersuchungen zu den enkomiastischen Gedichten Theokrits*. Diss. Kiel.

Merkelbach, R. 1952. 'Bettelgedichte (Theokrit, Simonides und Walther von der Vogelweide)', *Rheinisches Museum* 95: 312-27.

1957. 'Sappho und ihr Kreis', *Philologus* 101: 1–29.

Molinos Tejada, T. 1990. *Los dorismos del Corpus Bucolicorum*. Amsterdam.

Monteil, P. 1968. *Théocrite, Idylles (II, V, VII, XI, XV)*. Paris.

Nöthiger, M. 1971. *Die Sprache des Stesichorus und des Ibycus*. Zürich.

Onians, R. B. 1951. *The Origins of European Thought*. Cambridge.

Page, D. L. 1955. *Sappho and Alcaeus*. Oxford.

Parsons, P. J. 1992. 'Poesia ellenistica: testi e contesti', *Aevum Antiquum* 5: 9–19.

Pfeiffer, R. 1968. *History of Classical Scholarship from the Beginnings to the End of the Hellenistic Age*. Oxford.

Pollitt, J. J. 1986. *Art in the Hellenistic Age*. Cambridge.

Puelma, M. 1960. 'Die Dichterbegegnung in Theokrits "Thalysien"', *Museum Helveticum* 17: 144–64.

Richardson, N. J. 1974. *The Homeric Hymn to Demeter*. Oxford.

Risch, E. 1954. 'Die Sprache Alkmans', *Museum Helveticum* 11: 20-37.

Rosenmeyer, P. 1992. *The Poetics of Imitation. Anacreon and the Anacreontic Tradition*. Cambridge.

Rossi, L. E. 1971. 'I generi letterari e le loro leggi scritte e non scritte nelle letterature classiche', *Bulletin of the Institute of Classical Studies* 18: 69–94.

Ruijgh, C. J. 1984. 'Le Dorien de Théocrite: dialecte cyrénien d'Alexandrie et d'Egypte', *Mnemosyne* 37: 56–88.

Sanchez-Wildberger, M. 1955. *Theokrit-Interpretationen*. Diss. Zürich.

Schwinge, E.-R. 1986. *Künstlichkeit von Kunst. Zur Geschichtlichkeit der alexandrinischen Poesie*. Munich.

Segal, C. 1981. *Poetry and Myth in Ancient Pastoral*. Princeton.

Sens, A. 1992. 'Theocritus, Homer, and the Dioscuri: *Idyll* 22.137-223', *Transactions of the American Philological Society* 122: 335–50.

1994. 'Hellenistic reference in the proem of Theocritus, *Idyll* 22', *Classical Quarterly* 44: 66–74.

1995. 'ΟΥ ΠΟΛΥΜΥΘΟΣ (?): Lynceus as speaker in Theocritus *Idyll* 22' in Harder–Regtuit–Wakker 1995.

Serrao, G. 1971. *Problemi di poesia alessandrina. 1: Studi su Teocrito*. Rome.

Smith, R. R. R. 1988. *Hellenistic Royal Portraits*. Oxford.

Thomas, R. 1995. 'Genre through intertextuality: Theocritus to Virgil and Propertius' in Harder–Regtuit–Wakker 1995.

Visser, E. 1938. *Götter und Kulte im ptolemäischen Alexandrien*. Amsterdam.

Walsh, G. B. 1990. 'Surprised by self: audible thought in Hellenistic poetry', *Classical Philology* 85: 1–21.

Weber, G. 1993. *Dichtung und höfische Gesellschaft*. Stuttgart.

West, M. L. 1982. *Greek Metre*. Oxford.

   1992. *Ancient Greek Music*. Oxford.

White, H. 1976. 'Three problems in Theocritus XXII', *Emerita* 44: 403–8.

Wilamowitz-Moellendorff, U. von. 1896. 'Des Mädchens Klage', *Nachrichten der. k. Gesellschaft der Wissenschaften zu Göttingen* 209–32 (= *Kleine Schriften* II 95–120).

   1900. *Die Textgeschichte der griechischen Lyriker* (Abh. Göttingen n.f. 4, 3). Berlin.

   1906. *Die Textgeschichte der griechischen Bukoliker*. Berlin.

   1924. *Hellenistische Dichtung*. Berlin.

Zanker, G. 1987. *Realism in Alexandrian Poetry: a literature and its audience*. London.

   1989. 'Current trends in the study of Hellenic myth in early third-century Alexandrian poetry: the case of Theocritus', *Antike & Abendland* 35: 83–103.

General index

Bold page numbers refer to a major discussion of a topic.

Achilles, 64, 79, 114, 137, 177–8, 192–3
Adonis, **116–38**
Aeschylus, 2
aetiology, 141–3, 149, 161, 164, 191
Agamemnon, 64, 79, 137
Agesilaos, 134 n. 79
Ajax, 137
Alcaeus, 55 n. 35, **171–6**
Alcman, 5, 152–5, 156, 157; 'Louvre
    Partheneion', 140, 152–3, 155, 158;
    language of, 153–5
Aleuadai, 103
Alexander the Great, 12, 96; funeral of
    124 n. 48; corpse of, 134
Alexandria, 2, 5, 49, 119; *see also* Library,
    Ptolemies
Amycus, 57, 58, 62–3, 64, 67, 69, 72, 142
Amyklai, 154, 193–4
Anacreon, 101, 167, 186, 187–8
Anacreontea, 187
Antimachus, 19, 188 n. 86
Antisthenes, 168 n. 9
Aphrodite, 127–38, 163, 182
Apollo, 46, 79, 84, 143–4, 186, 192, 194
Apollonius of Rhodes, 17, 74; *Argonautica*, 2,
    30, 46, 55, **141–9**; and Theocritus, 14,
    59–63, 74
Aratus, 17 n. 67; *Phainomena*, 1, 57; echoes of,
    14, 55–6, 81 n. 19
Archilochus, 24–5
Aristarchus, 192
Aristophanes of Byzantium, 6
Aristophanes, 122; *Clouds*, 171; *Ecclesiazousai*,
    8, 126; *Frogs*, 98 n. 61; *Ploutos*, 6 n. 24
Aristotle, 110; *Poetics*, 119
Arsinoe II, 14, **116–38**, 163
Artemidorus, editor of Theocritus, 91
article, 'omission' of, 39–40

Asclepiades, 10 n. 37, **19–22**, 27–8, 111, 173,
    177 n. 50
'asclepiad' metre, 19, 172–3
Athenaeus, 7
Athens, 2–3
'Attic correption', 9 n. 32, 30

barbitos, 101–2
Berenice II, 92, 132–5, 163
Bion, 16, 127
books: poetry books, 28–9, 31; book-trade, 7
brother–sister marriage, Greek attitudes to,
    79 n. 11

Callimachus, 1, 5, 7, 10, 17, 18, 19, 23, 28,
    65, 170 n. 16, 185–6, 196; and
    Theocritus, 82 n. 21; *Hymns*, 46, 47, 49,
    51, 70, 73, 77, 82, 127, 142, 156; *Iambi*,
    1; metre, 29–30; *see also Index of passages
    discussed*
Castor, *see* 'Dioscuri'
Catullus, 29, 73, 152
Chamaileon, 97, 153
charis, 90, 97, 98, 100, 105, 179; *see also*
    Graces
chorus, in drama,, 139
Chremonidean War, 157
colometry, 6
Comedy, 11–12, 89, 111–13; Middle, 4, 5, 7
Corinna, 149
Cos, 14, 17, 18, 80
Cypria, 59, 64, 65, 72, 74
Cyprus, 131
Cyrene, 37

dance, 3, 139–40
Daphnis, 50
Demosthenes, 168

Index of passages discussed

Bold page numbers refer to a major discussion of a particular passage.

DUE